Wallace Stevens:
A Lacanian Reading

Wallace Stevens

A Lacanian Reading

CHETAN DESHMANE

McFarland & Company, Inc., Publishers
Jefferson, North Carolina, and London

Library of Congress Cataloguing-in-Publication Data

Deshmane, Chetan, 1968–
Wallace Stevens : a Lacanian reading / Chetan Deshmane.
p. cm.
Includes bibliographical references and index.

ISBN 978-0-7864-6457-9
softcover : acid free paper ♾

1. Stevens, Wallace, 1879–1955 — Criticism and interpretation. 2. Stevens, Wallace, 1879–1955 — Psychology. 3. Psychoanalysis and literature. 4. Self in literature. 5. Stevens, Wallace, 1879–1955 — Literary style. 6. Lacan, Jacques, 1901–1981. I. Title.
PS3537.T4753Z6247 2012
811'.52 — dc23 2012003269

British Library cataloguing data are available

Cover design by David K. Landis (Shake It Loose Graphics)
Front cover image © 2012 Shutterstock

Manufactured in the United States of America

McFarland & Company, Inc., Publishers
Box 611, Jefferson, North Carolina 28640
www.mcfarlandpub.com

To
my parents,
wife Supriya, and kids Hindavi and Saunved

Contents

Acknowledgments

This book has its origin in my doctoral dissertation submitted to the University of Pune, India, and I am indebted to the University for permission to publish it in a book form. Research is not possible without the individuals and institutions that help, sympathize, empathize, and cooperate with the researcher. Therefore, although this research was carried out without any grant of scholarship or financial assistance, or even any kind of exemption from college duties, there are yet some persons and institutions that I owe immensely.

I am particularly grateful to Dr. B. S. Valke, who supervised the research and guided me through its various stages and tempered my views and expression. I am indebted to Mrs. Aparna Kshirsagar-Mahapatra for English translations of the French in Stevens' poetry. Mr. Sanjay Kharate has been a friend in need indeed. He lives in the United States and acquired those recent books published on Lacan that were not available in India.

It was Osmania University Center for International Programmes (OUCIP; formerly American Studies Research Center) and the English and Foreign Languages University (EFLU; formerly Central Institute of English and Foreign Languages), both in Hyderabad, that provided the reference materials necessary for this study. The management of Gokhale Education Society and HPT & RYK College, where I now work, and Maratha Vidya Prasarak Samaj, the educational institution where I previously taught, have helped me immensely in the course of pursuing and publishing my research.

My greatest debt is to Wallace Stevens and Jacques Lacan, whose works are highly cerebral and poetic at once; this kept appealing to and challenging me as well as suggesting that their works are still not fully utilized. I am equally grateful to those who have written on Stevens and Lacan for the insights they provided. In much the same way, I am indebted to all my teachers and friends for their support and encouragement.

I am greatly obliged to Alfred A. Knopf (USA), Random House (USA), and Faber and Faber (UK) for permission to quote from the following works by Stevens:

The Necessary Angel: Essays on Reality and the Imagination. New York: Alfred A. Knopf, 1951.
The Collected Poems of Wallace Stevens. New York: Alfred A. Knopf, 1954.
Opus Posthumous. Edited by Samuel French Morse. New York: Alfred A. Knopf, 1957.
Letters of Wallace Stevens. Edited by Holly Stevens. New York: Alfred A. Knopf, 1966.

Guide to Abbreviations

All parenthetical and bibliographical documentation of sources follow the MLA style.

Most citations of Stevens' poems are from *The Collected Poems* (abbreviated as *CP*). The poems not included in *Collected Poems* are cited from *Opus Posthumous* (abbreviated *OP*). Stevens' letters, unless otherwise specified, are cited from Holly Stevens' edition (abbreviated *L*); his book of essays, *The Necessary Angel: Essays on Reality and the Imagination*, is abbreviated as *NA*. Holly Stevens' *Souvenirs and Prophecies: The Young Wallace Stevens* is abbreviated *SP*; the biography of Stevens by Peter Brazeau, *Parts of a World: Wallace Stevens Remembered*, is abbreviated as B. For information about specific words used in Stevens' poems, I have relied on the *Oxford English Dictionary*, 13 vols. (Oxford: Clarendon, 1933), abbreviated as *OED*.

References to Lacan are from the English translations of his *Écrits* (abbreviated *É*) and Seminars. Except for Seminar VI ("Desire"), the "Seminar on 'The Purloined Letter' " ("Purloined Letter"), and Lacan's presentation before the colloquium at Baltimore ("Structure"), the seminars are referred to by the letter S followed by a Roman numeral designating the number of the seminar (i.e., S I). Ragland-Sullivan's *Jacques Lacan and the Philosophy of Psychoanalysis* is abbreviated as ERS. Juliet Mitchell and Jacqueline Rose's *Feminine Sexuality: Jacques Lacan and the École Freudienne* is abbreviated *FS*. All references to the work of Sigmund Freud are to *The Standard Edition of the Complete Psychological Works of Sigmund Freud*, translated from the German under the general editorship of James Strachey, in collaboration with Anna Freud, 24 volumes (London: Hogarth Press and the Institute of Psycho-Analysis; New York: W.W. Norton, 1953–73).

Full references for these texts are given in the bibliography.

Preface

It is the personal in the poet that is the origin of his poetry. (*L* 526)

During the latter half of the previous century, criticism on Wallace Stevens showed interest in his personal life, but it was fraught with the fear of what Wagner calls "corrupting the pure act of literary understanding" in using the "'personal' elements" to provide illuminations on the poetry (83). A few instances worth mentioning: Jacqueline Vaught Brogan tried to avoid the personal in Stevens' poetry as much as possible, and chose for the title of her essay "Stevens and Sexism" instead of "Sexism in/of Stevens"; however, while she described the "problematic between feminine and masculine" *of the poetry* (6), she had to confess, "If Stevens suffered (and I think he did suffer) from a schism within himself, he also seems not only to have been aware of that but to have tried to 'cure' himself" (her parentheses; 15). Arensberg acknowledged what others had suggested apropos of the "central mind" in Stevens—namely, the "phallocentric nature of the 'central mind'"—but she rued the repression of "the centrality of the feminine *in the poetry*" (emphasis mine; 27). Following Doggett, who saw "the symbolic woman of Stevens' poetry" as "either mother or beloved" (43), Rosenmeier characterized the feminine figure in the poetry as "undifferentiated 'maid ... and mother'" (153), but imputed it to the poet's (conscious) use of the Wisdom paradigm and called the poet's work where it pursues the feminine "his androgynous creativity" (143), suggesting thereby that the masculine poet-scholar and the feminine figure of Wisdom become one in the work. Apart from Wagner, who equated the feminine in the poetry with Stevens' mother and/or wife, most other commentators seemed to deliberately turn away from seeing the poet's personality in the poetry, as if there could be no relation between them; though there were some, like Lisa Steinman and Joan Richardson, who saw the poet's "desire to appropriate the feminine" in his actual life (Steinman 200; Richardson, *Early Years* 239–40), they did not seem to really see it in, or to apply the idea to, the poetry, which made their account almost purely biographical.

Critics who wish to keep the personal in Stevens away from entering into their criticism on the poetry would point to certain things in the poetry—such as impersonality in Stevens' work, or his humor, or the use of intellect or wit—to suggest that it is unlikely for these to have been present in the poetry if there were so much "personal" in it. But how can we be so sure that these are not devices, functioning more as masks that hide the poet's true face? Good poets have always known that the tool of disguise profits both themselves and the reader, that it allows the reader to enjoy the work more than he would otherwise by enabling him to easily participate in the experience contained in the work. Freud has rightly suggested in his "Creative Writing and Day-Dreaming" that such disguise is an artistic necessity since the artist, being adult, is ashamed of revealing his "day-dreams," which he therefore imputes to the alter ego ("Creative Writing and Day-Dreaming" 153). We should also not forget that disguise may be fabricated for defense against criticism getting too personal, to the extent of harming the writer's social status or image. We cannot commit the mistake of believing that writers are not shrewd, that they cannot use the tool of disguise to hide what they do not want revealed. And Stevens was both a very good and a very shrewd poet.

Today, an understanding of the personality behind a work is no less than a literary crime or even a sin. The psychoanalytic approach is feared to commit this malfeasance through displacing its "object of analysis from the text to some person" (Brooks 335). Consequently, there is a general scarcity of such attempts, owing to the threat of becoming author-centered; the threat looms ever large, especially in this age of disbelief in the author's life. This study of Stevens believes that the "death of the author" is an extremist belief; at the same time, it does not attempt to restore the place of the so-called "author-god." Let it be said that this work tries to strike a balance between the "author-god" and the "place of the reader." The belief in the author's death tends to forget, after all is said and done, that the reader is still at the mercy of the language-as-Other that he follows as he reads—that there is no reader without the writing, that the reader's responses are ultimately governed by the suzerain language that he reads, and that the language of a work is peculiar in the way in which it combines the various codes, elements, or discourses of a language. Thus, while it was necessary to read Stevens' poetry "practically," it seemed no less important to observe the peculiarity of its language, the way it combines various codes of the English language, and to account for the peculiarity. Stevens believed in "pure explication de text" (*L* 793). I, too, found that there was no need to go beyond and make my own presence as commentator more conspicuous than necessary. The purpose behind this approach was to allow the reader to see Stevens as independently as possible and also to be more true to this strange poet's progress from patient to a sort of psychoanalyst, from — to use his own words — "neurosis of winter" to "the rock." For the same reason, I have tried, as the study progresses, to be less and less dependent on the poet's personal history and to concentrate more on the language of the poetry. After all, as Stevens wrote Elsie, he was more himself "on paper" than "in reality" (*L* 80); his biographer, Joan Richardson, also feels that Stevens declared "himself through silent black ciphers rather than in direct utterance" (*The Early Years* 44).

To understand Stevens' poetics better, a close reading of his works from a psychoanalytic perspective is essential; unless one adopts this Cyclops' eye, as Seamus Heaney would say, his poetics will remain "bottomless" like a bog-land.

Chapter 1

Prolegomena

Personality must be kept secret before the world. (*L* 44)

Despite many discussions of Stevens' poetry in relation to his life, one major aspect of his character has not received as much attention as it probably deserves, and it seems to be the key to resolving much of the difficulty and/or obscurity inherent in his poetry. The reason of its neglect is probably that it is too obvious, or perhaps it goes deliberately unnoticed out of a commonly held view of artists as eccentric people. It is like Poe's "purloined letter" that, despite its centrality to the investigation, lies openly hidden. This aspect, for all its being open for all to see, still waits to be rediscovered. Once located, that "letter" might well enhance our understanding, enjoyment, and appreciation of the poetry. Therefore, it is worth looking at Stevens' character from a new angle insofar as it is helpful in finding out what the subject of Stevens' poetry is. That is — to imitate the question Rose asks apropos of the "body" of Sylvia Plath's writing (29) — what is the subject that Stevens describes? Stevens was aware that a vast majority of poets did not have a subject (*NA* 120). In this sense, one is certainly interested in the central concern(s) of his poetry. In another, who is the subject in his writing? Who is it that he writes about? This study proposes to show how the poet found the subject for his poetry by providing an answer to the "who" of the second question.

A few of Stevens' critics have expressed doubts regarding Stevens' psychical health[1]; but others either stayed away from triggering "explorations of his psyche and the unconscious" (Martin, "She and/or Sea" 95) or, despite noticing the schizoid phenomena in his poetics, declared on a very infirm ground that he did not "literally suffer" (McCollough 101). Wagner goes a little deeper and is correct in his observations on the poet's crisis of self. Yet this is insufficient to make the poet's most obscure poetry yield to the satisfaction of a tenacious reader. It is necessary to find the cause of his crisis. A study of his personal life would be an advantage here since it was a particular "event," which in Freud is almost always "the paternal threat of castration" (*FS* 13), that seems to have been the origin of the crisis.

From whatever is known about Stevens' early life, he led a normal childhood. The Stevens brothers were playful and mischievous (see *SP* 8–9; also see *L* 125, 126). At the same time, however, Stevens was coming forward as a very good student in the Reading Boys' High School. "Elocution" seemed his favorite subject even as he took it during the first term of his final year at the school, 1896–1897. At the "Alumni night" on 22 December 1896, Wallace gave a speech and was awarded the prize for oratory (*SP* 12). At the end of that academic year, he gave another speech on "The Thessalians." The report in the *Reading Eagle* of 24 June 1897 referred to his attempt as "a splendid effort" and praised him as a "veteran speaker" (*SP* 12). Stevens himself recalled that he won "*all* the prizes" (*L* 125). Wallace was not a bookworm, though; he was popular among the schoolboys. When he won the gold medal for oratory on that "Alumni night," the local newspaper reported, the schoolboys "broke loose, clapped their hands and applauded ... the winner is ... a favorite in the school, as was proven by the send-off his classmates gave him"; they also gave him "the school yell and a cheer" (*SP* 12). Who could have believed that this same boy would be afraid of speaking in front of people when grown up? Would it have been possible for anyone then to believe that this playful and mischievous boy would live the life of a loner later?

Stevens studied at Harvard College, Cambridge, between 1897 and 1900. Some of the most important things of this period are his otherwise taciturn father's eloquent letters to him. Full of "strictures and advice" (*SP* 13), and often watchfully inquisitive, they do not lack shrewd suggestions amounting almost to warnings. The puritanical message of hard work and study keeps resounding through them (see *L* 14, 16, 18, 20, 26).[2] Though Stevens wrote his niece in 1943 that his father was not wont to push his way (*L* 454), Garrett's letters to him reflect how he was keen on pushing his say. The father's anxiety of influencing his children bore fruit, as all three sons decided to become lawyers like him.[3] The poet wrote his niece that as a young boy he always thought that he got his practical side from his father (*L* 454). Had Garrett not been given to pushing his way, he would not have interfered with his sons' marriages to such an extent as to seriously harm relationships (see B 258). In fact, Wallace suffered most from his father's actions; he had the feeling that his father was trying to control him (*L* 49).

After the Harvard years, Stevens lived in New York between 1900 and 1916. This period of his life proved very crucial in the sense that it shaped his future life as poet, lawyer, and person. In 1904 he went to Reading, Pennsylvania, for a long stay at his hometown, where he fell deeply in love with Elsie. The courtship, however, soon found itself in troubles. From the preserved correspondence, one sees that Elsie did not write Stevens as often as she should have or as the lover expected of his beloved. Her (seeming) indifference began to show as early as September 1904.[4] Stevens had started feeling that she was not exactly the sort of girl he wanted, or at least wondered whether she was.[5] Yet it was his attachment to or love for her that kept the relationship going. Her indifference must have had a certain unconscious effect on the sensitive Wallace often seen in a love affair — that of the expectant person getting more obsessed about the one who seems or is indifferent. One remarkable feature of the Wallace–Elsie courtship is that he felt more comfortable with her when they were not together (*L* 96). Strange though it may seem, the only reason could be that when together he could quarrel with her as to why she behaved the way she did, thus upsetting her and spoiling their reunion. Without her, he could allow his imagination to paint only a happy relationship, for then there would be no quarrels. In his imagination, she was more perfectly herself to him, which made him more perfectly himself to her; in his imagination, she did not make him "beg" (*L* 96), and would grant every demand Wallace might make. Thus, it is easy to see how Elsie became the fantasy object of the poet's desire.

This very desire complicated and jeopardized Wallace's relationship with his father, who put up a strong resistance to their marriage. The parents' strong views about their children's marriages created problems. Before their eldest son's proposed marriage with Sarah Stayman, they sent someone to check if the bridesmaid's mother was good enough (see B 258). Ultimately, they were satisfied with her family's connections. Thus, in a letter of 17 November 1907, when Wallace was contemplating marriage with Elsie, his father shrewdly wrote him about how Wallace's eldest brother was benefiting from the connections of his wife and her mother (B 259). However, Elsie came from a desolate background; there was nothing in it that could have cheered Wallace's parents — she did not belong to the class they had worked hard to join.[6] It is not difficult to imagine that Wallace must have foreseen his father's resistance to his marriage with Elsie long before their engagement in December 1908.

Although disturbed by Wallace's resolve to marry Elsie, his father preferred not to "butt in" (B 262). However, owing to ill health and financial difficulties, Garrett Stevens lost self-control and did interfere. Sometime between March and November 1908, before Stevens' engagement with Elsie in December, the father and son had a quarrel over the matter. On a rare occasion, Stevens confessed that he would be in a hurry to go to Elsie's house and would not see his family until it was time for him to leave for New York again, and when this started happening again and again, his father scolded him, saying that their home was not a hotel or a place to bring laundry to and if Wallace thought differently he should never come into the home at all (B 256). Wallace must have been hurt by his father's negative approach (*CP* 319). It was probably at this point that Wallace swore never to come back into the parental house (B 262); he kept his word, never spoke to his father again, nor did he have any relationship with any other family member — apart from his financial help to his elder brother during his illness — until his younger brother John Stevens' death in 1940. Wallace had to choose between Elsie and his family, and he preferred Elsie. However, he was a very sensitive person; his father died on 14 July 1911 without ever having spoken to him and the poet kept regretting and brooding over this for a long time (B 256). Perhaps he felt guilty, as is expressed when he wrote that the son's life is a punishment for the father's life (*CP* 323).

This is not a simple expression of the guilt feeling of what he felt as his "revenge" on the father (*CP* 319); it is a rare instance of the melancholic's mourning in Stevens, one that is very hard, almost impossible, to overcome, since the lost father cannot be substituted in adult age. In fact, owing to precisely this possibility of overcoming the loss, Freud distinguishes mourning from melancholia, which defers recovery from the loss. Moreover, this loss was marked with a sense of guilt in Stevens' case.[7] This must have had a tremendous psychological impact on Stevens since it is directly related to the problematization of the resolution of the Oedipal complex. Normally, in resolving this complex, the son finds a substitute for the mother. Elsie was going to be the substitute. Unfortunately, it was at this time that Garrett interfered, barring his sensitive son's access to manhood. In this way, the one who was supposed to teach his son manhood finally ended up by resisting it. In *Esthétique du Mal,* Stevens seems to describe Lacan's idea of a "No" implicit in *Name-of-the-Father* as he writes about the sad repercussions of his father's refusal to approve the marriage, suggesting that it annihilated him from within (*CP* 320, 319). Perhaps Stevens' tragedy started at this point (*CP* 320), since the poet kept regretting the quarrel and remembering his father until as late as *Auroras of Autumn* of 1950 (*CP* 411–21), and even after. Did he give vent to his feelings about his situation when he wrote that he had almost attained perfect manhood but then miserably failed (*CP* 318)? In the first section of "Stanzas for 'Examination of the Hero in a Time of War'" of 1941 (*OP* 83), are "they" Stevens' parents? Can the "sun" be replaced with "son," who wanted to be virile against the parents' wishes, thus destroying them? Is the son's desire for virility antique, or antic, since it destroys the parents? It seems that the enigmatic guilty feeling kept the poet occupied until the very end of his life (*CP* 419), for even in the last volume we find him lamenting about the supposed guilt (*CP* 504).

Crime and/or guilt have always been central to neuroses. In *King Oedipus* and *Hamlet*, it is crime that initiates the action and is responsible for the protagonists' crises. In both plays, delayed or insufficient mourning over the father's death and the suddenness of that realization accentuates the onset of crisis. Freud discusses the case of a 17th-century painter, Christoph Haizmann, whose wish to become a painter was probably opposed by his father. After the father's death Christoph did not practice the art; this "deferred obedience," preventing the son from "earning a livelihood," was "an expression of remorse and a successful self-punishment" ("The Devil as a Father-Substitute" 88). Lacan knew a Muslim patient whose father had been accused of theft. Islamic law advises cutting off the thief's hand. The right hand of this patient had an unusual writer's cramp—a self-punishment (S II 129–30). Strangely, the sons take on punishment for the crimes they have or have not committed; somehow they feel guilty. This is the mainstay of castration, and hence neurosis. Elizabeth Grosz writes, "The real father's authority is never so strong as in his absence or death. The dead father, murdered by the primal fraternal horde, founds an inexorable law, more powerful and effective than his supervising presence" (68). No wonder, then, that the father continues to remain alive on the son's imaginary plane. However, the castrating father cannot be the neurotic's ideal; thus, on the structure of neurosis, Lacan says that it is "subjective and intersubjective," adding that this is conducive to constructing the loss as a sort of ideal into the unconscious, as an Other of the neurotic desire (S III 288).

Wallace married Elsie on 21 September 1909, and the couple lived in New York until 1916. Stevens did write when he was at Harvard, but nothing of that period seems significant. It was only after the deaths of his father (1911) and mother (1912) that anything of significance started issuing from his pen. He himself said that his interest in poetry got revived ten or fifteen years after he went to New York in 1900 as he met his Cambridge friends in the city (B 8). It was during or around those years after leaving Harvard that the most unsettling events of the poet's life took place. In 1914, Walter Arensberg and some other friends formed a small literary circle in New York. This group of young writers merely provided an opportunity for the irruption of Stevens' suppressed, secret emotions and feelings. At Harvard, he had impressed "literary eminences" like George Santayana and his English professor Barrette Wendell with his "literary aptitude" (B 8). But the real strength of this aptitude started showing when he was well over thirty. His "Songs for Elsie," and a "book of verses" that he presented to Elsie in 1908 on her twenty-second birthday, suggest that "he made a new start in 1907"; however, "it was only in 1913," after his marriage and the deaths of his parents, that he began to try to write poetry again (Rehder 46; *L* 180). There are strong psychical implications in the poetry written after this time that must be heard, the roots of which point invariably to the events that took place over a period between 1908 and 1912.

In fact, it was not only his poetry—he himself had also changed due to those events. Richardson feels that this change began with his father's death (*The Early Years* 380); I think it had begun much earlier, with his father's authoritative intrusion into several of Stevens' decisions, which must have brought about tremendous changes in the poet's mind (*CP* 455). Thus, we see a considerable difference between the poet's personality in childhood and in adulthood.

Peter Brazeau's oral biography of Stevens is full of stories about him, narrated by persons who worked or came in contact with him. The general picture of the poet emanating from these stories represents him as one who remained aloof from people—a whimsical man, "a loner," a "sane schizophrenic" (B 27, 28). He spoke very abruptly, almost insultingly, to or about people. One of the most important aspects of his behavior that these things betray is his egotistic attitude. His general manner itself was like a man having a strong ego; one often suspects that he did it conspicuously and deliberately, for the whole effort seems to have been directed toward letting others know that he was "different than the common herd" (B 13). He often downplayed his superiors or equals, both in office and in literary circles. He did not want anyone to hold an upper hand, hated the idea of being dominated by others. One wonders why he would behave like an egotistic or arrogant person, or love to shock people, or try to impress them in bizarre ways. Was he trying to prove something, perhaps to himself? A couple of his colleagues have made a far more accurate observation on this side of Stevens: Herbert Schoen opines that the poet liked to play with words to attract attention (B 59). Arthur Polley expresses a similar opinion when he says that Stevens liked to shock people "just to see their reaction" (B 64). A comment by Clifford Burdge, Jr., that Stevens was a very shy person would look odd considering the way Stevens spoke to people, but what Burdge says next is more important from a psychoanalytic point of view: to cover up their shyness, shy people assume an attitude that resembles "arrogance, aloofness ... coldness" (B 29). Now, far from being shy, Stevens was very bold and self-confident in his childhood, as suggested by some of the things he did. Where had his boldness and self-confidence vanished? And if—as Stevens says in a poem—two opposite things depend on each other (*CP* 392), then did he feel something lacking in him so that he had to put on an air that would cover up the lack? If yes, when did it all happen? The answer to the last question invariably points to the period between 1908 and 1912, during which time Stevens underwent the most difficult events of his life, ones that changed him almost for his entire lifetime. Besides, the poet was concerned about his social image. Richardson says that his "insecurity about identity and his resulting need to display himself were intrinsic to his personality" and connects them to the degeneration of "social and moral orders" of the time (*The Early Years* 305, 73); however, the personal reasons cannot be overlooked.

Interestingly enough, the French psychoanalyst Jacques Lacan has something that approximates Burdge's comment about shy people. Lacan uses the term "castration" for what is very vaguely and generally referred to as the inferiority complex. When this complex, which everyone has to some extent, exceeds a certain limit in a subject or person, he is referred to as a neurotic whose "castration" is purely imaginary. Lacan writes that this castration is very strong and even the subject's proper name becomes an "inconvenience" to him because he is "Nameless"; he further argues that in an effort to deny castration, the neurotic hides it beneath this strong ego (*É* 323). The "Nameless"-ness that Lacan refers to here can be replaced by "signifierless"-ness since, in his thought, neuroses result from the repression of a signifier. Lacan could also be referring to the neurotic's proper name: because the phallic function is responsible for the subject's sense of "self" or his identity (which is usually evoked by the "proper name"), its lack in him is suggestive of his "Nameless"-ness and thus of imaginary castration. The ego becomes strong in the absence of phallic function since the neurotic hopes to hide his castration beneath his egotistic attitude, which thus functions as a protective cover. Whatever we know of the poet's personality, especially from Brazeau's biography, Stevens' egotistic attitude stands out from the rest of his characteristic features. I believe that in Stevens' case it was the signifier *Name-of-the-Father*, or the phallus, that was repressed.[8]

The obvious question that arises is, why would the neurotic hide his castration instead of admitting and confessing it with a hope to recover? Lacan has an answer: The neurotic does not want his castration to become the cause of the Other's *jouissance*; he feels that "the Other demands his castration" (*É* 323).[9] Lacan uses two terms here to situate the neurotic: Want-of-being (*Manque-à-être*) and Too-much-of-being (*En-Trop*). The "Too-much-of-Being" is a reference to the obsessional, who himself experiences the *jouissance* of the Other (i.e., the Other as *jouissance*) since he considers himself to be the phallus, which is thus responsible for the "Too-much-of-Being"; however, the neurotic (hysteric), who places himself far short of the signifier in question, feels the want of being.[10] In the former case, the subject himself experiences the *jouissance*, whereas in the latter he has little of it but imagines the Other to be capable of experiencing it at the cost of his own castration. Where do we put Stevens, then? His behavior exhibited traits indicating that he was strenuously avoiding the "sacrifice" of his "castration"; he did not want the Other(s) to enjoy his castration.[11] This suggests that the general air of superiority that Stevens put on was intended to hide his castration. This is precisely the essence of Freud's statement revealing the secret behind this kind of behavior: "*Sie leben also den Wahn wie sich selbst*"—"Thus they love their delusions as they love themselves" (qtd. and trans. in S III 214).

Stevens avoided not only people but also discussing his poems or poetry. He never told anybody that he wrote poetry. People always knew it from other sources. Through a Company business Stevens met Judge Arthur Powell in early 1922, with whom he enjoyed the closest friendship of his mature life. Although their friendship was very "intimate," Powell says he had no idea about the poet's involvement in creative literature until 1927 (B 103). Even as late as in 1947, when Stevens was being questioned by José Rodríguez Feo, who wanted to translate his *Esthétique du Mal* (*CP* 313–26), Stevens was very cautious, coy, and reserved (B 139). Many others tried to open him up on his poetry, with little success. He obviously did not want to make people privy to his poetry. He deliberately avoided the men in the literary circles—even once close friends like William Carlos Williams.[12] One wonders, what was there in the poetry after all? Once he cautioned his wife to keep his literary endeavors secret (B 48; *L* 180); similarly, a lawyer from the insurance business was prevented from publicly speaking of Stevens' literary work (B 48). However, there were reactions from people who read his poetry indicating that they did not understand it; moreover, though Stevens must have felt aggrieved due to the lack of response to his *Harmonium*, he might have, ironically, felt relieved that people found his poetry difficult and incomprehensible. He then merely had to try to avoid discussing it with people or giving clues to understanding, which he did. Something there was that loved the wall of obscurity; something there certainly was in the poetry that he did not want to give away, to let others know. It was his personality. "Personality must be kept secret before the world," he once wrote (*L* 44). There is a solecism in the statement; notwithstanding the absence of the indefinite article, for it to be grammatically correct either the word "secret" should be followed by the preposition "from" or the word should be spelled "secretly," making it an adverb. And what the poet did was both; he tried to keep it secret and also kept it before the world secretly—through the poetry.

To conclude, he was definitely trying to avoid letting others know something, and his poetry contained or revealed, despite himself, the very thing he was hiding: his castration, his neurosis. This is precisely why his ways of behavior looked strange—he did not want to be inimical to others, but he had to guard himself somehow; this seems to be the most probable reason why he avoided discussing his poetry. He might have explained some things from his poetry to some people like José Rodríguez Feo or Latimer, but he either explained those things where he did not have to reveal his secret or explained them in a way that would accomplish the purpose of secrecy. Much of his poetry deals with his own reality, his mental crisis and his struggle to overcome it, and the experiences thereof; hence Frank Jones' feeling that Stevens had lost his touch with the "actual ... real world" (B 124), and that the loss of reality was caused by some mental disorder. Stevens' "poetry of reality" seems an outcome of this loss. His dissatisfaction over the surface of reality and the desire to see through and beyond it—to approach the unmediated, pure reality—bear the hallmarks of his illness.[13] After all, as Stevens himself said, everything came to him from within himself, where he was as he was (*CP* 237). *As what* was he? Or, to return to the question posed at the beginning of this chapter, *who* is the subject that Stevens writes about in the poetry? The rest of this study will try to find an answer to that question, but not conclusively, for his poetry might be described as "music without *a* subject" (emphasis mine; *NA* 120).

Chapter 2

Neurosis of Winter

> I long for ... the solitude of self. I want to know about myself, about my world. (*L* 80)
>
> The mirage of this monologue ... and the forced labor of this discourse without escape. (*É* 41; Wilden 10)

Village grows into town, town grows into city, city grows into industrial capital, industrial capitals unite into cyberworld ... and the native keeps alienating within it. Even when a village population increases a little too quickly during a particular period of time (and) because of new settlers, the native finds that, apart from the other natives, he does not know all the people; he sees and feels that the newcomers, who now seem to form the majority, have created their own society, different from that of the natives. A strange feeling comes over him: he enters *métoikos*,[1] feels apart within his own house, as it were. And if he happens to be a poet, he creates a world of his own in his poetry, a world alienated within a world. Does it stop there? Does it suffice? Did it for Eliot's Prufrock, for Pound's Mauberley, or for Auden's Mr. JS/07/M/378? Hardly; existence always has the background of the sense, the sordid weight, of that alienation, since the radical *otherness* it develops has already become an inevitable part of the spirit, mind, and body of the native who thus keeps *geron*ing. The question is, can he "wait for the rain"? (Eliot 39). He can; there are two clear ways out of this situation: he may seek to reduce that otherness, have desire for it, learn to love it, and thus merge with it; or he may choose to compete with it, to be its equal or even be to it that which it is to him. The former, which is really a way *in*, is a rather meek submission, almost psychopathological, while the latter is the "rain" itself that Eliot's protagonist awaits. One recalls, and distinguishes between, the neglected lot of Umuofia, having sought refuge in the church, in Achebe's novel, and Okonkwo, who follows the latter path.[2]

Most of the poets writing in the first half of the twentieth century could have wished for the latter way out suggested above, but their poetry indicates that they only occasionally followed the first way, the way *in*, and that most of the time they remained pent up in their *métoikos*, resentful yet resigned. All this may be observed in the industrial and spiritual waste strewn through Eliot's poetry, lying therein as if on a sickbed like the "evening" in "Prufrock"; in the cultural waste in Sandberg's poetry; in Hart Crane's attempts at acclimatization of industrial complexities into life and poetry; in the wreckage of human civilization in different periods of Pound's *Pisan Cantos*; and in Auden's numbered citizen, who remains a perfect gentleman on paper. Stevens also shared the predicament of these poets, but with a difference — he seeks a resolution of the two ways. He begins where the otherness has become inevitable, has penetrated into the depths of the psyche and, having acquired a speech of its own, has started expressing itself and wielding authority. To use Wyndham Lewis' comment made apropos of Eliot, if the earlier Eliot was "a figure entering the portals ... of [a] Heartbreak House" (qtd. in Chandran 11), Stevens began as a member of that "House" (*CP* 507) who may be found either loving its strange coziness or trying to escape it and be its master, as would befit the son within the Oedipal triad who, by his sheer desire of strength, overthrows and usurps the father's authority. It is due to the want of such desire that the other poets of the *métoikos* seldom break or even create a breach in that "House of Castration"; at least it may be said that their desire never found the right path — with the possible exception of Eliot. The strange or suffocating coziness of, and the assumption of authority in, that "House" are replaced in Stevens with the symbols of "winter" and "summer," respectively, emblematic of the polarity of psychical seasons or moods.

Stevens loved this summer; he celebrates it in many poems. But the way he enjoys it seems a childlike excitement; there, he is more than jubilant — it is almost like the jubilant mood of one who has just escaped the harshness of "winter" and finds himself bathing in sunshine (*CP* 371). And this is not without reason. Stevens had his own "winter." Therefore, in a sense, not only the early poetry of *Harmonium* and *Ideas of Order* but all of his poetry is the outcome of his mental winter. Thus, even almost at the end of his career and life, when Richard Wilbur sent him a postcard with a comment by Gaston Bachelard, the Sorbonne philosopher and aesthetician, implying that the human imagination simply cannot cope with polar conditions, Stevens wrote back emphasizing the importance of polar conditions in people's lives (*L* 740; B 170). The artist's creativity finds this condition conducive to itself because, perhaps, as Nietzsche's Zarathustra said, "all profound knowledge flows cold" (Nietzsche 105); in other words, the creation does not merely remain an enjoyable thing but also facilitates knowledge. And Stevens was an intelligent and scholarly poet, always on the lookout for both joy and new knowledge; otherwise, the question of comparing his poetry with philosophical tradition, or of calling him (or even denying him the status of) a philosophical poet, would not have been raised in the first place. If one wishes to call him a philosophical poet, one has to look for the new knowledge that might be there in his poetry. At the same time, however, one must not forget that he was a poet and not a philosopher; naturally, the knowledge that might be there in the poetry would not be given in a systematic way but in a poetic way — through the arcanity of experiences and the baroque-ness of the poetic language, disguising the experiences still more.

There would hardly be a better beginning to a longer study of Stevens, therefore, than to explore his "winter" experiences. In this respect the first thing that comes to mind is the difficult, harsh "The Snow Man" (*CP* 9–10), which is both an experience in winter and a "winter" in experience. The poem continues to be an enigma chiefly because of the question of the speaker, as well as the "listener" within the poem, and also because of the intriguing last line. Most of the poem's commentators recognize these difficult points. Some have offered their opinions on the question of the poem's speaker and the "listener" within it in order to arrive at an interpretation. Despite all these attempts, every critic of the poem knows inwardly that neither his interpretation nor anybody else's is in any sense authoritative. The question of a final word on the poem remains out of reach — though, of course, the desire to arrive at a final word keeps criticism alive and going strong. David Hesla is, however, the only critic to my mind who seems to have read the poem and the last line well enough to attempt to claim to have arrived at a final word on the poem. Yet, surprisingly, his interpretation tends to circumvent the question of the speaker and the "listener," which is extremely essential for the poem's reading, and for the poet as well. If and once they are properly identified, this poem, which has bothered so many for so long, will hopefully yield to a greater extent.

Hesla rightly observes the importance of linking the "and..." part in line 7 with the poem's preceding section (249). Discarding the imperative or implicative readings of the poem, he suggests that the poem's single sentence is inferential, enabling him to read it thus: someone does not or cannot think of any misery in winter and therefore the person has a mind of winter (250).[3] However, some problems immediately arise regarding this inferential reading. This poem does not refer to any single person; in fact, it denies the specificity to both the speaker and the "listener" that the inferential reading must grant generously. The "one" of the poem is impersonal; or better, it is an open space waiting to be filled up by any noun or pronoun — in the first person or second or third, irrespective of singular or plural form. Thus, it is at once personal and impersonal. One uses this pronoun when what follows it goes beyond the stage of "I" and then of "you," and then of "he" or "she" or "it," or even of "they" or "we," since all these pronouns are subject-specific and point to a particular person or persons. "One," on the other hand, can take on the pronouns either one at a time or all at once. In short, this pronoun is used to generalize or to make applicable to each and all individuals what follows it. Hesla's reading is essentially with reference to either second or third person; it excludes the "I," the first person. His final comment also makes this clear, as he says that the poem's tone is that of a person who is "bemused ... appalled" by people who remain unaffected by a winter landscape (251). It leaves out the one who is "bemused," the "I," which the pronoun "one" does not exclude; after all, one can be bemused or appalled by one's own strange behavior.

Another problem arises from Hesla's comment just quoted: it suggests that it is the speaker of the poem who is bemused and appalled, and that "people" represents the idolic "snow man" of the title, but it shrewdly avoids the mention of the "listener" within the poem. Hesla himself argues that the "Nothing" that is absent is "the something that is" and the "nothing" that is present is the "misery" (251). It is the "listener" within the poem who sees both of these nothings. That is, the "listener" cannot avoid the pathetic fallacy. Going by Hesla's comment, it is the speaker of the poem who cannot avoid it, "bemused" and "appalled" as he is by those who can or have avoided it. This creates a confusion regarding his understanding of the poem's speaker and the "listener." At best, one can see that he literally identifies them. However, it shocks the reader of the article, for Hesla commented earlier in his article that the speaker does not suffer from the pathetic fallacy (245). If we accept this, then why is the speaker "bemused" or "appalled" by those "people" who are able to avoid the pathetic fallacy? It raises the question of why—if the speaker is able to avoid or has avoided the pathetic fallacy—Hesla bothered to welcome Bloom's comment that the poem's speaking voice "urgently seeks to avoid any indulgence of the pathetic fallacy" (qtd. in Hesla 245). After all this scholarly attempting to read the poem, Hesla fails to either distinguish or even identify the speaker of the poem and the "listener." This is why he has carefully avoided any direct mention of the speaker or the "listener" in his final comment.

This is not to suggest, however, that Hesla's inferential reading of the poem is wrong. It is, after all, an outcome of the insufficiency of the previous imperative or implicative readings. Nevertheless, the imperative or implicative readings are not wrong either. In fact, all the readings, scholarly as they are, are correct. The only exception one might take to them is that they do not provide any legitimate solution to the problem of the speaker and the "listener." Of course, Hesla has some valid reasons for rejecting some ways of imperative reading; in order to reject some of them, he also rightly thinks of what Stevens wanted to say. However, he forgets one important imperative way of reading, but before coming to this, I would like to emphasize the importance of what the poet wanted to say.

What Stevens wanted to say, or says, is indeed important. For all our emphasis on practical criticism, it is simply impossible to dismiss the intentional pressure that gives rise to a work of art. Despite the belief in "the death of the author" that seeks to avoid any "intentional fallacy," the "dead author" does remain "a reader's *fantasy of perfect mastery*.... A *fantasy* for the critic who would identify with such *mastery as reader-writer*" (emphases mine; Gallop 182). Robert Con Davis has a similar comment when he writes, "One comes to literary texts to find and take hold of the father" (189). Like the "dead" father, the "dead" author does remain alive in the reader's fantasy; it is the reader-critic's fantasy to achieve the same mastery as the author himself had (or *has*, since here his death could be biological or metaphorical). Gallop asserts that the author and/or what he wanted to say are very much the objects of desire in the fantasy of the reader or the reader-critic, who desires to rise to the author's level by showing his own understanding of the author's work. She seems correct because without that desire, there would be no reader or reader-critic; thus, he would be in the same position as the dreamer-son Freud describes as having "nursed his father through a long and painful mortal illness ... [and] wish[ed] for his father's death (as a release)" (see "Formulations on the Two Principles" 225–26). Thus, though he did not want the father to die, he still secretly wished for it — this morally painful and unbearable wish was immediately repressed, and then returned in the form of a dream as a result of the sense of guilt; to overcome it, the son often "dreamt that *his father was alive*" and "*was talking to him in his usual way*" ("Formulations on the Two Principles" 225). Lacan describes the son's ruling passion in terms of his preference for death to occur before the father could know that he was dead (*É* 300). The son's criminal desire is reflected in the reading practice that is in vogue today. The dreamer-son did not want the father to know about his guilt, and so preferred to die before his father. Reading and criticism today, however, have no scruples about their guilt; "killing" has been sane-itized. With such a reader, the ruling passion is "Rather than have the author say it, I'd know/read"; with the reader-critic, the passion can be described in terms of a preference to explain before the author speaks anything, thus brazenly wishing for the author's "death" and desiring to occupy his place. Lacan glosses this further as "Being of non-being" (*É* 300); that is how the dreamer-son came at the place of the dead father. This is also how the reader-critic comes at the place of the "dead" author — by being the author's "being."

Jane Gallop wonders whether the kind of disseminative, polysemic, or skeptical procedures in current criticism are "a defense against something more threatening," perhaps against "a fading author" (182). The reader-critic does not really want the author to die, but unconsciously wants the author to see what he has done to his work; nevertheless, the reader-critic's desire to come to the place of the author betrays his anxiety (recall Barthes' anxiety about restoring the place of the reader), enabling one to interpret Gallop's expression "fading author" also as the reader-critic's sense of his own fading authority, or his "I." This is no less than believing in the traditional "I," with its supposed authority and centrality, thereby committing the fallacy of believing in the "self" as a substance, a static entity. Lacan subverts such a notion of the human subject in the essay "Subversion of the Subject and the Dialectic of Desire in the Freudian Unconscious" (*É* 292–325). Shutting up the author, killing him, seems to be a defense against the subversion of the reader-critic's "I," which therefore emerges at the cost of the author's death. The chief reason for this is obviously the prominence given to intellect as opposed to the desire (though, in reality, this move resists the very purpose of the reader-critic's desire to occupy the place of the author, since a sudden achievement of desire—which, ironically, the intellect is supposed to bring about—leads to problems). Hence the enlarging rift between what the author wanted to say and what the reader-critic believes he said. "In this activity" of criticism, "direct (what Lacan calls 'real') knowledge of the father ... is outside of articulation and impossible, as signification begins with absence" (Davis 189). However, instead of remaining purely intellectual, if this activity makes or accepts desire as its base, the contemporary critic would not be far from his goal. Stevens' poetry might have used wit and intellect, as Eleanor Cook shows through her two works,[4] but what it promotes is the human desire, because the poet knew that the human subject was subverted and decentered, and that the traditional concept of the self as a united entity was an illusion. At the same time, he shows the awareness that desire alone can hold the decentered subject together.

"The Snow Man" is a poem that does not explicitly lay the human subject before us, but it implicitly convinces us of its ex-centric, decentered nature; to use Litz's words, it "lays bare that irreducible reality upon which the poet builds his fictive structures" (100), though it is difficult to tell the fictive from the real. Stevens was a careful artist; he structured his poems while paying meticulous attention to every detail. The single sentence of "The Snow Man" is intricate enough to give rise to multiple readings. Two major divisions noted among its readings are David Hesla's inferential reading and the imperative or implicative readings of other critics like Miller, Keyser, Weston, and Cameron.[5] It is worthwhile to see if and how the poem can be read unequivocally as bearing an implicative or imperative meaning. This may be accomplished by sensing the urgency in the addition of the "and..." part; it is as if the prescriptions in the first two tercets, regarding what one must have or must have been exposed to, can also, on the contrary, induce the thought of misery, which the "and..." part warns of. However, language proficiency was not the poem's intention; the ambiguity that Stevens favors in this particular poem is not in the poem's sentence. Vendler believes that "Stevens' allusions, in his briefer poems, are more often to content than to language" (*Words Chosen* 48). The ambiguity of "Snow Man" must be found in its content; the poem's single sentence seems to hide it. The "listener" within the poem is not simply someone who is there as a necessary part of linguistic communication. There is something more to him than that. After all, one cannot fail to wonder why, if the "listener" is so clearly mentioned, the speaker is kept in hiding. And who is the man in the title? All the three figures are in question. Accordingly, critics have a difference of opinion regarding the identity of the speaker who dwells in darkness, of the "listener" who is in gloom, and of the titular "snow man": Litz identifies the poet-speaker with the "snow man" (100); Cameron treats the "one" of the first line as the speaker and distinguishes him from the "listener" (584, 585); Bloom identifies the "one" with the "listener," whom he also identifies with the "snow man" of the title (29); and Macksey, in suggesting that the "listener" refrains from committing the pathetic fallacy, identifies him with the "one" (198).

It would be better to approach the problem beginning with the levels of experience. It has already been mentioned at the outset how the pronoun "one" comes into use — it has a lot to do with levels of experience. One thinks of an experience at three levels: at the individual or personal level ("I"), at the level of other individuals (second- and third-person pronouns), and at the level of each and all individuals collectively (all pronouns including the "I"). At the last level the experience attains universality since, of course, it repeats itself in time, space, and person. While relevant to an individual, this universality is also twice removed from the individual. Thus, the speaker must have seen misery in his earlier experience of a winter landscape. Removed once from it, he knew that others see it too. Removed twice, he realized its universality,[6] and this objectification helped him to embark on finding a way out. Of course, all this happens unconsciously, which is why the thought of misery seems to hit from the back of the poem.[7] What we read in the beginning is, therefore, the speaker's conscious discourse, when he has started thinking consciously of "how to get rid of it." Grotesque as his solutions might seem, he also prescribes them. It is a different question altogether of whether he himself follows these prescriptions; what is more important is to see that the "listener" is helpless to accept them. Unlike the speaker, he is not able to objectify himself from the experience since he *does* listen the sound of misery, and *does* see both of the nothings. This is where Bloom's comment may be happily welcomed *and* applied to the speaker as distinct from the "listener": "The voice speaking *The Snow Man* ... urgently seeks to avoid any indulgence of the pathetic fallacy" (54); Sharon Cameron echoes Bloom when she refers to the speaker as "a person not guilty of committing the pathetic fallacy" (585). Yet this does not answer the question of the "listener." If the nothing is the misery, as Hesla says, then the obvious question is whether the "listener," who thinks of and sees it, indulges in the pathetic fallacy. If, as Hesla quotes from James, the nature is "not wholly inert," then the human mind is not at all inert since it functions; thus, the "listener" is human and he does think of the misery. To conclude the argument: from the speaker's desire to avoid the pathetic fallacy and from the inability of the "listener" to avoid it, one might infer that the speaker and the listener are different, and that they need not be identified.

Interestingly, Hesla does realize that "the self and its world" are central to Stevens' poetry (247). Had he thought a little more on "its world," he might have come to see the two worlds — the external world in which the self finds itself and the inner world of the self. Although they are not mutually exclusive, Stevens was a poet for whom there was a greater abyss between them than for any other poet of the *métoikos*, and which he strove to reduce. "The Snow Man" deals with both worlds. The external world perceived by the self is the winter landscape, vividly described in the poem. But the inner world of the self goes largely unnoticed. The poem gives enough clues for its discovery, though: The speaker's attributes are that he speaks, regards, beholds, and thinks; more importantly, he seems to have a sort of control over these functions or, at least, has such a desire — this is explicit in the "must" and the imperatives. The "listener," however, can simply "listen" and "behold," as if helpless. Both of these are purely receptive functions; thus, he has no control over them. Hesla equates the "nothing" with misery since it is "nothing, no thing, not a thing" available to the senses as the sound of the wind and leaves are (Hesla 251); similarly, the "listener" is also nothing, no thing, not a thing available to seeing or hearing but, like the misery, very much present. The "listener" can be distinguished from the speaker, whose ability to speak makes him available to hearing, and thus makes him tangible.

Here is where Stevens and Lacan come close on the nature of the human subject, the "I." In the three poems — "The Snow Man," "A Dish of Peaches in Russia" (*CP* 224), and "Of Modern Poetry" (*CP* 239–40) — Stevens seems to have thought deeply on the nature of the human subject and resolved to divide it into the speaker and the listener, which are comparable to Lacan's *je* and *moi*, respectively.[8] Lacan's *je* is the speaking subject, and the *moi* is like an object and a narcissistic subject. Stevens' "listener" in "The Snow Man" is also narcissistic in the sense that he is capable merely of receptive functions like listening and seeing. Likewise, observing the verb forms in the final stanza, he is clearly treated as a third person, almost as an object. But he is not static like an object; the *moi* is "an Imaginary function," "a specular subject," "evanescent" (ERS 60, 61, 43); Lacan is against thinking of the ego as a thing (*É* 131). Stevens' "listener" is also no-thing; it is not available to hearing or listening like a thing, but is perceived clearly at points of emotions and feelings, which are imaginary functions. If Lacan's representation of the *moi* is difficult to grasp, so is Stevens' delineation of the "listener." This is obvious from the fact that Stevens' critics have not paid serious attention to his "listener" despite no less than three direct references to him in the poetry; in fact, he is at the center of those poems.

Ragland-Sullivan glosses the two Lacanian subjects, the *je* and the *moi*, as "two modes of meaning fighting to occupy the same place" (43). In Stevens' poem, the winter landscape is that place, which the speaker and the "listener" both try to cope with and interpret, but in different ways. This is when the split between them becomes more prominent. The *je* is able to objectify itself from the experience since it can adhere to "cultural stipulations" (ERS 43); it recognizes the ways of the external world and bends accordingly, makes the necessary adjustments, conforms itself, and hence can find ways out of adversities; it can think mechanically even in situations of stress. The *moi*, however, is limited in its response to the external world since, in this responding, it can "*only experience itself*" (emphases mine; ERS 43). This speaks of the narcissistic tendencies of the *moi*, and also of the limitation of its potential to merely receptive functions. The *je* "translates" the *moi* as well (ERS 43); thus we have the last eight and half lines in "The Snow Man" where we read the *je* account of the *moi* response to the winter landscape. In this way, although the speaker of and the listener within the poem differ in their response to the external world, and thus *are* different, they still belong to only one person; they are the composite parts of the same human subject.

Now, who is the man of the title, the "snow man"? He is one for whom there is no fight for meaning (as) between the *je* and *moi*, one whose *je* is powerful enough, as it were, to make his *moi* agreeable to itself. Such a man will have the mind of winter that will not think of any misery despite staying in the cold for a long time. The speaker of the poem (*je*) perhaps hopes that staying in the cold for long will finally make the "listener" (*moi*) adhere to the stipulations of the external world, thus ending the war between them — so that there will be no thinking of misery. Nevertheless, the practical question is, can such a man exist? Will a man ever be the "snow man"? When? The poem does not provide any clues or answers in this regard. Fortunately, as Cameron has put it, "there is no such thing as a man purged of misery and empty of illusion; there is no such thing as a man of snow" (585), suggesting that the "snow man" of the title is an illusion, an imaginary construction, made into an object of desire. The conclusion, therefore: The "snow man" does not exist. However, neither does any man exist who is, as Cameron says, "empty of illusion." So, after all is said and done, the "snow man" exists — albeit as an illusion — in the fantasy of those who find themselves in a reality conducive to illusions. This also indicates that misery will always be there, or (broadly speaking) that there will always be emotions and feelings. In brief, human beings will always be human, or will always have the "hue" of "man" and not of the "snow." In a sense, therefore, "The Snow Man" does not seek anything. It simply is a statement on — or rather *of*— human condition: Stevens presents the world without, the world within, and the split in the world within along with the *je* speculations and the inevitability of the *moi* response to the world without.

As said before, Hesla's inferential reading could be proved correct, but it is possible only if the whole poem is considered as the *moi* speculation. It will then be as if the *moi* says, "From the fact that the *je* can think of not thinking of any misery, it can be inferred that it has a mind of winter." It is only then that Hesla's final remark comes right — that is, the *moi* is bemused, even appalled, by the fact that the *je* seems to have forgotten its humanity so as to remain unaffected by the winter landscape. However, then another question arises: Is the *je* not moved? The fact that it can or has a desire to "regard" and "behold" proves that it is indeed moved. These verbs or the functions they represent suggest a contact with the external world; Lacan's *je* is the subject that is in immediate contact with the outside world, and it conforms to that world's stipulations. Thus, the *moi* has no reason to think this way about it. Then, about whom? This is the same as asking who the "one" in the poem is. Is he the "snow man" of the title who, supposedly, has a mind of winter? If yes, why is he referred to so obliquely? And if he has a mind of winter, he cannot possibly be a human being, for there is no human being empty of illusions or without misery — inhuman, in short. In any case, this leads to equating the "one" with the "snow man," as Bloom has done (59). But Bloom equates him with the "listener" as well. If it were possible to equate them like this, why did Stevens toil at all to use different significations? He could have, in that case, straightaway started the poem with just about any singular personal pronoun and abided by it until the end of the poem. The heart of the matter is that the "one" keeps substituting in its place the speaker of the poem, the "listener" and the "snow man," thus complicating the poem's dialectic beyond hopes of satisfactory reading.

In fact, no amount of such investigation would suffice unless one sees the problem that Stevens poses. It is a problem that has no solution but one in which Stevens was indeed interested. Plainly stated, the problem is, who speaks? It interested Lacan too. Both the poet and psychoanalyst problematized the question of the speaker. For a better understanding of the problem, it would be necessary to refer to Lacan's *Schema L*, through which he delineates the human subject (though not in its totality). *Schema L* is a Z-shaped figure whose four corners represent parts of the human subject: he writes *je* (also called "S" or Freud's "Es") at the upper left corner, the "other" at the upper right corner, the "Other" at the lower right, and *moi* (the ego) at the lower left (see S II 243). Thus, the "other" and *moi* are at the ends of one diagonal while the remaining two form the other diagonal of the figure. Lacan tells us that there are two subjects, S and Other; both have two objects — the ego (Lacan's *moi*) and the other (*É* 139). The *moi*, in fact, is both subject and an object of its own experiences (thus it is also an other to itself), the other and the Other being the sources of the experiences. The Other — with "O" in the uppercase — represents the unconscious, and the other — with "o" in the lowercase — represents the outside world of actual objects and things with which the *moi* seeks to identify itself, while the S denotes the subject of speech, the *je*. There are two triangles: one is constituted by *je*–other–*moi* and the other by other–*moi*–Other. The imaginary predominates in the first while the symbolic dominates the second. The S or *je* is on the level of the other, and hence is related with the *moi* as an other. The Other is the subject of the unconscious. It can speak *to* the *moi*; it also speaks *through* the *je*, as is observed in slips of tongue, jokes, and so forth. The line between *moi* and other divides the conscious and unconscious domains; it is, let it be said, a thin line, since the imaginary activity is also responsible for the other's coming to reside in the unconscious. Thus, later, the other crystallizes the Other's impact upon the *moi* (ERS 3). The Other, therefore, is of capital importance.

There is a close relation between the ego and the other. However, the Other is the aim of the subject's speech; it is never achieved since he always attains the other "through reflection" (S II 244).[9] This is what happens in "The Snow Man" and "A Dish of Peaches in Russia." In the former, the "one" who is supposed to have a mind of winter is aimed at, but it is the "listener" as the other that is attained in the end; in the latter, the one who speaks *despite the speaker of the poem* is sought, but what is achieved at the end are the peaches and curtains.

It was suggested earlier that "The Snow Man" keeps the speaker in hiding. Even though the present analysis has so far assumed that the *je* is the speaker and the *moi* is the "listener," such watertight distinction will not do: Hesla's inferential reading cannot be dismissed precisely because he shows that the speaker and the "listener" may not be distinguished, even though his final comment on the poem, already quoted, creates confusion. His inferential model for reading the poem leads us to believe that the *moi* speaks the whole poem, whereas the present analysis involves the *je* in the act of speaking as well. This is a catch-22. It is difficult — in fact, impossible — to get out of it; what can be done at best is to change our very goal to knowing the nature of the whole imbroglio and thus to understand why we face this impossible situation. In order to achieve this goal, it would be worth making a tour de force, which is not really so, and see what light "A Dish of Peaches" can shed on the problem at hand.

The very first couplet of "A Dish of Peaches" resists the intelligence: How can one possibly taste anything with one's body (the foregrounding of the body is unmistakable) when the function of each sense is peculiar to a particular part of the body? We learn that the "I," presumably the poem's speaker, has a body. If this "I," with a concrete physical existence, is speaking, then why does he ask, "Who speaks?" This question occurs immediately after the very first sentence spoken by the "I," who has begun speaking the poem and is now suddenly interrupted. This is interesting indeed: Is the first sentence spoken by the answer to the "who" of that question? And thus, is there someone else who is listening to what that "I" says, and then asks the question? If it is the listener who asks that question, then he too speaks in the poem. The poem's reader expects some kind of dialogue might take place at some stage. To his amazement, there is no dialogue in the poem; to his confusion, the poet does not use quotation marks anywhere in the poem that began on such a dramatic note. The reader wonders whether it is a dramatic monologue. After that surprising question in the poem's second line, however, the "I" resumes his speech. But the question again appears in the seventh line. This time it is accompanied by a realization regarding the identity of the "who" in "Who speaks?" The reader's confusion is not resolved yet: Who realizes? The speaker of the poem (if it is a dramatic monologue)? Or the listener-questioner? As if to compound the matter, this realization is enigmatic in itself; instead of a second- or third-person pronoun, there is the first-person singular pronoun, suggesting that the "who" of the question is the "I." Then who is the "I" that began speaking the poem? The pronoun "that" identifies and yet distinguishes the following "I" from the listener-questioner. Fortunately for the reader, there is a reference to two selves in the poem's last line, and the penultimate line has a reference to their tearing apart. The reader is now free to conclude that there are two selves involved in the poem's dialectic. Yet the problem of who speaks and who listens remains unanswered, since the listener speaks too.

Even if it is assumed that there is only one speaker who speaks the whole poem, the fact that he encounters someone else's speech even as he himself speaks cannot be ignored. The absence of quotation marks may be a good reason to believe that the poem is a monologue, but the answer to the speaker's question of "Who speaks?" clearly points to someone else ("that" in "that I") as one who speaks, or even as one who began speaking the poem. In any case, the reader finds himself in an inescapable labyrinth.

To approach the problem in a better way, fragmenting the poem into two parts might help. Let us assume that there are two parts — one is a speech by a speaker (part a) and the other is an inquiry into the speaker's identity (part b). The first appearance of the question "Who speaks?" and its second appearance further on belong in part b. It is important to note the occurrence of the question in (b) immediately after one strain in (a). Apparently, both the parts seem to be spoken by different persons or speaking subjects. The questioner, in (b), realizes that the speaker of (a) is a part of himself ("that I"); the "that," however, indicates the distinction between the questioner in (b) and the speaker of (a). The questioner treats the speaker of (a) like a second or even third person, even though he locates himself into the speaker. Lacan says that the "I" is situated in the "you" (*É* 299). Thus the questioner, in realizing that the speaker of (a) is "that I," recognizes that (a) is also his own speech. It may also be noticed that his question is not answered by anybody else but by himself. Now the question is, cannot the speaker of (a) hear that question? If not, why? Lacan would answer that the Other, the subject of the unconscious, speaks, but that he cannot answer the question "who is speaking?" since he neither knows what he speaks nor whether he himself speaks (*É* 299). This is because he only speaks, forever, and "never stops talking" (S III 126; ERS 197); it is through such speech that the Other makes its presence felt. In short, it could be the Other who speaks the poem, which is punctuated by the listener's question and his own answer to it.

Now, who could be the listener? The fact that he listens to the Other and maintains his objectivity from the Other should be enough to identify him as the *moi*. In the very act of listening to the Other, it becomes the object of the Other's speech and also objectifies the Other, since it dislikes the idea of its "origin of identity in the Other" (ERS 149). This is why the listener in the poem repeatedly uses the pronoun "that" in lines 6 and 7.

For all this discussion, such watertight compartmentalization immediately vanishes, for even a casual glance at the lines in part (a) reveals that this is what is properly called the process of identification with the other, as Booker also observes (494). The whole body and/of the "I" is involved in tasting, touching, smelling, absorbing, and seeing the other (the peaches). That is, the body, the self and almost all senses are involved in this act. This is a movement that seeks to bridge the abyss between the "self" and the other as the "self" identifies and merges itself with the other. The *moi* tries to satisfy its narcissistic desires through identification with the other. In other words, one can say that part (a) has to be *moi* speech. However, the *moi* cannot speak, as it is "nonverbal" (ERS 43). Thus, one might impute the identification process in part (a) to the *moi,* but since it is "nonverbal," the question is how to account for the perfect language that is available for reading. Well, as quoted earlier, it is the *je* that "translates" the *moi*—obviously, into the particular language spoken by other men around. Besides, though Lacan often said regarding the structure of the unconscious that it is "like a language" (*É* 234), his use of "like" suggests that the grammatical rules of a language spoken by men are not necessarily applicable to the Other's messages. In brief, if the *moi* and the Other do not know the English language, it must be the *je* who is speaking the poem.

Thus the problem of the speaker persists; the analyst cannot get over the inherent discontinuities of speech in the poem. Yet these discontinuities point to the unconscious and to the intrasubjective intersubjectivity—even as this intersubjectivity has the last line in the poem. The essential characteristic of the speech in the poem is that it shifts in the economy of intersubjectivity from one subject to another to yet another—all of whom belong to the "I," or to only one person, or rather to one body, since the traditional concepts of the self, the subject, and the person are rendered invalid here. Lacan took note of these observations and eventually introduced the concept of the "fading subject" (*É* 299). The very structure of "A Dish of Peaches" speaks to the idea of the human subject as discontinuity (*É* 299), owing to the "cuts" or "interruptions" in the poem-as-signifying-chain. What can be said of the speaker of the poem at best is that the "fading subject" speaks the poem; this is the reason why there is such difficulty in identifying the speaker, or why it is not possible to make a precise distinction among the *je, moi,* and the Other. The poem's dialectic is interrupted and compounded by the Other, who speaks (who *only* speaks) and controls the *je* and *moi* discourses as well (see *É* 163; see also ERS 3). The *moi* is better off as compared to the *je,* for it maintains its objectlike status or separate existence; however, the *je* not only participates in both the conscious and unconscious systems but also "translates" the *moi* while adhering to the social norms and stipulations. Thus, the *je* has to make a tremendous amount of adjustments and therefore is—shall we say—inconstant, a "social chameleon" (Baron and Byrne 168).

Perhaps the stage is now prepared to go back to "The Snow Man," which is not as conspicuously discontinuous as "A Dish of Peaches." Nevertheless, the less discontinuous nature of the former poem makes it more problematic. The reader has to discern the "fading effect" that takes place as the poem progresses. The poem begins with a rigidity of outlook even in the adversity of the winter landscape. The "must" that is explicit in line 1 becomes implicit in line 4, and by the time the poem reaches line 7 it becomes impossible to be sure that the "must" exists there at all. It is here that the rigidity of outlook seems to have melted; the cause is obviously the thought of misery. The world without, once again, is seen as one normally sees it. And with the last stanza returns a sort of emotional illness, an inevitability. The poem's progress is clear, then: from a fantasy or illusion through a realization to reality; or, to use psychoanalytic terminology, from aggressiveness through regression to frustration.[10] In fact, one could say that in "Snow Man," regression begins with the title and stops at the end. Lacan defines regression as the phenomenon that occurs when the ego, at every stage of its decomposition, reconstitutes the fantasy relations; this is realized in the discourse (Wilden 14). The fantasy relations and decomposition mark the poem's beginning (title included) and the rest of the poem's gradually declining rhetoric. The psychoanalyst further adds that regression is found in "inflections" and "turns of phrase" that resemble "baby talk" (Wilden 14). The three segments of "The Snow Man," separated by the semi-colons, are to be read with inflections owing to the modal "must," the imperatives, and the suddenness of the "and..." part, while the poem's first half resembles a fantastic baby talk. There are also some turns of phrase worth remembering: one at the end of the first line and the others in the final line.

The ego, the *moi* of Lacan, is the locus of these phenomena. In a bid to identify with the other (here, the winter landscape), it creates the "snow man," a "monumental construct" of its narcissistic tendencies (Wilden 9). However, it is unaware of the fact that in creating this imaginary construct, it has also alienated its desire and placed it into the "snow man." It then goes about seeking a satisfaction for that alienated desire. However, Lacan warns that the subject is alienated from his *jouissance* more and more if he exercises his desire.[11] This breeds frustration, which is brought on by the object of desire (*É* 42; Wilden 11). Thus, both "Snow Man" and "A Dish of Peaches" end with what cannot be referred to as anything except frustration. In both poems the *moi* seeks something impossible: to be the "snow man" in one, and to know who speaks—and also to see itself in the Other ("that I")—in the second. What will happen if it succeeds in achieving what it seeks? It will become the "snow man" and will become one with the Other. However, it is nothing but a metaphorical death of the "self," for in Lacan's thought the "self" is merely an effect that the *moi* is responsible for creating. Thanks to the ending of the poems on a note of frustration, the *moi* is thus able to maintain its separate existence.

In his "Function and Field of Speech and Language in Psychoanalysis," Lacan suggests that aggressiveness follows the frustration caused by an object in which the *moi*'s desire is alienated; he further adds that this desire really hides the desire for death (*É* 42; Wilden 12). Both of Stevens' poems begin with elaboration of an alienated desire, hence with a sort of aggressiveness, which is followed by a gradual regression (poetic regression, as I would prefer to call it). This clearly implies that some kind of frustration must have caused that aggressiveness. Thus, in fact, one could conclude that it was the frustration that is revealed only at the conclusions that initiated both poems on a note of aggressiveness. If the aggressiveness of a subject reflects his desire for death, then the desire to have a mind of winter or to identify with the Other is a desire for death. This is not a biological death, but metaphorical, since that identification, as such, brings the *moi*'s another-ness, its sense of separate existence, to an end; with this must come the end of the sense of "self." The psychoanalyst further comments that the slightest intervention may incite aggressiveness to denounce and dismantle the intended object that the subject has constructed to satisfy his desire (*É* 42; Wilden 12). This desire is obvious in both poems: identification with the "snow man" in one, and with that radically Other "I" in the second. In one poem, the thought of misery causes the intervention; in the other, it is the curtains and peaches.

The intervention results in dismantling of the constructed fantasy object: the "snow man" vanishes, and the Russian self is not even mentioned in the last half of "A Dish of Peaches," except perhaps obliquely in that unspecific reference to two selves. Stevens does not directly say anything about how the aggressiveness responds to these interventions,[12] but frustration is very obvious after the points of intervention. At the point of intervention, the subject's relation with the Other is disturbed and the Other's presence is withdrawn, bringing on the feelings of alienation and pain that lead to frustration (S III 127). However, there is a consolation in this frustration. It may be observed that in "Snow Man" it is the thought of misery that brings the "listener" into focus, and in "A Dish of Peaches," the movement of the curtains violently separates the two selves. To be precise, it is the *moi* that is separated, brought into view; in fact, it is restored, for it is only through such intervention that the *moi*, with whom lies our sense of "self," regains its "objectlike" status, its another-ness, therefore restoring the "self" by barring or deferring its "desire for death."

As the two poems are being compared, the "snow man" and the Other have been juxtaposed in the preceding paragraph. The temptation to compare these two objects of desire is unavoidable. Scanning Lacan's views on the Other gives a hope that the comparison might yield fruit. Lacan compares the Other with God, who has nothing to do with the human subject's needs and emotions (S III 127; ERS 197). The desire to have a mind of winter is a desire to be (one with) the "snow man," who, supposedly, does not even think of thinking of misery since he has a mind of winter. Thus, it is possible to persist with the thought that the "snow man" has no feelings or emotions, that he is purged of illusions and emotions and feelings. Do not sometimes our circumstances force us to think of God as having no emotions or feelings, as inhuman? Witness Milton's "On His Blindness"—like Milton, Stevens' descriptors in line 7 of "A Dish of Peaches" also declare the Other-God's inhumanity. Although Lacan emphasizes the Other as largely nondeceptive, in Seminar III he does speak of its deceptive nature since it has its own subjectivity and can falsely convince others and lie (S III 64). Have not the "snow man" and the answer to the question "Who speaks?" deceived the *moi* first by convincing it of their own presences and then suddenly tearing it apart from them, by promising and then repudiating what it sought to achieve—namely, identification with them?

A comment by Safouan will justify Stevens' poetic rendition of the whole imbroglio as observed in the two poems: he writes that the subject believes himself "to be loved by the Other" through "signs" that are "minted" by himself. However, in analysis, this "certitude" of the subject is "suspended"; the analyst reveals to the subject the "regressive character" of those "signs." In this sense, "the analytic way is that which leads towards anxiety" (qtd. and trans. in Wilden 101). Both of these poems express the desire of/for the Other through "signs" that reveal a love of/for the Other. However, the structure of both poems manifests the regressive character of the "signs"—the signs of the *moi* "certitude" of the Other's existence, if not of the Other's love for itself. And finally, as said before, the poems end on a note of frustration and alienation from the Other, which must breed anxiety—so that they begin with the aggressiveness commensurate with that frustration or anxiety. Thus, one comes to a stage where the dilemma of whether to call Stevens a "patient" or "analyst" looms large over the reader-critic.

One of the prominent features of the speech in these poems is the "fading effect," as noted before. Lacan, in order to bring this effect into a sort of definition that would be an answer to the question "Who speaks?," says that "the subject speaks *to himself with* his ego" (his emphasis; S III 14); that is, the subject speaks to himself *and* along with his ego. Lacan also says that usually the ego speaks about the subject to another, making the subject (S) the third person (S III 14; recall Stevens' use of the pronoun "one" and the noun "listener"). However, since the ego is nonverbal, it is the subject of speech (the *je* or S) that "translates" and directs the ego's response in the form of discourse to another. Thus the *je* speaks *to* another *with* the ego. Lacan often uses the word "another" to refer to the ego because of its dependence on the other, without which there is no ego.[13] The ego's division into "self" and "another" is thus clear. This is how the ego ("self") speaks through the agency of the *je* or S to itself as "another"; put another way, the S speaks along with the ego-as-"self" to the ego-as-"another." This explains the enigmatic formulation that "the subject speaks *to himself with* his ego."

In a psychotic case, as opposed to the neurotic, imaginary relations gain unusual prominence and create grave problems in the simultaneity of discourse. Lacan says that hallucinations are the most characteristic form of these imaginary relations. In such a case, the subject (S) experiences complete identification with the ego, so that the triplicity implicit in "the subject speaks *to himself with* his ego" changes to a duplicity; thus, the subject speaks with his ego (S III 14), where the "subject" represents the unity of *je* and the ego-as-"self,"[14] and the "ego" represents ego-as-"another." In "The Snow Man," the "snow man" itself is the hallucination, but the poem does not seem to have identified the speaking subject with the ego owing to the fact that the ego is referred to in the third person, as the "listener," and not in the second person, as is implied in the duplicity mentioned above that characterizes psychosis. The reason why the subject of "Snow Man" cannot be called psychotic may be found in Lacan's comment where he says that, in psychosis, hallucination is perceived as reality and the subject speaks with his ego, and that it is like some third person speaking about him (S III 14). The hallucination of the poem is not within it but rather in the title; besides, the sense of reality reflected in the poem is that of the external world — the winter landscape, the other — and not that of the existence of the "snow man," the hallucination. And as long as the other is there, existing to be "regarded," "beheld," or loved by the ego without excessive imaginary relation, and as long as it imparts "misery" by frustrating that love, there is neurosis, not psychosis; indeed, reading the first six or six and a half lines of the poem do convince the reader of the subject's normalcy in comparison with clear psychosis.

Of course, if one believes that the *je* of the subject in the poem is identified with his ego as-"self" (the "one," since the pronoun does not exclude the "I") and that it speaks with the ego-as-"another" (the "listener," which is free to exclude the "I," though one cannot be sure about this), and that — whether within or above the poem — the "snow man" does exist as reality for the poem's subject, then it may be proved to be a case of psychosis. From this viewpoint, it may be seen that the *je* + ego-as-"self" (the "one") is commenting like a third person on the ego-as-"another" (or the "listener"). Lacan believed that in psychosis proper, the subject becomes the object of the Other's speech. In the case of the poem's subject, what speaks to him is *je* + ego-as-"self," which could be reformulated as S + ego-as-"self," where the S represents both the *je* and the *Es* (i.e., the *je* and the Other). This is why it is possible to say that the poem may be an instance of psychosis. Thus, we have two conflicting interpretations. Owing to this ambiguity, the best we can do is to say that the subject of the poem is on the verge of psychosis. A similar ambiguity can be observed in "A Dish of Peaches," where the listener-questioner would be the ego-as-"another," who is spoken to by the S + ego-as-"self." The S could easily be the subject of the unconscious (the Other, or Freud's *Es*). When the Other speaks, the ego-as-"self" is not in question at all; in this case, the ego is "another" in relation to the Other-as-speaker. This experience of being an object may be the reason why the ego does not directly refer to itself as "I" in the poem but only vaguely as "that I."

The possibilities of speaker-listener couples in the two poems may be outlined as follows:

"The Snow Man":
i) S + ego-as-"self" ("one," speaker); ego-as-another (listener)
ii) Other (speaker); ego (listener)

"A Dish of Peaches in Russia":
i) S + ego-as-"self" ("that *I*," speaker); ego-as-another (the listener-questioner)
ii) Other ("*that* I," speaker); ego (listener-questioner)

In "A Dish of Peaches," Daniel O'Hara hears the "unconscious voicing" that he feels is "close to psychosis" (72); however, the problem of the speaking voice persists in many of Stevens' poems, even the longer poems like *Chocorua to Its Neighbor* (*CP* 296–302). The ambiguity surrounding the answer to the question of "who speaks?" cannot be resolved satisfactorily. Both the poet and the psychoanalyst preserve it. Lacan thus says that the Other functions as the locus in which the phenomenon of speech between "I" and the other takes place; whatever is spoken is in itself the reply as well, and the other hears the speech whether the "I" has spoken or not (*É* 141). Here, in using the pronoun "one," Lacan already makes it impossible to clearly see who speaks: the *je*, or the ego-as-"self," or the Other? From the viewpoint of literary criticism, the author is the locus in which the reader-critic's "I" speaks to himself who listens; whatever is spoken is also the reply, and the listener hears it whether the "I" has spoken or not. The reader of a literary work decides to hear as an other, irrespective of whether the "one" has spoken or not, where the "one" could be himself-as-a-critic or the author of the work or both simultaneously.

Having realized the "dialogic relationship" that insists on the economy of the human subject (Booker 495), Stevens sees it imaginatively in the form of romance in "Re-statement of Romance" (*CP* 146), thereby abandoning the regressive character of the discourse that led to anxiety in the two poems discussed above. The term "romance" has had varying meanings for literary generations. From Stevens' point of view, its meaning may be aligned with that which was used by Wordsworth, for whom man's mind was a favorite haunt. But Stevens' approach and procedure echo Coleridge of *Biographia Literaria*. This is to suggest that although his predecessors had given the term a psychological touch, Stevens extends the scope of its psychical connotations and "re-states" it.

For romance—as between lovers—to take place, two living organisms are necessary (even if both of them belong to the inanimate world, they are treated as animate), and for it to flourish a noncongenial background is more conducive. Without such a background, there would perhaps be no romance, since it must depend upon something unromantic—its opposite, like day and night (*CP* 392). "Day" is very often "desire" for Stevens (*CP* 167), but "night" has several connotations. It is a threatening and consuming darkness in "Domination of Black" (*CP* 8–9) and "Valley Candle" (*CP* 51)[15]; it is "sleep" in "The Blue Guitar" (*CP* 167); and it is "beautiful" in "God Is Good. It Is a Beautiful Night" (*CP* 285) since the "brown moon" (i.e., the Other—for this interpretation, see the discussion of "Study of Images II" in the next chapter) as God appears in the "night" as he does in *Chocorua*. Despite the several connotations, it is certain that the poet viewed the night throughout his work as something where everything is beyond the human (*CP* 62) and, as Doggett puts it, "out of which reality emerges" (44): one of Stevens' colors for reality is green, which is the hue of the night in "The Candle a Saint" (*CP* 223). Like Stevens' contrasting feelings of the pressure of and love for reality, his view of "night" keeps oscillating between threat and goodness. In "Re-statement," however, it is neither threatening nor good, but is rather met with a sort of indifference characteristic in a choice between two equally cogent things. In any case, what it signifies in Stevens is perhaps best expressed in its description as the internal world of a human being in "A Word with José Rodríguez-Feo" (*CP* 333); this appears as a question, lending uncertainty to the remark, but even "questions are remarks" for Stevens (*CP* 462). However, there is a certainty about the night's nature in "Prelude to Objects" as the hue of man's self (*CP* 194), but it must be remembered that the poet believed in the multiplicity of the self (*OP* 164).

If the "night" is merely one's internal world, then the question is this: How could it be conducive to the "romance" of the "I" and "you" of the poem? In what way does it oppose that "romance"? Obviously, by being unaware of both, as the poem's first line suggests. The night's ignorance of the commerce between "I" and "you" is seen as knowledge. However, this knowledge, this life, is enveloped by the "night," so that the reader will not have the knowledge the poem contains and conceals without entering the internal world (*CP* 333). In the poem's second line, the declaration of "I" brazenly ignores the knowledge of the "night" in reciprocal opposition, and also of himself. Emulating God's answer to Moses—"I am that I am"—he seems to elevate both night and himself to the level of the Judeo-Christian God. However, the difference between "that" in God's answer and "what" in the declaration-cum-confession of the "I" is crucial. God knew or knows the full meaning of "I am," whereas the question "what am I?" exists in that declaration in the poem. The difference between the certainty in God's answer to Moses and the uncertain assertion in Stevens' line is suggestive of the lack of full knowledge of "what I am"; it points to the human-ness of the "I," to the "bad time" the human being is caught in — in a late poem Stevens inquires about and answers the bearings of man (*CP* 426). On the same line, Stevens' question seems to both ask and answer the question without really answering: "What am I? What I am I am. But what?" At the time of writing "Re-statement," Stevens could not be as assertive as he looks in "In a Bad Time." During the gap of time between the two poems, Stevens might have overcome to some extent the question of "what am I?" so that in the late poem the question of "what have I?" becomes prominent. However, at the moment he is not able to answer "what am I?" Although in both, "what I am I am" and Stevens' uncertain assertion in the second line (the question of "what am I?") exist, the difference in the syntax of the two statements polarizes the meanings. The significative term or the term of significance changes the meaning altogether: "what I am" and "I am," the significative terms appearing at the end with which both sentences attain meaning, if any, suggest that "What I am I am" is more emphatic despite its poverty in comparison with "I am what I am." All the same, the "Re-statement" does want to assert the existence of both the "I" and "night." The "night" *is* because the "I" is not God, for whom it *is not* since He does not have the problem of what or who He is. However, being human, Stevens has to search for an answer in this night of ignorance.

What is heartening is the perception of this very ignorance, which must be removed for the "I" to be able to assert himself like God. Yet the poet-speaker does not completely deracinate the "night," he merely reduces it to background in the final stanza. And this is no small achievement since the very distinction he is able to make between "night" and himself is sufficient, perhaps because it is the best that humans could do. The perception of this difference enables the poet-speaker to know his self, and he immediately begins to concentrate on the self. At the very thought of the self, and within the gap between the first two stanzas, he perceives yet another presence — the "you." An exploration in this introspection reveals an intro-retro-active presence of the "you."

In "The Snow Man," this presence was vaguely perceived or specified; in "A Dish of Peaches" it was recognized, but as "that I" and not as "you." These two poems were perhaps reluctant to accept the crass otherness of that presence because they could not establish a relationship with it. In "Re-statement," however, the "I" (presumably the poet) not only recognizes its otherness but is also able to establish a relationship with that presence, which is the Other. This relationship between self and Other, this commerce between "I" and "you," is what Stevens calls "romance." This romance is essential throughout Stevens' poetry; it gives the sense of the mother-child unity. The loss of (or the sense of) unity with the mother, this otherness, is what motivates the unconscious; this is what starts building the Other, the term that unites the sense of alienation and otherness and is written also as (m)Other. Human beings are thus, right from the birth, caught in an eternal struggle to eradicate their alienation from the (m)Other. However, since the birth itself and the subsequent imposition of language on the child ensure its entry into the symbolic order of language and culture,[16] the human desire for the unity with the (m)Other remains unfulfilled. The meek, because inevitable, acceptance of the symbolic order leaves the struggle for that unity entirely on the psychic level; even a sexual relationship with the mother cannot take one back to the pre-natal state as unity. The struggle for that mythic unity is compensated, through the agency of the *moi*, by the struggle of making the outside world the *moi*'s alter ego (the other), the purpose of which is to eradicate the distance between the self and the other in order to attain that unity, which is also referred to as *jouissance* by Lacan. This search for *jouissance* is indeed the hub of human relationships. Nevertheless, these external relationships are only one way of seeking that *jouissance*. Besides, apart from "Owl's Clover" (*OP* 43–71), which Stevens preferred not to include in the *Collected Poems*, the poet does not show keen interest in social issues. And it is probable that the external world may not always be congenial.

What if the world without does not conform to the *moi* desire of making it its alter ego? Or, to use Stevens' language, what if the *moi* fails to make the world its mirror or cannot find its mirror image in the outside world (*CP* 383)? This is when one becomes an introvert, since the only way that remains to seek *jouissance* is to look within. This is when the introse relationships develop and are accentuated. There are many terms to refer to a person who thus becomes introverted or an "introspective voyager" (*CP* 29): schizophrenic, paranoid, hysteric, neurotic, delusional, psychotic and so on. Lovers of Stevens may not like the idea of calling him by any such name; however, it is impossible to reject outright the fact that much of his poetry reveals various psychic phenomena observed in persons suffering from some mental disorder. The possibility that Stevens suffered from some mental disorder has already been verified in the chapter "Prolegomena"; one needs to go deeper, though. Jahan Ramazani imputes the "morbid interests of *Harmonium*" to the three deaths in the Stevens family (570); referring to Freud, he makes another but more important comment that "the melancholic mourner," which the Stevens of *Harmonium* certainly is, "is more likely to grieve over an unconscious than a conscious loss" (569). *Manque*, or "lack," is Lacan's word for such unconscious loss. This occurs when the "mirror" of the outside world is shattered; the shock thereof penetrates into the unconscious too. However, this lack not only develops morbid interests but also gives rise to all kinds of interests in the hope of filling it (e.g., fetishism, voyeurism, day-dreaming, hallucinations, etc.) or creates a complex of emotions and feelings akin to mistrust and phobias. No human being is an exception to these phenomena, but in certain cases they are raised to a higher level as compared to the so-called normal person, and are thus called patients. Thus, the variety of interests and the complex emotions and feelings — accentuated as they are — of *Harmonium* owe their impetus to some lack in the poet himself; they are, moreover, further pursued throughout the rest of the poetry. These things need not offend Stevens' devotees since in spite of the early psychic abnormality he was a good psychoanalyst himself; if he did not recuperate himself, he came very close to doing so, as his later poetry testifies. Abandoning the pathological introversion, his poetry shows a positive movement toward finding what will suffice to make the outside world the mirror of his *moi*. If *Harmonium* reflects unhealthiness, it is because Stevens had become "too rigidly attached either to reality or to unconscious processes"— this is how a practicing psychoanalyst accounts for the "unhealthy" state of the psyche (Feirstein 437). Stevens begins to create "health" after *Harmonium*— with "The Blue Guitar," to be more precise. It is no coincidence that the process of creating "health" begins with this poem; Feirstein points out that Susan Den's model of "health" is "the artist in the act of creation" (437). One would do well to recall the pose of Picasso's "Old Guitarist" that the poet seems to assimilate with his own guitarist: "bending over" his instrument "to improvise" (Patke 81), in the act of creation. In fact, Lacan emphasizes the need for reconstitution of the psychic patient's imaginary order if he is to recover, and "the blue guitar" in Stevens represents imagination — again, it is not a coincidence that the poet's view of the imagination comes close to Lacan's imaginary order.

When the relationship with the other, the outside world, is disturbed, the subject undergoes a mental upheaval, and is forced to look "within." Thus, the "you" of "Re-statement" cannot be found in the world without. It reminds one of the famous case of President Schreber, in which both Freud and Lacan showed great interest (see Freud's "Case of Paranoia," *SE* 12: 1–82; and Lacan's S III). Lacan locates Schreber's crisis in his inability to become a father, in the lack in him of the signifier *being a father* (S III 293).[17] It is indeed an effect created by his inability to find himself as part of the cultural exchange (i.e., copulation with a woman and becoming a father). Fortunately, Stevens did not have this problem. However, the poet did suffer from the loss of some signifier. There are many instances in the poetry when he speaks of a vaguely specified signifier that is referred to as "syllable" or "alphabet," which is qualified with adjectives that speak of its loss (see *CP* 113, 179, 260, 267, 268, 294, 516, 530).

The signifier that seems to have been lost in him must be the *Name-of-the-Father*, or the phallus[18]; note that Stevens also refers to this signifier in various disguises: it figures as "cock" (*CP* 75, 82, 377) and as the "bean pole" in section IX of *Credences of Summer* (*CP* 377) (which resembles the human phallus), and the description of the "X" in the last stanza of "The Motive for Metaphor" (*CP* 288) evokes the image of the erect human phallus. It is also important to see that Stevens does show an understanding of the significance of both its loss and recovery. This has to be imputed to the great disturbance that occurred in his family over his marriage with Elsie Moll. The period between 1908 and 1912 was a crisis period in the poet's life, and his *Harmonium* was largely composed between 1912/1913 and 1923. If the deaths of his father (1911), mother (1912), and sister (1919) were responsible for the poet's interest in death as reflected in *Harmonium*, then certainly there must be other items in the volume that owe themselves to things that happened during that period of crisis; it is necessary to explore these things, for they kept haunting Stevens throughout his life. Most, if not all, of the secrets of his poetry, thus, may be found in *Harmonium* years. It would be a mistake to say that he had no problem because he became one of the most successful surety-claims lawyers, for his success in the business could be looked upon as an attempt to cover over what he lacked — namely the *Name-of-the-Father*; that is to say, he lacked the signifier phallus. This signifier is the pivot of (sexual) identity, and hence of the sense of "being." His search for an answer to the question "what am I?" is part of the question of "being."

Lacan says with reference to Schreber, who lacked the signifier *being a father*, that the signifier "procreation" or "paternity" can mean something to a subject only if he or she has some understanding of or relation with the signifier "death" (S III 293). The same can be applied to almost any term or signifier precisely because death forms an opposition to everything that *is* and that is symbolized by the human being. Thus, for "to live" to have its full meaning, one must have some understanding of death. Schreber's wife's abortions were his closest connection with death (S III 308), and the three deaths in the Stevens family were the poet's closest relation with it. One thus might feel that they know the significance of what it is *to be*, but it must be remembered that by an understanding of or relation with death, Lacan is merely suggesting a vague understanding of death that all of us have. A closer relation with it — for example, the death of a loved one — is likely to strip one of even the vague understanding of it, for then one finds it very difficult to account for the death; such loss of the meaning of a signifier is the signifier's repression into the unconscious, from which it dominates the subject, as in the melancholic. One would not grieve too much over the death of a loved one if one could account for this phenomenon. This accounting is nothing but a kind of symbolization of death, which makes it mean something. We know there were races that celebrated death because they accounted for it as an entry into a better world, or heaven, as closeness with God. Even today, the concept of *fiadeen* in Islam, meaning an entry into a happy world of Allah's grace after one's death in religious action, is respected by the community; the messages or communications of the persons involved in the 9/11 tragedy bear out the proof. Accounting for death in this way does alleviate the grief over and fear of death — not only for those who willingly involve themselves in these actions but also for their relatives. For those who fail to "apprehend" and account for death, even the thought or mention of it can prove baneful, since for them death has become a signifier without meaning; more deaths around such a person would make this signifier more meaningless and thus grab him or her by the neck, as it were, and rule him or her that much more forcefully (S III 185). Stevens' interest in death, hence in "being" or "self," suggests that the recurrence of death in the family gave rise to and sustained it.

What made him ask of himself "what am I?" is a more important question here. This is where his father's death attains its full significance; it has to do with the Oedipal complex in the poet. Although we do not have as much knowledge of Stevens' relationship with his mother as of that with his father, some remembrances — and the poet's references to his mother in his poetry — shed light on it and are useful. Stevens' mother, Margaretha Stevens, took good care of young Wallace because he looked sick and delicate (B 264). This is suggestive of the attachment between Wallace and his mother. Wagner has already discussed this attachment as pathological. Stevens' situation here reminds of the relationship between Gertrude and her son Paul in D. H. Lawrence's *Sons and Lovers*. However, Paul's father is a moron, which is why the son remains attached to the mother until his own death. Stevens' case is different. His father was an impressive and respected person. He was very practical, as his letters to Wallace indicate. He enjoyed a respectable social standing; Wallace certainly respected him. Thus there was no question of the resolution of the Oedipal complex. In fact, Wallace's love affair with Elsie was the sign of its resolution, because usually the son replaces his mother with another woman in resolving the complex. And unfortunately, it was at this important stage of Wallace's life that his father interfered. As long as Garrett was giving advice, everything was all right. It was at a time when the son was acceding to manhood that the father started showing signs of resistance to Wallace's attachment with Elsie. In a letter of 17 November 1907, even though he merely offered an indirect suggestion, Garrett wrote Wallace about how good it was to marry a girl from a family having "useful" connections (B 259).

However, Elsie came from a poor family. Wallace could have foreseen at this point in time what was coming, could have anticipated his father's resistance to his marriage. The relationship between Garrett and Wallace has a lot of importance from a psychoanalytic point of view. It is true that they had a quarrel in 1908 over Wallace's probable marriage with Elsie, after which they never spoke with each other again, but this does not mean that they had rivalry between them — at least, the son did not look upon his estranged relationship with his father in that way. It is true that Garrett was a sort of person who would impose himself on the important decisions of his sons' lives, decisions regarding their careers and marriages, but this represented the father's love, care, and concern for his sons. Yet his opposition to Wallace's marriage with Elsie made the Garrett–Wallace relationship look inhuman to the sensitive son (S III 204). Garrett's aggressive behavior might have had the same castrating effect on Wallace as in a story Lacan tells us of a woman whose permanent aggressiveness gave rise to homosexual tendencies in her son (see *É* 10).

Reflecting on Lacan's thoughts now gives us a different view of Garrett's character with respect to Wallace, suggesting what an imposing person Garrett was. His incessant suggestions, advice at times bordering on warnings, were perhaps part of his authoritarianism to some extent. Wallace once wrote Jerald Hatfield that he became "a lawyer, a Presbyterian, and a Democrat" because his father was all these things (qtd. in Rehder 7). This implies that it was the way shown by his father that Wallace took. Rehder further adds here that Garrett had a similar effect on Wallace's brothers; however, the father's influence on Wallace was comparatively greater, for, apart from other things, both were interested in reading and writing poetry. This greater intimacy could also have played a part in accentuating Wallace's suffering. The son living under the shadow of the influential father, says Lacan, undergoes a psychopathic crisis, forcing him to take the feminine position (S III 204). The description of the "father" in the concerned passage in Lacan more or less suits Garrett Stevens. However, Wallace did not look upon his father the way the psychoanalyst describes here: had the poet looked upon his father as authoritarian, as behaving in a unilateral and monstrous manner — even though Garrett indeed behaved in this very manner with Wallace — then there would have developed the feeling of fear breeding rivalry in his mind, whereby the son could have turned a blind eye to the father (S III 205). In reality, Stevens' regret for what happened between them suggests that this was not the case, that he still had the same respect for his father in his mind throughout the rest of his life as before 1907: he could assert in 1943 that his father was not wont to push his way, that the Stevens children loved him and also were afraid of him (*L* 454). In such a situation, the subject finds himself in an "imaginary capture" by the paternal personality (the father), whose image functions as a reference point for the subject to see his own image (S III 205, 204). This self-image cannot identify itself with the father; it rather identifies with the mother or anything that would serve to establish a sexualized relation with the father (S III 205).

Since Garrett Stevens manifested himself through his fatherly relationship with his son and not through an authoritarian position (see S III 205; Garrett used the phrase "our home" while scolding his son about rushing to Elsie's house every time he came to Reading [B 256]), there was no question of fear or rivalry—at least not from Wallace's side; instead, the letters exchanged between the poet and his father, the father's influence on the poet, the poet's alienation from him and subsequent regret about the quarrel and the guilt-feeling thereof, are indicative of his "imaginary capture" by the father's image. This could have led him to adopt a feminine function with reference to his father's image, possibly through identification with his mother or with Elsie or more probably with both simultaneously (the last seems most likely because Wallace's desire for Elsie was yet to be legalized or to be brought into the symbolic order of culture). And since the son replaces the mother in his unconscious with another woman in resolving the Oedipal complex more fully and legally by marrying, the lack of legalization in Wallace's case at the time of the quarrel left his mother and Elsie virtually on the same plane and place in his unconscious, almost without any conflict between them, and conflict is necessary for the complex's resolution. In short, Wallace's desire for Elsie, who had almost supplanted the mother, was threatened with non-legalization by the father's resistance, thus leaving the replacement suspended on his psychic plane indefinitely. This is why Wagner seems absolutely correct in observing that the "wife and the mother were joined in Stevens' unconscious" (91).

The other side of the story—namely, Stevens' psychical relationship with his father—deserves equal attention. They were certainly alienated from each other. From the son's point of view, it was "dehumanizing"; Lacan suggests that this is symptomatic of the loss or repression of some signifier, for which the subject will try to compensate throughout his life (S III 205). The signifier in question here is the *Name-of-the-father* (or that which it stands for: the phallus). Stevens' poetry confirms that he suffered from his dispossession of the signifier; from the Lacanian perspective, he failed to realize the signifier *father* at the symbolic level, leaving himself with the paternal function that was no longer part of the Oedipal triad (S III 204–5). The father's alienation from the triad leaves him meaningless on the subject's imaginary plane, yet functioning as a pivot for the subject to see and recognize himself through the father's question with regard to the subject's identity: "What are you? A man, or a woman?" In other words, it is what enables the subject to ask of himself, as Stevens did, "What am I?" Lacan comments that despite this situation the subject can lead a compensatory life with apparently normal behavior for a long time; however, suddenly, this normalcy may be shattered due to the irruption of the Other, interrupting and disturbing the internal (romantic) discourse (S III 205). Stevens showed all these traits in his life and poetry. He did live a compensated life for the most part, with intermittent decompensations in which the Other irrupted suddenly and, at times, even spoke to him; his poetry is studded with instances of this. His adopting a feminine position led him to the question "What am I?" or, similarly, "What it is to be a man?" or "Am I a man or a woman?" or even "Am I?"

Thus, in "Farewell without a Guitar" (*OP* 99), we see the poet lamenting in his characteristically oblique and secret way the lost masculine identity that *was.* Stevens could only retroactively conceive of his lost masculinity (this poem was composed in 1954): he not only remembers the lost masculine identity, but his words also betray the desire for remembering; the memory is painful, though, since remembering is like getting hit with blows (the Old French *bufe*, from which "buffet" is derived, also means "blow"). Due to this situation, Stevens indeed felt like a patient who, he says, constantly suffered from a question (*CP* 331). In fact, what was missing in him was the signifier *Name-of-the-Father*; the basic question therefore was "What is the [*Name-of-the-*] *father*?," which gave rise to a string of related questions quoted above, culminating in or leading to the question of "being" itself. Lacan believed that neurotics are faced with a question that is concerned with the lack of the signifier, and that the question is addressed to the Other (S III 202). This question has its origin in the loss or lack of a signifier and, since a signifier is always related to other signifiers, the question may involve the whole set of those signifiers (S III 205), or there may be a string of related questions involving the concerned signifiers. These signifiers or questions are in fact related to *being*, the most primal signifier (S III 170).

The lack of a signifier is nothing but its repression into the unconscious. And since the *Name-of-the-Father* is responsible for subjectivity — for the subject's sense that he *is*— its repression in Stevens led him to the question of being itself. When Lacan suggests that the question may first ask itself (S III 202), he means that it is from the field of the Other, where the signifier is repressed, that the question interpellates the subject ("What are you?"), who then asks of himself "What am I?" in his attempt to (find an) answer (to) the question coming from the Other; however, says Lacan, the answer to the question cannot come from the Other, as has already been discussed in this chapter in relation to "who speaks?" from "A Dish of Peaches." The Other is the other of speech (S III 168), but one who does not answer the subject's question, thus creating the mirage of a monologue. In reality it is at least a dialogue, even though the possibility of a trilogue is never out of the question. Stevens' mention of the "you" or "he" in many instances is a reference to the Other; that is why it has been difficult to see who the "you" (for example, in "Hymn from a Watermelon Pavillion" [*CP* 88–89] or "Re-statement" or in the epigraph to the *Notes*) is, or who the "he" in "The Bird with the Coppery Keen Claws" (82–83) or *Chocorua* (*CP* 296–302) is. The discourse between the subject and the Other is one that is aimed at *being* (S III 138), for it is this discourse that sustains the subject at the level of "being"[19]; any failure in it threatens his sense of being, the reason why such subjects love their illness (S III 214).

It is this discourse, which the patients love, that is romanticized in "Re-statement." The word "romance" in the poem's title is puzzling. However, the poet's own question of "What am I?" or "What it is to be a man?" seems to solve the reader's problem. When sexual identity, conferred upon the subject by the symbolic world and cherished by him as part of his being, is threatened — and the poet's case very much goes this way — the subject opposes it with all his being. This happens such that the subject undergoes, psychically, a change of sex — as a mode of resistance — to protect his or her virility, for basically it is castration that he or she fears and hates.[20] Insofar as realization of the Oedipal complex is concerned, normally the subjects of both sexes have to go through identification with the father since the phallus, which they think of as being with the father, is a unique symbol (S III 176).[21] It is only at the time of the resolution of the complex that their paths diverge: the male subject's path does not change, but the female subject seeks to identify with the female sex — the (m)Other. Nevertheless, when, after the successful resolution of the Oedipal complex, the male subject becomes neurotic due to some "accident" that threatens his sexual identity, he gets identified with the female sex in order to protect his virility. The phallus is lost or repressed, and becomes the Other of his desire, because it then attains a certain grandeur with respect to his ego, which is identified with the female sex. Lacan further comments that in such a case, the subject is faced with the "other," who is worthless in comparison with the Other of his desire; this is extremely frustrating — the other with small "o" is nihilating for the subject (S III 209).

This explains why Stevens behaved with people (the other), in general, in a strange manner; his imaginary alienation from them almost always made him suspicious of their intentions toward him. It also answers why the question of reality (as the other) became so important for him that he sought to make it bearable or even pleasant, and to see himself against it, as one lion against the other lion (*CP* 175). Thus, Stevens' position was one of being captured between the Other and the other, a position that problematizes not only the subject's discourse but his acts as well (S III 209). Such discourse may also be observed in a normal subject, but in psychoses where the *moi*-Other dialectic gains prominence, it becomes more articulate as compared to that in the normal subject and hinders the subject's own speech. Stevens showed these symptoms in his speech. Elder Olson, a poet on the faculty at the University of Chicago, observes that Stevens often meditated and, when he spoke, did not make "connected argument," making his speech "a series of ... remarks"; he further comments that Stevens did not think consecutively and his speaking style was like his "Adagia" (B 211). Wagner thus feels, "There was a strong component of primary process thinking in [Stevens'] secondary process discourse ... probably symptomatic of neurosis or some developmental failure" (86). Here, one can make out the "interruption" or "interpellation" in the poet's speech; what must have been responsible for it was the "discourse of the Other" that he had become fond of hearing, which, Olson says, disturbed him.

Therefore, the "you" of "Re-statement" is to be treated as masculine, as the "paternal imago" (S III 209), as the Other bearing the phallic signifier (S III 194); this obviously means that the "I" in the poem (who speaks it) is to be identified with the female sex that is the poet himself (Stevens' probable restructuration as feminine is further discussed in chapter 4). Without this kind of reading the poem would not be a re-statement of romance that it claims to be. In the poem, Stevens positions himself as the woman of the "you," the Other (see S III 77), like Schreber. Schreber's repugnance to adopting a feminine position toward his father replaced the latter with the Other, whom he referred to as God (S III 89). Stevens' strong opposition to his father's wish that he should not marry Elsie suggests his reluctance to be the father's woman. However, whereas Schreber's father is replaced with God, Stevens' is replaced with "you," the Other of speech. Stevens had within him a man and a woman, best expressed in "Burghers of Petty Death" (*CP* 362), where the man was his Other, from which the phallic pulses originated, and the woman was himself (his *moi*), who trembled before those pulses like Nanzia Nunzio before Ozymandias (*CP* 396). And the mode of this romance between him and his Other is, invariably, speech, as if in the Other's speech he touched his being. Hence Rosenmeier's reading of Stevens' work as an "androgynous creativity" (143). Stevens had accepted the feminine position with regard to the Other so completely that he even boasted of feeling completely virile without the phallus, and also of being important for the Other's perfection (*CP* 396). It is not a mistake, therefore, to see a romantic, even erotic, relationship between the "I" and "you" of "Re-statement"; it is nothing but the I's attempt to get an answer to the question "Am I?" in the sense that there he is testifying to himself, and to the "you," through the relationship, that *(s)he is*. The "you" also speaks to the "I" through what Lacan refers to as "procession of forms and emanations" (S III 67). Thus, there is a relationship of exchange and influence between the "I" and "you." Freud saw that such an erotomaniac relationship exists in the paranoiac and based it on the utterance "*I love him* and *you love me.*" On the basis of the ways to negate the utterance — suggested by Freud himself as characterizing the ways of the subject's delusion and deciding the precise variety of the paranoiac disorder (see "On the Mechanism of Paranoia" 62–65; S III 41) — Lacan interprets Schreber's erotic relationship with what Schreber believed to be God: "*I do not love him, I love God,* and *God loves me*" (S III 89), where the "him" is the father and God represents the paternal imago as raised, elevated to a vital form of grandeur. This is because the subject hates castration, the pivot of which is the father (thus, *I do not love him*); in a case like this, the subject removes the father, who now exists merely as a nihilating other, and places his affection onto something more sublime, and hopes to obtain satisfaction from this delusional relation of grandeur (S III 89) (thus, *I love God*).

In Stevens' case, there is no need to replace the "you" with God; retaining Freud's "you," Lacan's gloss can be read thus: "*I do not love him, I love you,* and (reciprocally) *you love me.*" The "I" is the subject who speaks these utterances; however, since it is not easy to point out clearly who or what part of the subject speaks, Lacan puts a question mark around him (S III 41). The "you," as said before, is the Other. Lacan seems to suggest that the "he" in the utterance is the other, who tries to be a master in relation to the subject (S III 93); it is clear that the "he" is the father in the cases of both Schreber and Stevens. Since the "he" is an other of the same sex, Lacan's interpretation also involves his view of narcissism (which is unmistakably one of Stevens' favorite themes — this is explicit in "Of Modern Poetry," which will be discussed later in this chapter; he also gives due attention to this theme at the end of the prose part of his essay, "Three Academic Pieces" [*NA* 79–80]). Lacan explains narcissism with an illustration of the male stickleback, who, when attacked by another male stickleback, displays erotic behavior when he is confused in relating himself with his attacking counterpart (see S III 94–95). The neurotic's situation in his relation with the father is similar. The father is like the attacking male stickleback, who tries to re-adopt mastery over the subject, forcing him to defend himself; this enforces a change of behavior reflecting eroticism. Though the other is thus necessary for the erotic behavior, there is a difference between the sticklebacks and human beings. Even though the neurotic adopts a feminine position before the father, he literally displaces his love onto someone more powerful than the authoritative father or the other; it is the Other whom he loves, perhaps in the hope of survival or of negating the other (or the father). For all this, the existence of the father is essential for the neurotic and so it is no wonder that Stevens' father continued to exist on his imaginary plane and in poetry.

The declaration of the oneness of "I" and "you" in "Re-statement" is the culminating point of the erotic relationship; yet both retain their subjectivity, their separate identity, because the "I" places a great deal of importance on his own specular image (being essentially narcissistic), and also because the Other keeps his own subjectivity, his otherness, and remains almost a stranger to the subject (S III 64, 274). However, the Other is the locus of recognition for the (neurotic) subject (S III 168); it is thus also the Other of desire. This is why the "romance" between "I" and "you" is so precious to the "I," so much so that he does not care for the father or for the other—the diminutive and annihilating reality—which is relegated to marginality and referred to as no more than a background of their selves. The reality's ignorance of the "I" and "you" is met with a reciprocal ignorance, since the relationship between them is sufficient for the "I."

All the romance in life is essentially centered on narcissism. "Of Modern Poetry" (*CP* 239–40) promotes narcissism, which should not be confused with the commonly understood, narrow meaning of egotism even though the ego is at the heart of narcissism. Thus, since the "I" appears too many times in the work of the Romantic poets, especially in Wordsworth, it would be a mistake to call them "egotistic" in the usual sense. Pearce and Miller seem to have realized the true meaning of narcissism in the Stevens poem and its centrality in human life, for they use its full text as an epigraph for their anthology of essays on Stevens.

Ann M. Gallagher is not sure whether the poet demonstrates "willingly or not" that one cannot leave the mind behind while describing the act of the mind (93), but a closer reading would reveal that he did it willingly, as he found it impossible to leave the mind behind. Yet Stevens *wanted* to leave the mind behind; the purpose was to free the mind once the act, the description, was completed, because only this would open the way for narcissistic satisfaction through looking objectively at the described act. While the literary world is divided on the issue of approach to reading/writing, Stevens strikes a balance between the two opposing lines of thought on the issue, which has given rise to the chief dichotomy of the subjective/personal/biographical and the objective/impersonal/textual approaches. If narcissism seeks to bridge the abyss between self and other, Stevens would prefer that literary work do the same. There can be no guarantee of (complete) success here; however, this can at least maintain a kind of balance between the subjective and objective forces. As Miller points out, such equilibrium is necessary, for if these opposing forces "were ever to coincide, the poem would disappear" (*Poets of Reality* 234); this "poem" is of both the "mind" *and* its "act."

Before actually coming to the theme of narcissism, it would be worth exploring the details that support it. To begin with, Stevens clarifies that all poetry is modern in its own time (*OP* 244); the syntax "has ... always had" makes this explicit. Modern poetry is viewed as a continuum of presentnesses, which is implied in the grammatically incomplete first sentence of the poem. Without the expected form of *to be*, the sentence lacks any indication of time, but shows the continuity of the act of the mind through the gerund form of "find." The second sentence speaks of the origin of modern poetry: the mind must "find," or it can "repeat," from the "script" in order to give rise to it. The use of these words commands special attention. "Repeat," from the context in which it is used in line 3, seems to suggest "imitation"—with almost a Platonic sense of "mimesis"—from the "script." It also seems to have been used as distinct from "find"; hence the rise of the notion that "find" suggests originality or inventive genius of the mind. This does not, however, relegate "repeating."

The word "script" may mean all the knowledge in the world, including both known and unknown. It could also be considered analogous to Barthes' concept of the "already-written," or the "general text" (*S/Z* 18–21, 82). Barthes' view is that the author cannot "express" anything but can only mix the chains of discourses that constitute the "general text," and that "the writer contains an immense dictionary" of discourses that "interweave in the text" (Selden 305); this "grouping of codes [or discourses], as they enter into the work, into the movement of the reading, constitute a braid (text, fabric, braid: the same thing)" (Barthes, *S/Z* 160). Barthes' interest was in decreasing the importance of the author and restoring the place of the reader. Stevens also shows keen interest in the activity of reading[22]; besides, writing and reading are analogous, respectively, to speaking and listening, functions with which Stevens' poem is deeply concerned. In fact, the poem seems to form alignments—reading-listening-finding and writing-speaking-repeating—that may further be aligned respectively with the subjective/personal/biographical approach and the objective/impersonal/textual approach. Being one of the first generation of critics who attempted to promote reading and poststructuralist tenets, one can understand the extreme conclusion of believing in the author's death that Barthes reaches. However, Stevens does not underestimate the author-ity of the mind. Thus, if "repeating from the script" is important to Stevens (and closer to Barthes' ideology), "finding" is no less so. And yet, the poststructuralist critic must see that Stevens does not allow the mind any scope for invention as such: the mind can only "find" or discover—obviously from what already exists, from what Barthes refers to as the "already-written." In support of Barthes, Stevens uses "find" in much the same sense when he writes that the mind has "to find from war..."; here, "war" is the "script," the "already-written" (the word "script" also appears with reference to war in "Gigantomachia" [*CP* 289]). At the same time, though, Stevens preserves the originality of the mind (as a movement away from repetition [*OP* 177]), since it alone is capable of giving the mind a measure of the satisfaction it seeks: the lines about war suggest that the mind has to be selective in order to meet the criteria that what it finds must "suffice" and give happiness; the mind's originality lies in selecting a particular part or aspect from out of the whole "script," for success or satisfaction depends on the selection. Thus, Stevens' use of the word "find" approximates the Aristotelian sense of "mimesis"; like him, Stevens gives due credit to the mind's creative vision, and thus to the subjective element in art. However, the selection alone will not suffice; merely "finding" is not enough—that is, subjective approach alone is not sufficient. The actual work of art is, in fact, a skillful "repetition" of what the mind "finds." It has to meditate, be slow and exact, and give greater scope to skill, to technique, to carefulness (hence to the objective approach to speaking or writing as opposed to the natural, emotional, narcissistic—that is, the subjective—approach). Stevens thus demonstrates that both subjectivity/personality and objectivity/impersonality *must* unite in a "modern" poem—*must* owing to his repeated use of "has to," which is impartially applied both to "find" (as analogous to listening/reading) in line 10 and to "speak" (analogous to repeating/writing) in line 13, which is closely associated with "repeat" of line 14.

Let us now see how the poem uses its own terminology to lead to a narcissistic satisfaction. Speech or writing is an act due to which "finding" becomes "repeating," a skillful process through which the "finding" is objectified and made into a "repetition" of the "finding." The author speaks or writes to objectify his "finding." There is a project involved in this objectification—that of narcissistic satisfaction. Those who "find" but cannot speak or write it out properly know how unfortunate or dissatisfied a lot they are. In Lacan's view, the human being is essentially fragmented and incomplete (*É* 2). He seeks the wholeness and completeness in and through the other, the world outside. The incompleteness and divided nature of existence is at the heart of narcissism. Perhaps this primordial fragmentation, alienation, or division has penetrated into other human phenomena as well: there is no speech without listening, no writing without reading, no "repeating" without "finding"; just as "monologue" is a "mirage" in Lacan's thought, so any part in each of the above pairs is a mirage without its counterpart. The *moi* needs the other for its own reflection, with which it identifies itself. However, danger waits on either side of narcissism: if identification is accomplished to its fullest, the subject's fate would be similar to what Narcissus faced in the end; if the other does not comply with the *moi* desire of making it its alter ego, the subject faces a sense of profound alienation. Similarly, if the *moi* speech or thought is not echoed, which it must hear, alienation will be the result. The subject will never be united with the other—that is, it will never be fully identified with the other; yet it is the illusion of identification that maintains the *moi*. The persistence of this illusion of narcissistic satisfaction itself is the state of equilibrium. Hearing the echo of one's speech from the other is part of narcissistic satisfaction; to this end, the other is essential. The work of art becomes the other for an artist or its connoisseur in which his speech and emotions are alienated and by which they are echoed, giving him or her immense satisfaction. Stevens recognizes the importance of this echo. "Hearing-oneself-speak" is very much at the heart of his poem. Stevens is clever enough to evade any mention of the speaker, who is also the listener, though for convenience one could call him the *moi*; like Lacan, the poet also kept wondering about "who speaks?" This is the reason why the ambiguity surrounding his use of the pronoun "it" cannot be resolved: Is it the "mind" that speaks or is it the "poem" as the other that speaks? Therefore, both the poet and psychoanalyst maintain the otherness of one's own speech, or rather, the half-otherness, since half of the total sense of speech convinces the subject that it is he who speaks. Yet the fact that he hears the same speech suggests that the subject is the listener; thus, he himself becomes the listener who listens to himself. This is how the (subjective) speech is received objectively. This is how Stevens integrates subjectivity and objectivity, forming an essential dialectic that he considers the mark of "modern poetry."

The human subject has no satisfaction unless his desires, thoughts, and opinions are echoed by and as of the other. Why would he need the other to be his alter ego? Because, using Robert Frost's words, "Eden has sunk to grief" (*Collected Poems* 272); because, as Stevens puts it, man's "disinheritance" after the Fall has brought on the "bad time" (*CP* 227, 426)—thereafter, the suffering of alienation became a permanent part of his being (*CP* 427). This is a poetic rendition of what Lacan believes to be the inevitable incompleteness in the human being, the "native insufficiency" (S III 95) that he refers to as a "primordial Discord" (*É* 4). As a result, the ego never attains substantivity, but always remains a specular agency, dependent on the other, seeking that wholeness-as-substantivity by attempting, with the help of the other, to resolve that discord (*É* 2, 4). This is the importance of the other, of the primary identification as in the pre-mirror and mirror stages, or even of the secondary identifications in later life. For this reason, when Lacan says that the structure of all subjectivity is essentially bipolar—that whatever maturity of subjectivity the subject attains, it is simply an anticipation—he is hinting at the native insufficiency (see *É* 10). The subject always attempts to meet this insufficiency, which is always found in the other and does give a certain measure of satisfaction. This is why hearing-oneself-speak is such an important activity, in which there are not two persons speaking, but it is *as if* two persons are speaking. It gives a narcissistic echo of the subject's emotion, as if two people are coming to an accord. The words spoken or exchanged between them give a sense that the subject and the other, to whom he speaks or listens, are one, identified. Since this feeling, this sense of identification with the other, is the *moi*'s ultimate goal, it desires nothing short of it or more. The achievement of this goal lends the human subject a semblance of unity, Oneness, which is one of the connotations of *jouissance*. The meaning of "satisfaction" thus goes well beyond the ordinary meanings of enjoyment or pleasure.

Stevens was perhaps conscious that the other, which the *moi* seeks, could also be one with a capital O — the Other. Like the stage "actor," who mediates between the author and the audience, the *moi* is merely an agency that fluctuates between the Other and the other. The first of the poem's two sentences in which the "actor" figures suggests that he "repeats" from the "script," as if objectively; this is, however, being conscious of the author's separate existence, of his intentionality (subjectivity). In the second occurrence, the "actor" seems to approximate the author; he is presented as a metaphysician-musician, who has no score or "script" before him from which he can "repeat." He is thus a sort of improviser reminiscent of the man with the blue guitar. His description suggests his (subjective) involvement in exploring the dark regions of the psyche, the unconscious itself, of which he has little knowledge. In Lacan, the unconscious is the place of the real, which can be apprehended — if at all, and to whatever extent — only imaginarily. Stevens also believed in imagination as "the only clue to reality" (*NA* 137). In order to approach and apprehend the unconscious or the real or the truth, the "actor/author" must work with the tool of his imaginary/imagination so that he may find that which will suffice. The object is not found as such, though, but it is apprehended in the form of the feeling of having heard the most right sounds. Stevens' love of sounds in poetry is of great importance since they are the origin and aim of feelings, emotions, and thoughts. In sounds, he finds something more than simply ordinary meaning (*CP* 352); for him, they are the means to approach the truth or reality.

What Stevens has done in the course of describing the "mind *in* the act" is that he has also written of the "act *of* the mind." The difference between the "in" of the poem's first line and the "of" of the final line seems deliberate; it is akin to the difference between the subjective "finding" and the objective "repeating" (finding is without a particular object as such, and repeating becomes possible only after the finding; the latter also involves objectivity in the sense that it requires a distance between the subject and the object). The "of" here is much like the Latin *de*, which separates a thing from its object — this is how St. Augustine, says Lacan, explained the word *Ex* by *de* to one of his disciples (S I 253). This is more or less true of most of Stevens' poetry;

he could separate himself from what he wrote and look at it objectively, as if to derive pleasure from it. This is important in light of his estranged relationships with other people. At the same time, though, it allowed him to test his own writing, whether it was good enough. It is akin to a philosopher or a scientist testing their own hypotheses. This is one of the reasons why, although his writing is necessarily poetic, it releases philosophical energy.

Stevens' desire for identification with the other is very much reflected in "Of Modern Poetry"; in fact, it is reflected in many other poems as well. He is not the only writer who shows the need of "hearing" in the other the "echo" of his own acts, but it is the intensity that sticks out in his case. In "Of Modern Poetry," one cannot fail to notice that he does not make the external (real) world the mirror of reflection; instead, he makes his poem the other in order to seek that reflection or echo and derive the satisfaction of Oneness out of it. Arthur Marotti welcomes Ehrenzweig's comment that the relationship between the artist and his work of art is a "good object relationship" since the work of art acts as "a good nursing mother" for the artist, and further remarks that this mother-artifact "accepts her child's aggression and, thus, facilitates his development as a whole person" (483). Lacan would starve first before accepting this since, in his view, such a dyadic relationship really prevents the subject's growth. There is no doubt that Stevens did precisely what Ehrenzweig or Marotti would appreciate—he felt more himself on paper. However, this is a clear indication of a discord with the real world around him. The self is related to the world imaginarily; it is a "mirror relation" (S III 87). If that relation were at stake in the poet's case, the problem was not with the reality but with himself—with his imaginary domain. For that relation to be meaningful, it is the imaginary that needs to be reordered. Is this why the *Ideas of Order* and "The Man with the Blue Guitar," which, respectively, reflect the poet's rage for ordering his chaos and his concern with the imagination, follow the mostly pathological *Harmonium*? The next chapter discusses the poet's views on the imaginary and its importance in human life; it was indeed important to him, for he was the sufferer.

CHAPTER 3

Bits of Blue

> In spite of the prevalence of the imagination in life, it is probably true that the discussion of it in that relation is incomparably less frequent and less intelligent than the discussion of it in relation to arts and letters. (*NA* 147)
>
> [T]he imagination ... tries to penetrate to basic images, basic emotions, and so to compose a fundamental poetry. (*NA* 145)

As one begins to collect Stevens' thoughts on "imagination," it becomes obvious that a sort of theory is evolving. Stevens was a poet and cannot be expected to have presented this theory in a coherent manner either in poetry or prose; however, imagination itself does not function coherently. In the absence of any coherence, the critic is left with the task of exhausting himself in bridging the gap between the demand for coherence and the utter irrationality of the imagination. The experience of Lacan's critics is no different. Both authors preclude consecutive presentation of arguments on the issues they handled, because all the issues they were concerned with, besides being evanescent, are so interrelated and interdependent that they closely inmix and become inseparable. It is only upon a keen observation that some aspect of an issue comes into the domain of the "inward eye," but not as unrelated to the other issue(s). A full view of a particular issue in isolation from the others is impossible. Hence, the treatment of such aspects of an issue might seem isolated, fragmentary, but still natural, since that is how one comes to know them. The strain caused by the conflict between the desire to preserve this naturalness and an awareness of the expectation of logical presentation might be reflected in a critic's account of these authors' thoughts on any given issue; it might look like a *rebus*. Both Stevens and Lacan's works have a style that is impossible to separate from what is stylized, and an understanding of which "involves an interminable analysis based more on the free associations of its parts than its cohesion as a narrative or totality" (Grosz 17–18).

The apparent lexical similarity between Stevens' "imagination" and

Lacan's "imaginary" attracts attention. Comparing their thoughts on the imaginary domain is a startling experience due to the innumerable similarities and closeness between them. Stevens was not equipped with psychoanalytic terminology, but he invented his own. A study like this requires using psychoanalytic terminology in order to methodize and enhance an understanding of Stevens' meditations on this human faculty that are presented in a poetic jargon peculiar to the poet. One has to first see how Lacan characterizes the imaginary before establishing its parallelism with the imagination as Stevens' *fecit*. Lacan's imaginary order is the domain of what Freud called the *imago*, the field of images and image formation, and of relationship interaction or relationship dynamics; the images could be imagined or conscious, real or unconscious. The imaginary functions are nothing but processes like introjection, projection, absorption, expulsion, substitution, displacement, and so forth. By means of these processes, the imaginary perceives the world through forming its images; it also establishes relationships between man and the world (its images), and between or among different images perceived, thus forming a kind of (imaginary) network.

Stevens' work shows the understanding implicit in what Lacan named the "imaginary order." Stevens himself was surprised by the relationship interaction that the imagination brings about when he observed that poetry itself is an "effect of analogy" (*NA* 107). One can easily say that any creative work is, without doubt, one of the effects of the imaginary.[1] More so than Stevens' poetry, his essays are a direct statement on this inevit-*ability* of the imaginary since most parts of these essays are devoted to its modes of functioning and its relation to (and significance in) human life. In "Three Academic Pieces" (*NA* 71–87) Stevens writes about resemblances between things. A passage from the essay, describing the scene of a beach surrounded on its sides by trees and the sea, with the cloudless sky above (*NA* 71–72), reveals that "resemblance" is one of the connotations of the "interaction" among things of the world established through the agency of the imaginary. The passage is not just about relations among things of the Not-Me world but also the relationship between that world and imagination, since Stevens is giving us *his* sense of the landscape (*NA* 119). And almost magically, his words make us speechless as they establish a relationship, in terms of samenesses or differences, with our (or the reader's) sense of the landscape.

The sense of resemblance is, undoubtedly, in the perceiving mind. This is a restatement, or substatement, of one of Stevens' observations: "[W]e live in the mind ... with the imagination" (*NA* 140). The second half of the observation is more important for Stevens, since it is imagination that is responsible for the activity mentioned in the first half; the "with" in that statement almost functions like a subordinating conjunction. The passage referred to above illustrates how things come together to produce a unified picture of themselves; if they do not combine, they can at least be said to interact (obviously by way of imaginary processes) and influence each other. This resemblance or interaction is, according to Lacan, the outcome of the imaginary drive for fusion and agreement with the "other," the goal of which is to deny the difference between self and other, to seek this impossible (sense of) Oneness. Throughout Stevens' poetry, we see his attempts at bridging the gap between self and other and the resultant jubilation or despair. Success in the attempt means obliteration of subjectivity, causing jubilation; failure in it restores, poignantly, the sense of the "abyss" between the perceiving subject and the object (*CP* 437). The poet's poetics is caught in the vicious choice of (not between) the two, for the loss of subjectivity almost means (a metaphorical) death even as the abyss between self and other is unbearable.

Although one cannot shake off the feeling that Stevens uses "analogy" or "resemblance" more as blanket terms, it is impossible to say that he was not particularly conscious of the basic imaginary processes. In fact, as will be discussed later, he did write poems that solely enact these processes. He was aware that the imaginary processes bring the unconscious within the domain of consciousness (ERS 190), as is made explicit in the image of "sheep without a shepherd" that he explores in one of his essays (*NA* 127). Before analyzing that image, Lacan's own illustration of the vase and the bouquet can be utilized for our purpose of understanding some of these processes (see S I 124–42). The images seen by the eye are stored in the unconscious (as) memory (ERS 143). This is the process of internalization or introjection.[2] One has already recorded in one's Other the image of the vase with a bouquet in it by way of introjection. At a later point of time, if the same person is shown a vase without a bouquet, he will imaginatively place one in it. This happens due to the process of projection, whereby the previously recorded image, which exists in the unconscious memory, is projected onto the image of the empty vase. Thus, for the Other, there is always a bouquet in the vase whether there is physically one in it or not. This must have been in Stevens' mind when, in "Hymn from a Watermelon Pavilion," he wrote about the subject of the unconscious that, for it, the watermelon always has the same color (*CP* 88). Here, Stevens uses the image of a cabin for the unconscious. In his poetry, images of home, house, building, theatre, room, cell, cabin, cabinet, cave, cloister, and chrysalis stand for the self or, more generally, the interior of man. He uses them to refer to the unconscious as well. Perhaps, like Lacan, he knew that following Plato's cave, the unconscious was commonly designated as a cellar or cave (S XI 187).

In "Effects of Analogy" (*NA* 107–30), Stevens deals with these processes as he quotes St. Matthew, who in his Gospel said that Jesus saw the people scattered like "sheep without a shepherd" (*NA* 113). As the poet says, the analogy here is certainly not provoked; rather, the imaginary has invoked it almost magically. What is interesting here is that Stevens is conscious that the imagination or the imaginary of St. Matthew chose the image of "sheep without a shepherd" almost without thinking, without deliberate effort (*NA* 113). That image had been recorded or introjected into St. Matthew's unconscious. From all such recorded images only this image was selected. This is nothing but "expulsion" (of other images), one of the imaginary processes. Stevens' interest in the fact that St. Matthew produced the image without deliberate effort shows his awareness of imaginary processes as also participating in the unconscious domain. Further, he shows the understanding of this process as imaginary projection when he compares imagination and reason in terms of the much shorter time required by the former for its "projections" (*NA* 114). All these things point to Stevens' interest in psychical phenomena; his discussion of that image from St. Matthew is essentially psychoanalytic.

Imaginary order is thus responsible for formation of images and relating them among themselves by availing of ever so slight similarity between them; "resemblance" is Stevens' term for it (*NA* 77; see also ERS 157), which lends unity to the whole world. Stevens gives a great importance to this act of relating and binding things together (*NA* 72). It helps one bind oneself to the world. This is its importance in the human life; one's relation with the world is vital, especially for one who has lost it. Stevens' unceasing praise of imagination is often a direct outcome of his alienation from the surrounding world; everyone suffers from this alienation, but in Stevens' case it became an "abyss" (*CP* 437) since he suffered greatly due to the separation from some long-lost unity, which he equated with life (*CP* 236). His elevation of the imagination as a principle that unites and binds together reflects a desire for that unity, and he hoped to "set up a transference paradigm for a cure" through imagination (Arensberg 28). Although the experiences depicted in his poetry of imagination are universal, they are nevertheless his own. Therefore, he was constantly drawn to observing the relations created among things through imaginary phenomena like resemblance, analogy, even unity, among them.

This kind of free play of association between or among things goes on continuously in the poetry. However, this does not mean that there is no limit to the imaginary activity. Stevens knew that the imaginary operates only on the basis of the data that has already been recorded in the Other as knowledge or memory in order to work upon nature, but it cannot create a "new nature" altogether (*NA* 74). Lacan gives importance to the "first images imposed on infant perception" for their role in creating the foundational matrices through which other images are interpreted by way of forming "'hallucinatory' networks of meaning"; it is these original images that build a frame of reference, which in turn is responsible for perception of reality along with hallucinations of signification or meaning in the rest of life (ERS 141–42). It may be said that Stevens' "resemblances" are no different from such "hallucinations," or that they are instances of daydreaming that, in a way, order the mind of a confused person (ERS 142). This obviously leads one to say that the poet is a confused person. Indeed he is, like one who is involved in intellectual work, trying to make things make sense (but he is not a psychotic insofar as he is able to perceive or create "order" out of *his* "chaos" and, more importantly, to remain unobsessed by it). As Stevens would have it, it is the imagination that enables us to find order in chaos (*NA* 153). This can be easily observed in the way poets resolve their confusion. Donne's attempt at "canonization" of lovers (57–59) or, for that matter, various poets' discovery of similarity in totally dissimilar things may be cited as examples. This phenomenon does not remain only at the level of perception; it comes into the poet's expression, especially in figures of speech. All figures of speech come into being as products of what Lacan terms "hallucinations," or what Stevens calls "resemblances." Consider these examples: Robert Burns finding resemblance between the beloved and rose (simile); a lock of a child leading toward imagining the child himself (metonymy) (*NA* 75). Therefore, Stevens even goes on to make resemblance the basis of all connotations (*NA* 75). One may thus generalize that all human beings, not merely poets or artists, perceive such resemblances, and this could be observed in their expressions.

Stevens had realized that dealing with imagination was not an easy task because of the difficulty of pinning it down or catching it in words that would represent some sort of theory. He confessed that it is difficult to justify the value of imagination or to theorize the role of imagination since it resists fixity (*NA* 149, 152). Its role as well as value cannot be fixed or justified except at particular points and in specific instances. He knew that any stable image of the world is a deformation or falsification of the intrasubjective dynamics (see Gallop 61). Portraying Lacan's imaginary, Anika Lemaire writes that "everything in the human mind and its reflexive life is in a state of flux before the fixation is effected by the symbol, a fixation which, at the very least, tempers the incessant sliding of the mutations of being and of desire" (61). Although Lacan could be said to have succeeded in theorizing it, yet the fact that he had to do so by always referring to the other two orders points to the difficulty of formalizing it (ERS 141). In saying that the imagination does not allow us to be content with any stable image of the world, Stevens also speaks of the control of imagination over the mind. Ragland-Sullivan likewise says that it is the imaginary processes that structure the mind and, in a way, control it (ERS 138). Even though Stevens admits the problem of justifying the value of the imagination, his habit of exemplifying it through his prose and poetry does evolve a kind of theory of the imagination and seems to assign a very important role for it, as in Lacan. The psychoanalyst, on the other hand, did not care for exemplifying his theories; he was concerned with basic structures and their dynamics. If Stevens was not particularly inclined to theorize, it was because he wanted to be a poet.[3] However, his keen observations of the working and modes of imagination are certainly enough to raise him at least to the level of a psychoanalyzing poet. And the joy for the critic lies not only in substantiating Lacanian theories with examples from Stevens' work but also in experiencing those phenomena both subjectively and objectively, thus enriching his sense of himself and of the world — to use Stevens' term — by "analogy."

Stevens must have searched for the impetus behind the insatiability of imagination, and he found it in desire. Helen Vendler has paid attention to the pervasive role of desire in Stevens' poetry in her book bearing a very suggestive title: *Words Chosen Out of Desire*. In adult life, the imaginary childhood experiences of repression,[4] which deny the child the sense of wholeness or Oneness (and the *jouissance* thereof), take the form of a substitutive imaginary text. This imaginary text is thus always marked with a sense of loss or lack of the primordial order. Hence the imaginary is a function of the desire for overcoming that repression or loss. The imaginary thus linked with desire becomes, like desire itself, object-oriented and object-seeking in order to fulfill the desire or to recover what has been lost. It is therefore obvious that the function of resemblance, being part of the imaginary relationship dynamic, is object-seeking. Thus, although resemblance is an imaginary activity, Stevens recognizes the desire for it (*NA* 76). In other words, the imaginary becomes a representative or a means of desire for manifestation and realization or fulfillment. If to remain insatiable is the very nature of desire, it follows that the imaginary also cannot be satisfied with "things as they are" (*CP* 165). This is the reason why the imaginary may be said to ground desire with regard to the desire's fulfillment (ERS 156); otherwise, desire would try to manifest and fulfill itself through unimaginable bodily violence, which would be a threat to the "other" as well as to the body itself, through which it must manifest in the absence of the imaginary. Its absence is, therefore, a fiction, not a reality (*CP* 503).

When Stevens emphasizes the study of resemblance as one of the ways to understand poetry, and goes on to state that poetry tries to quench the human desire for analogy or resemblance (*NA* 77), he is also linking the imaginary with the symbolic order, which is the sphere of culture, ethics, law, language, and so forth. Poetry, as belonging to the symbolic order of language, tries to "catch" into words what the imaginary has "captured" in the perceiving moment. Hines perhaps confuses Stevens' use of "catch" and "capture," and equates them as "term[s] for verbally catching something" (230). The intensity of struggle that is obvious in the word "capture" as the poet uses it in section VII of *Credences of Summer* (*CP* 376) is not quite there in the "catch" of *Notes* (*CP* 398), where that struggle regards the image, not the word "catch," and not so much in the act of "catching" the image in words, even though the "catching" is also difficult owing to the irrationality of the moment of the image. The difference in the intensity of the struggle is also supported by the relatively slow-paced cadence of the passage from *Notes* in comparison with the fast, broken — as if gasping — rhythm of the last six lines in that section from the *Credences*.[5] Besides, in the *Notes* passage, the preposition "from" separates the "catcher" from the image. The moment of the image is not rational since the image is transient, momentary.[6] The "catcher" does not "catch" this "moment," so its reasoning into words must be equally irrational, rendering the description itself unreasonable. In the passage from *Credences*, on the other hand, it is the very object that is to be "captured" *an sich*. It does not separate but brings the "catcher" and the object together. This "capturing" is, nevertheless, imaginary since it is "the only clue to reality" (*NA* 137). In short, "capture" for Stevens belongs to the register of imaginary activity; it means perception (perhaps a little more than perception) of an object, which is prior to the further displacement of the perceived object's image through and in the symbolic act of verbally "catching." In the *Credences*, Stevens indeed places the symbolic activity after the imaginary "capture." In the passage from the *Notes* as well, the capture has already taken place, the image is already there; what remains, or what is next, is to "catch" it into words — language. However, this symbolic act is not easy to accomplish since the irrationality of the "moment" of an image carries over into the expression.

While this discussion distinguishes between "capture" and "catch," or imaginary and symbolic, it also establishes a link between the two in the sense that there would be no poetry (language) without imaginary perception, no "catching" without "capture." Thus, poetry is not simply language. It is more than even the imaginary perceptions legalized or fixed by the symbolic order of language. The image is composed of "things as they are" and what the perceiver thinks of them (*CP* 165, 180); it may not be exactly the thing it represents, but that thing is nevertheless a part of it. Therefore, reality is an indelible aspect of poetry. Yet the reality depicted in poetry would have no particular value if it did not represent the "real" real: Stevens writes that the resemblances between things that have the power to affect our minds metamorphose the things through their transfiguration or sublimation (*NA* 77); this state of things is their "real" real.[7] This view of reality, which poetry provides in abundance, gives a more vivid experience of it; it exalts our idea of the reality (*NA* 77). In this way, all three orders — imaginary, symbolic, and real — inmix and become inseparable in poetic discourse (ERS 190). Poetry is valuable insofar as it unites the three orders and enables the subject (reader/writer) to experience *jouissance* to the point that he forgets his divided nature. This is the true value of poetry in Stevens; this is the essence of section VI of *Description without Place*, where he glosses "description" as reconciliation (CP 345).

In "The Blue Guitar," the guitarist finds it impossible to describe reality as it is, but that is what the audience demands. Both find it impossible to see or say things as they are. The guitarist declares at the very outset that the guitar changes them. Here, the poet shows the realization that the imaginary itself is a principle of *méconnaissance*, or mis(re)cognition, in the sense that it functions as a sort of blindfold that resists clear perception of both "self" and other (ERS 148). Yet he praises imagination since the unclear perception of an object gives rise to hallucinations; he refers to this process as an "extension" of the object. The imaginary activity "extends" an object by essentially making it ambiguous, unclear, thus rendering clear perception of it impossible; the object itself attains "the moment of impossibility" (*FS* 31) where imagination falters. He further says that this ambiguity, far from being a hindrance, is conducive, as poetry originates from it (*NA* 78–79). Stevens was a poet who would not relegate the imagination or imagine its absence; instead, he valued transformation of the real into the imagined (*NA* 79). Our imagination and languages both are incapable of holding reality verbatim, which may be the cause of our imperfection and the bitterness thereof; yet this insufficiency or imperfection is also the cause of our desire for reality or truth or perfection (*CP* 194). And what makes the truth or the perfect what it is if not our imperfection? For this reason, Stevens values both imaginary *méconnaissance* (*NA* 114) and the insufficiency of our language (*CP* 194). Toward the end of "Poems of Our Climate," one wonders whether Stevens elevates our linguistic poverty, since it has the potential to afford us *jouissance*. If he does, he will find Freud with him, who pointed out our irrational interest in the strange, and often apparently meaningless, language and sounds that manifest themselves in jokes, slips of the tongue, dreams, symptoms, and so forth. If our imperfection has any value, it is because it alone establishes the possibility of there being something like paradisiacal perfection or truth (*CP* 194). In this sense, the ambiguity, the imperfection, the "flawed"-ness that is inherent in our perception, expression, or existence is not unreal, but a reality in its own right; it *is* and creates a human reality through which we wish to attain to a higher reality, to truth, to perfection. As opposed to our incomplete view of reality, at times our sense might exceed reality itself; even this is a reality in its own right (*NA* 79). The incessant drive of the imaginary is toward perceiving things in their ultimate real state (*CP* 168). Each time the imaginary perceives the same object, it forms different image(s) of it in the mind and each time affects the mind in a different way. The desire to know the real of that object is behind the drive of the imaginary; it is as if there exists a predetermined real state for every object and every image of the object leads toward it; if this is so, the images cannot be separated from either the object or its reality; their total effect is like a complete view of the object, of reality itself (*NA* 114). This is akin to what the poet says apropos of the proliferation of resemblances leading to a heightened sense of reality.

Like Lacan, Stevens recognized the vastness and complexity of the field of images and activities of the imagination. He realized the importance of the image as a formative value. He was also constantly aware that the external world is an inevitable part of images; that, in fact, the external world provides images, which build the general character of a person or people living in a particular geographical area or environment. He knew that the place in which we live defines us, contributes heavily in shaping our character or personality. "Anecdote of Men by the Thousand" (*CP* 51–52) is a specific statement of the relation between man and the external world. In a beautiful image at the end of this poem he speaks of how the "place" is an inevitable part, if not of the soul as such, then of one's overall character or personality ("dress") (*CP* 52). Costume for Stevens is a realization of imagination as a "social form," or as identity (*NA* 146).

The place in which one lives provides basic images that form the rock-solid foundation on which man's personality is built. The role of the imaginary is vital in this context since it seeks fusion or unity with the external world. In the infant stage, the first images create a frame of reference so that each image perceived later will be interpreted through it and added to this frame. Thus, that frame of reference, originally created by images derived from the external world, provides a basis for studying one's personality as unique (ERS 145). Therefore, from the images of a poet, or of any man, one can understand his personality. The illustration is found in a passage from "Imagination as Value" (*NA* 133–56), where Stevens bids the reader to imagine two blind persons discussing *their* images (*NA* 140). In fact, it is impossible for us even to imagine this discussion. The images of the blind would be different from those of anyone who can see, and the difference creates the stumbling block—not only in our way of imagining their discussion punctuated with their images but also in our understanding of their sense of the world. Such a stumbling block between two persons gives rise to what we call a communication gap, which is suggestive of the difference between sensibilities, and hence between personalities.

However, if to bid the reader to imagine something unimaginable is itself a stumbling block in the way of the point that Stevens is trying to get across, the poet furnishes another illustration in which he imagines a Parisian and a

Ugandan, two quite differently grown persons, and asks what will happen if their imaginary texts are interchanged (*NA* 140). Far from helping, this suggestion mystifies even more. Apparently, it is difficult to answer the question Stevens asks here. However, in light of Lacan's theory of introjection and projection, which has been briefly discussed in this chapter, one is in a better position to arrive at an answer. The imaginary operates in two major ways: first by introjection, and then by projection, which includes phenomena like creating resemblances. The introjected images are recorded in the Other, and projection then uses these previously recorded images — as in the case of St. Matthew, who used the image of "sheep without a shepherd." By transmission of the imagination Stevens means transmission of the Other-recording of images as well. This is the only way the Parisian with the Ugandan imaginary would conceive — if at all — of the football as something unusually strange. However, his description of the football might parallel the normal Parisian's description of the Muenster at Basel, just as in normal circumstances the Ugandan's description of the football is likely to parallel any normal Parisian's description of the Muenster. On the other hand, the Ugandan (with the Parisian's imaginary) might initially find his experience at Basel confusing, even disturbing; he would be hard put to conceive what is happening around him (especially on suddenly confronting the gargoyles) if the experience is not already recorded in the borrowed Parisian imaginary, or he might feel extremely thrilled as a result of the previously recorded experience of a similar kind ("delirium" means "mental disturbance" or "excited happiness"; here, one has to imagine that facing things like gargoyles or being in a mysterious and frightening setting is not very unusual in Uganda). That is, his description of the experience at Basel might be similar to the normal Parisian's description of his "delirium" at, say, the final of World Cup football with France as one of the two contenders.

In the case of such transmission, the Parisian would not remain Parisian but would become the Ugandan, and the Ugandan would become the Parisian. With the transmission of their imaginaries from one to the other, their identities would also be interchanged. The study of the personality is, therefore, the study of the imaginary. Ragland-Sullivan refers to this study as "unraveling," which reveals "the way identity was composed as a 'self'-text," like "the reverse side of a tapestry" that reveals how the work of art was made (142). "Personality," "identity," and "self" are therefore fictions, "tapestries," "works of art" — in short, "fables," not real.

For all our attempts to get a full view of the imagination and images, it is impossible to exhaust the field in order to make up a theory that would be complete. Stevens, therefore, never got tired of elaborating this field. Lacan, too, found the domain of the imagination and images unfathomable (ERS

144). Therefore, despite the wide recognition that Stevens' imagination has received from his critics, it seems worthwhile to make an attempt to bring together the poet's observations of the imaginary.

It is interesting to see how Stevens brings his theory of imagination into poetic practice. It is not desirable to separate theory and practice in this way; however, all the aspects of the imaginary are so inmixed with the other issues that explaining them from a Lacanian perspective while discussing a particular poem by Stevens would break the rhythm of discussion into several diversions. It seems necessary to first deal with the theoretical perspectives of the imaginary from Stevens' viewpoint as they are manifested in his poetry, so that, at opportune moments, they may be compared with the corresponding views of the psychoanalyst.

Previously in this chapter we began with the imaginary as a functional set of various processes. Accordingly, we now pick up with "Study of Two Pears" (*CP* 196–97), in which the imaginary processes are very much directly involved. Shape being one of the most prominent aspects in the perception of any object the eye sees, the poem's first section dwells on the shape of the pears. The Other memory of the observer has a record of a large number of images introjected from the beginning of one's life. Shape is one of the categories in this record. The moment the shape of an object is perceived, the imaginary invokes from the Other memory certain similar shapes through "expulsion" of the non-similar ones. The imaginary seeks to create a resemblance by relating the perceived shape with each of the invoked shapes alternately; this is the process of "projection." This happens fast enough so that the perceiver does not perceive perception as a flux. In this projection, another process is also involved — that of "substitution" of the recorded shapes for the object that is being perceived. The desire to perceive the object *as it is* is continually "displaced" in the process. It is these displacements that are rejected in the first section of "Study of Two Pears." While the desire to see the pears in their essential nakedness, in their real state, causes these displacements, the desire is never quite satisfied, partly because the search for their real state shifts attention to their other details — to color, for instance. This further complicates the problem since the same imaginary processes would be operated again for color perception.

Perhaps the poem began with a view to touch the real state of the pears by rejecting imaginary intervention since it caused deviation in perception. The rejection of resemblances of the pears with other objects in section I could be a result of this view. Now, there remains only one possible way to know or perceive the real pears: the reason, the realistic point of view. Stevens, therefore, changes his stance and, in sections II and III, attempts to see them in the "square hated" fashion of the realist (*NA* 133; *CP* 75), solely concentrating on their physical reality. Here, the description may be very accurate, but it is almost in the vein of the radical advocates of the "dehumanization of Art/Nature" cult. The question is, does this satisfy the mind? Perhaps not. One always desires more. Reason is not the proper "light" in which to study the pears since it is like the "snowy light" that can reflect only snow (*CP* 193) or, as more appropriately described in "Common Life," the light of reason is "morbid" (*CP* 221). The mind remains dissatisfied with such "realistic" perception since reason makes the pears look cadaverous. The so-called realists do not seem to believe that, apart from reason, man has other faculties as well (*CP* 351). Hence, Stevens again resorts to the "light" of imagination in section IV; the imagination cannot be repressed for long (*NA* 152). The "realistic" viewpoint gives way to see the way the pears are modeled. The observer senses the role of imagination in the creation of the pears. Indeed, the process of creation is highly imaginative, whether it is artistic or scientific. Was it not first *imagined* before actually coming to the conclusion that the earth has a force that attracts objects?

The verb "model" itself seeks resemblance — this is what was rejected in section I — between some "model" that is still unknown and the pears. If the imagination is involved in the way in which the pears are modeled, then the search for the "model" itself (i.e., the "real" pears) must proceed along with or through the imagination. As Stevens himself accepts, imagination is "the only clue to reality" (*NA* 137). Although this is a return to what was rejected at the beginning of the poem, the imagination at least makes the pears come alive and shine instead of making them look cadaverous. By virtue of standing in the light of imagination, the pears acquire a kind of reality since they create impressions in the mind. This does not happen in the light of reason, and hence they do not even remain objects of desire, like the woman in "Common Life," who, having no shadows, is not a man's desire (*CP* 221). The pears, as section V describes, have various shadows. In other words, an object is essentially perceived through the possible resemblances of its features and aspects with those of other (similar) objects. That is, perception of an object is always with reference to the other, already known or recorded, images, due to which the object acquires plurality at the level of perception itself. The plurality forecloses the real object to human perception. This is why Stevens has cause to be dissatisfied even with the imaginary perception; therefore, the poet writes in the final section, the reality is distorted, tainted, by imaginary perception of the pears, so that pure perception of reality finally eludes the observer. The poet might also have benefited from what Santayana said: "Each image breeds a hundred more.... The mind, exercised by its own fertility and flooded by its inner lights, has infinite trouble to keep a true reckoning of its outward perceptions" (*Interpretations of Poetry and Religion* 7–8).

In a letter of 17 March 1937 to J. Ronald Lane Latimer, Stevens wrote about the problem of seeing things as they are and as one thinks they are—he calls this the "painter's problem of realization" (*L* 316). "Study of Two Pears" attempts to see the pears in both ways, but it also enlarges the scope of the problem and makes it universal by making it the problem of perception. The imaginative-artistic (painting) and the morbid-realistic viewpoints are to be compared. A study tries to reach the truth by comparison of the analyses carried out using different available means and tools. In this case, imagination and reason are used, but the truth that emerges is bittersweet. Bitter, because no available means allow clear perception of reality that would satisfy the mind, and sweet, because there is at least the respite, provided by imagination, that makes perception a desirable activity, though not absolutely satisfying. One wonders at the end why there are two pears, and not one. One wonders whether it is not a study of two *peers*: Imagination and Reason. Rehder seems to have come close to this idea, though he ultimately avoids the point by limiting his interest to the two people—painter and perceiver (206). Stevens himself said that there is a constant struggle between reason and imagination to apprehend reality; here, he further remarks that this struggle has no outcome and therefore is of no interest (*NA* 141). However, "Study of Two Pears" is not without outcome, for it proves the significance and inevitability of the imagination in reality perception. And, though Stevens rejects any interest in the struggle, he does not resist its use in his poetry: for example, the sixth of the "Six Significant Landscapes" (*CP* 75), "Study of Two Pears" *(CP* 196–97), and "Common Life" *(CP* 221) depict the struggle in such a way that it ends in the imagination's triumph; the poet's line of resistance to reason is obvious in his prose and poetry as he elevates the quality of imagination, which satisfies desire.

Although reality is affected by the "blue guitar," Stevens prefers, over reason, to play it to see reality as it is (*CP* 165). It is in this "play" alone that the mind has any chance to grow. This growth is essentially related to the images the mind is capable of forming with the help of the imaginary, since they comprise a frame of reference that is responsible for perceiving the world. It is images that compose the rhythm that the poem of the mind has, as Stevens suggests through "Poem with Rhythms" (*CP* 245–46). Here the hand, wall, candle, space, and light seem to be loaded with symbolic value. The hand is between the candle and the wall, and the mind is between light and space. Both grow large; the wall and space function as the background of their growth. The position of both is that of an agency that grows large by mere intervention. If the hand and mind are thus similar, then the candle and the wall may be equated with light and space respectively. In fact, the first two stanzas may be equated by their apparent similarity in form and in their respective perfect end rhymes. However, one must note that all the elements in the first stanza have concrete physicality, whereas the mind, light, and space of the second stanza do not, though their existence cannot be doubted. That is to say, one is in a position to believe that the two stanzas deal respectively with the real world of objects and the abstract and evanescent.

Obviously, the second stanza deals with something that is complex—hence the complexity in its structure in the form of the increased number of lines that are, moreover, parenthesized. Yet it is difficult to believe that for a poet like Stevens the real world of things is not complex. In fact, for a reader who has some familiarity with Stevens' poetry, the second stanza will not be strange, but the first might be. He will therefore be immediately on his guard against the trap of the first stanza's apparent simplicity. In short, both the stanzas are complex. The mind is the masculine presence within the room,[8] and the woman waiting for him might easily be called Stevens' imagination; she could be, as Riddel would say, "Penelope-imagination" of "The World as Meditation" (*CP* 520–21), whose lover, "Ulysses-reality," keeps coming close to her "but never to consummation" (Riddel 247). A similar treatment is observed in the second and third stanzas of "Poem with Rhythms." However, the roles seem to be reversed. If "we live in the mind ... with the imagination" (*NA* 140), then the mind and the imagination are always together, so there is no need to use the pronoun "this" for the man and "that" for the woman. These pronouns in the second stanza not only distinguish the man and the woman but, more importantly, also distance them. As I would like to read the lines, the "man-mind" is on the near side whereas the "woman-reality" is on the far side.[9] It may further be argued that the woman, being an object of desire, has to be away from the man, for there will not be the desire otherwise. Besides, Stevens seems to be personifying reality in more than merely a literary sense, for he seems to seriously believe in its anima (this issue will be taken up later). Thus the "woman-reality" awaits the "man-mind," her lover.

One more problem is raised by the use of these pronouns with regard to light. The mind is not simply between light and space, but either between "this light" and space or between "that light" and space. This creates a placement problem for space. Where would it be? On "this" side of the mind or "that" side? One has to approach the problem cautiously, since the mind remains "between": if "this light," then "that space"; if "that light," then "this space." That is, the mind is either between "this light" and "that space" or between "that light" and "this space." And yet the space seems to evade this logical approach since it is the light that is variable and changes its place; the space is a constant. Stevens does not involve the space in the logic of either-or as he does the light. The same is true of the mind: it does not change its place and seems to be constant. It seems that there are two lights. Adhering to Stevens' use of the pronouns "this" and "that," it may be assumed that "this light" is that of the imaginary (Stevens' "imagination" as that which is always with the mind — on this or near side of the mind — and that illumines), and that the "that light" is of the reality (of the corporeal world outside, which, when perceived momentarily "beyond itself," affects the mind and heightens our sense of the world — just as the effects of actual light regarding reflection, refraction, or dispersion affect our view). After all, the Real can be felt or accessed or seen only in the effects it creates (ERS 189). What is interesting in the poem is that either "this light" exists or "that" light. To understand the (un)reasoning behind this, it is necessary to imagine the situation before imaginary perception. Prior to imaginary perception, the external world is nothing to the perceiver; there is the vast space in front of the mind, a meaninglessness, nothingness, even though the imagination is with the mind, because it illumines only when at work — while perception is taking place — whether of real things or of the meditative kind. This situation may be represented temporarily as light(imaginary) — mind — SPACE.[10] At this moment, the state of the mind could be best described as "the creator having yet to create anything" (*CP* 169) or, better, as perpetuating through imbecility (*CP* 172), since, metaphorically speaking, there is space even within the mind owing to the absence of any activity of imagination.

As the imagination engages in the act of perception, the situation becomes LIGHT(imaginary) — mind — SPACE. If, though momentarily, the mind approaches the real of what it perceives, the perceived becomes "that light"; it is the "light of the real" or "real as light." This can be represented as SPACE — mind — LIGHT(real). These representations justify how the mind is always between light and space; it also justifies the poet's use of the pronouns "this" and "that" concerning the light. However, the space changes its place in these representations, which does not match its characterization as constant, all-inclusive and pervasive, and unaffected even though things inside it glow and grow. To justify this, the above representations may be modified: SPACE — LIGHT(imaginary) — mind — SPACE and SPACE — mind — LIGHT(real) — SPACE. Since the mind also enlarges, its growth must be reflected: SPACE — LIGHT(imaginary) — MIND — SPACE and SPACE — MIND — LIGHT(real) — SPACE. Thus, the mind *is*, whether it enlarges or not; the space *is*, whether it diminishes or not. The light, however, exists either as the imagination-in-its-act or else as the effect of the real on the perceiving mind.

As the image of an actual object is formed in the mind, one feels the effect on the mind and is able to perceive the object beyond itself, in its enhanced or "real" state — though for a moment only; or, as Stevens has it elsewhere, the effect goes beyond the grasp or reach of the mind (*CP* 436–

37). This is a moment of the *jouissance* of the union of the mind and object, of the self and other. It is semblable of the experience, however fleeting, of the achievement of the object of desire, when the imaginary function of object-seeking comes to a momentary halt and the mind experiences enlargement or, if the coinage is allowed, an "accompletion" (*CP* 512), closing the abyss between self and other; the mind's growth gives a sense of the diminution of the space. This is how the space or, to use Riddel's expression, the "nothing" works out as a "productive principle" in Stevens (qtd. in Jarraway 176),[11] curing or covering the native insufficiency or the primal discord in man's relation to his being.

Now it should not be difficult to see the importance of the first stanza. It is not as simple as those hypothetical substantive arguments the metaphysical poets kept inventing throughout the poem in order to hammer home their conviction, though it must be conceded that the parallelism between the first two stanzas gives such an impression. I am more inclined to view the "hand" as representing the external reality.[12] Stevens uses it in much the same way in "The Hand As a Being," where the dame represents the asocial, unsymbolized real, while her "hand," as Lacan would say, is the humanized or symbolized reality (*CP* 271); even "The Candle a Saint" describes the unsymbolized, unknown real as the queen who is seen by the clairvoyant who can look beyond the physical reality (*CP* 223). The movement of the "hand" is the doing of the will of that "dame." I will discuss how the "real" hallucinates or animates the actual world for the subject, such that it grows beautiful on the mind's wall. However, suffice it to suggest here that the same image is used in "Poem with Rhythms" with a little variation: the "hand" is made to appear, move or grow due to the light of the candle. This thought invokes comparison between the wall and mind, since images are formed on them, so that the comparison made earlier between hand and mind seems fallacious. In this way, the first two stanzas are connected through the associative link between the wall and mind. To grasp the whole discussion, the following representation might be useful:

Imagination ("this light")-Mind/Wall-Hand-Candle ("that light")

All the things and phenomena in the above representation take place within the all-inclusive "space," and are therefore included in it. At the same time, all of the things have their own existence apart from (yet within) the "space." The slash between wall and mind separates the internal world of the self (on the left of the slash) from the other world (on the right), which — for all its magnificent internal changes and growth — would be nothing if there were no self or mind to appreciate it; there would be no "space" either. It is because the mind is there, forming images of the world on itself as on a wall (but not insensitive like it), that the objects from the real world not only grow large but also, as the poet says, acquire a desire for enlargement on the mind's wall. This is where the "wall" in the above formulation collapses and the "wall" in the poem appropriates the "mind," such that the "hand" seems to grow ever larger.

However, if we listen to Doggett's suggestion that the "hand" in Stevens represents creativity (24, 44), then it also evokes human intervention in the outside reality, and this again takes us back to the assumption that the "hand" is linked with the "mind." Now, if the candle is taken to represent Christianity, the wall would represent all other human constructions, political, social, and so forth. However, since Stevens' art is secular, the candle would suggest the world of faith that is not essentially religious; let us therefore say that it represents faith in the Lacanian real. From this viewpoint, the wall could also represent the religious structures, since they are of human making. On the first reading, the poet already gives the impression of similarity between the wall and space through the poem's dialectic. To sum up, Stevens seems to be suggesting that the world of actual objects or creativity ("hand") can defy the largest possible structures, whether man-made or natural, by virtue of "this" and "that" light. Relying on the poet's humanistic procedure in his work, it may be said that the central issue in "Poem with Rhythms" is "this light," the imagination, whose presence makes everything else in the poem possible. Stevens' genius is manifest in his ability to make the volatility of his symbols into a virtue of versatility; they serve the prism through which a spectrum of meanings opens up like a treasure trove and one simply enjoys looking at it, imaginarily.

While discussing "Study of Two Pears," it has already been mentioned that Stevens seems to have been seriously thinking of the anima (even desire) of the real world of objects. This is one of his many assertions that are qualified because he had his own reservations about them or their acceptance.[13] In "Poem with Rhythms," the above mentioned assertion is qualified with "must." The poet's suspicion regarding the anima of the objective world persisted until the end of his life. In a late poem, he writes that everything (which includes the inanimate world as well) has the ability of and desire for transformation (*CP* 514). In "Poem with Rhythms," this assertion could have been stronger since the reality has the desire to grow large, and heavy and strong as well. However, the "growth" of the object does enlarge the mind in terms of the effect its image has on the mind. Realizing this, toward the end of the poem Stevens writes that the image is a union of the mind (ego, or Lacan's *moi*) and the real world (the other of Lacan). Like Lacan, he had realized the important role images play in the construction of the sense of "self." Though Lacan did recognize this, his emphasis was more on the relationship of the subject to the language he hears and speaks in terms of the evolution of the "self" (see ERS 145). This is how the mind grows large, and it is in this growing large that the "man-mind" really perceives the image and understands its significance. And it is in thus being imagized that the "woman-reality" becomes complete as a result of "her" effect on "his" mind. But the "man-mind" never actually goes out to her or, if Stevens is playing with "come," it never achieves the desired consummation, that unity with the external world since, as Stevens writes in "The Well Dressed Man with a Beard" (which is placed very close to "Poem with Rhythms"), the mind always remains unsatisfied (*CP* 247). It is in this remaining always unsated, in this mercilessly impossible desire alone, that the self attains "vitality." This vitality, a kind of fullness or completeness that Stevens describes in "The Poem That Took the Place of a Mountain" (*CP* 512), is not the result of imagination, but of a more fundamental and powerful principle: desire. It is a sense of satisfaction resulting from the realization of desire. That this is not actual oneness or unity with the outside world is what Stevens suggests through the use of "as" in the penultimate line, qualifying his assertion once again.

Going back to Doggett's suggestion — that "hand" in Stevens represents creative art — opens another dimension of "Poem with Rhythms." It addresses a basic issue concerning art; it also explains why the poet would not discuss his poetry with others or give clues to its meaning. Lacan's concept of the "gaze of the Other" supplies a valuable addition to our understanding of Stevens' view on the function of his poetry with regard to himself. Gaze is generally defined as "seeing oneself seen," though Lacan glosses it variously in Seminar XI. The gaze of the Other has the same effect on the subject under it that a bright light has on the eye. The eye retreats; this obstructs its relation with an object between the eye and the source of the light. However, says Lacan, a small screen introduced between the two, which cuts into the object that is not seen clearly due to the bright light, makes the light "retreat" and allows the emergence of the concealed object (S XI 108). We know that Stevens was sharply aware of the gaze of other people, under which he visibly writhed. By presenting his poetry ("hand") to their eyes, he could make them abandon their gaze (S XI 101). This is satisfying to the subject under gaze since it allows his emergence in terms of the strength of his relation with reality; it has a certain soothing, balming effect on the subject (S XI 101), which Stevens enjoyed. He wanted his poetry to be a challenge to the readers, so that their gaze — which he imagined to be fixed on him — could be laid down as their eyes would be fixed on the poetry. The "hand" in "Poem with Rhythms" grows larger precisely because the poet wanted to (re)establish his relation with reality by avoiding or screening out the gaze of the Other. This may be viewed as one of his ways of "emerging" as a subject, of (re)making or (re)composing himself.

Stevens was in no doubt at all that it is perception in the form of images that composes the "self." Lacan subverted the traditional notion of the self as substance and called it merely an effect (ERS 145), an imaginary construction, a myth. Stevens' views were no different; he had realized the meaning and understood the role of imaginary identifications in "self"-construction. Lacan's view that one's primordial fusion with images builds up layer upon layer of representations that create a frame of reference suggests that studying a person as a specificity, as a personality, is nothing but the study of the person's images. Lacan thus agrees with others on the "formative value" of images (S III 165). Stevens illustrates this concept in a passage already discussed from "Imagination as Value" (*NA* 133–56), where he bids the reader to imagine two blind individuals' discussion. Their discussion would be the discussion of *their* images of the world, *their* sense of the world, which would be peculiar to them. However, this is an extreme case. And, as if it were impossible, and must be, for us to imagine the images of the blind who have no knowledge of the images of those who can see, Stevens provides another illustration involving a Parisian and a Ugandan. In discussing this illustration, it has been suggested that the study of personality is the study of the imaginary. Ragland-Sullivan refers to this study as "unraveling" of the "self" text, and suggests that "personality," "identity," and "self" are "tapestries," "works of art"—that is, fictional and not real. These thoughts might have crossed Stevens' mind, for he refers to the "self" text as an "artifice" existing inside the human being (*NA* 141), which is the doing of imagination, the maker of her world (*CP* 448, 129); it is by virtue of her "singing" that the "I" grows (*CP* 448), which is the world in which "she" sings. This is the reason why Stevens meditates on its artificial nature in the second of his three academic pieces (*NA* 83). The title of this piece is "Someone Puts a Pineapple Together"; the whole poem, however, is not so much a contemplation of either the "someone" or the "pineapple" as of the act of "putting together." The whole poem could be read as an exercise in unraveling the imaginary, a study of the *way* the "pineapple" is "put together." If the poem speaks of the "someone" of the title at all, it does so through the way the "pineapple" is "put together." The poem reveals the way the "I" is composed, like a work of art.

If personality or "self" is artificial, an imaginary construct, a myth, then the only way to study it is to go beyond it to the images, since they are the substantive elements of this myth. And, since the ego is the center of the imaginary identity as the "self," it is the study of the ego; therefore, by referring to Freud, Lacan compares the ego with an onion, which can be peeled to see how it was constructed (S I 171). However, images are derived from the actual world outside as the imaginary processes work upon it, effecting the profitable commerce between self and world; therefore, the study inevitably and invariably reflects the "region" in which the images are formed. This is the subject of Stevens' "A Mythology Reflects Its Region" (*OP* 118). Morse thinks that the poem might have been written in 1955 (*OP* 300), almost at the end of Stevens' poetic career and life, which was perhaps the most mature period of his poetic practice. Looking at the high degree of brevity, maturity, and compactness of thought in the poem, Morse's guess appears valid.

A casual glance at the title might make one wonder how and when the poet — rather, a strong advocate — "of modern poetry" developed liking for mythological past, especially when one has read Stevens' avowedly "anti-mythological" long poem, *The Comedian as the Letter C*, or after getting fairly acquainted with his "line of resistance to the past" in general.[14] One might recover by taking the first sentence, which is the same as the title, on strictly denotative terms, and thinking that Stevens will soon revert to his anti-mythological stance. With the first part of the tripartite second sentence, however, comes the real jab, as the poet regrets his absence during the time when the mythology of Connecticut was being created. One almost commits the mistake of interpreting Stevens as becoming nostalgic for the past at the end of life after all his previous resistance to it. Further, the conditional second part, "But if we had," would support such a view. However, all these things set up and function as a nice trap that may not have been specifically devised to mislead the reader, though he might feel caught in it. In fact, Stevens is contemplating "new and local mythologies" (*NA* 17).

Myth, with "imaginary person" as one of its meanings, points to "personality," "character," and "identity" — that is to say, to the "self." Mythology — the study of myth(s) — is, therefore, the study of the "self." Studying or creating "mythology of self" was one of Stevens' greatest interests (*CP* 28). He proposes to undertake such a study in this poem by way of "decreating" the self.[15] His understanding of the significance of images helped him to make them the means of the study. Since images are products of the conjunction of the mind and the real world outside, it is a study of both. Thus, "mythology" for Stevens is the study of both mind and "region," and he presents it through the last six lines of this ten-line poem — a considerable amount of lines to have been spared to it in such a short and compact poem.

Before returning to the poem's second sentence, it is necessary to see Stevens' thoughts on the Connecticut of his present. In "Connecticut" (*OP* 294–96), which is a convincingly argued statement of the significance of "place" in Stevens' conception of the self, he describes one of his railroad journeys from Hartford to Boston, which he glosses as a journey "through the character" of Connecticut (*OP* 295). This suggests that the "personality" or the "myth" of the state had already been established. Further, it may be noticed that Stevens studies it through the images of farms, barns, orchards, houses, and so on; these images are mostly "acts of culture" (Doreski 152). It follows that the general character of the people living there had also been established, that the Connecticut Yankees had already acquired and assimilated, as part of their characters, the miserliness of the environment (*OP* 294). This is emphasized when he further says that the first people who came to live in Connecticut must have "endured and mastered" what he calls the "primitive difficulties," thus giving rise to a state tradition; he also comments that the Connecticut people are now living in the same tradition and equates it with mythology (*OP* 295).

One would do well to recall Conrad's Mr. Kurtz in Africa. It must have been the barrier of the native language and culture that made him face and, more importantly, assimilate into his character a primitiveness that would enable him to cope with the primitiveness of the land. For his part, he must have first been exposed to the primitiveness of the land, like Marlow. However, he had to put up with it longer than Marlow had to. That is, while the native culture and its development among the tribes had alleviated the monster of the primitiveness of the land for them, and thus of the primitiveness within themselves, for Mr. Kurtz it came in its pristine form. This, added to the greed involved in the trade culture and the supposed supremacy of his whiteness, made his character all the more monstrous, even more monstrous than that of the unfriendly native tribesmen and primitive Africa; that is to say, more monstrous than the hostile tribesmen and primitive Africa could have actually made it. Thus, the natives had a different tradition and Mr. Kurtz developed a unique one, peculiar to himself. Sheshadri-Crooks argues that "dominant racial identification — or whiteness ... when threatened ... is susceptible to uncanny effects" (353). Surely, before the Russian's arrival, away from the "Central Station" and deep in the heart of the African forests, Kurtz must have been the only white man among the native tribes; his whiteness itself must have been the cause of that threat, the "uncanny effects" of which are obvious in the novella. For a lack of "the sedimentation of the 'we' [white race] in the constitution of [Kurtz's] 'I,'" his imaginary must have suffered in its "phantasmatic efforts" of identification with the environment (Sheshadri-Crooks 359).

The example of Kurtz brings into view the scope of the implication of "primitive difficulties," of "tradition," of "mythology," and of the changes that take place as time passes and culture develops — all of which figure in the Stevens essay. Stevens, too, had come to live in Connecticut from a more "abundant" state: Pennsylvania. However, for him, unlike Kurtz, there was no barrier of language, which proved conducive to his assimilating the Connecticut culture easily. This justifies Lacan's emphasis on the role of language in the creation of the "self." In short, the people of Stevens' Connecticut were living in a tradition — which he equates with mythology — that had already been established through the past; a tradition, as Eliot would say, is continually added to or modified. William Doreski describes Stevens' regret for his absence when the mythology of the state was being made as a "coy disclaimer" (164); if Doreski had in mind both "modest" and "secretive" as meanings of "coy," then the description is apt. The "secretive" part of Stevens' line is that mythology, as a study, is still possible; moreover, as tradition, its creation is an endless process.

The key expressions in Stevens' essay are "gray, bleached and derelict," and the initial "primitive difficulties." It is these difficulties that the poet seeks in the poem's "— But if we had —." These dashes, ellipses, hiatuses in Dickinson and Stevens are extremely important since they are significations beyond the range of cultural language.[16] Both poets prefer them to verbal expressions, which seem "inadequate and paltry" for catching their "private experience[s]" that are "ineffable" (Corn 3); both convey much through these marks by saying nothing. In these two dashes Stevens answers when and whether mythology was or is possible. Stevens' ride through the character of the state is timed when the external world is unfriendly: the weather was gloomy and wintry; everything seemed "gray, bleached and derelict"; the landscape was harsh and almost hostile. The fact that he could study the personality or mythology of the state in difficult times, or in difficulties that are essentially "primitive," suggests that mythology is possible in such times and places alone — in times and places that are not familiar or humanized — so that there is a fair chance of observing how the imaginary functions to perceive them in images that build up the basic imaginary text that is generally referred to as the "self." For this reason alone — that is, in order to study and/or to evolve the self— Crispin moves away from the place that had been familiarized through his dwelling there before embarking on his voyage: from Bordeaux to Yucatan to Havana to Carolina (*CP* 29), from "South" to "North," from the familiar and humanized to the unfamiliar and nonhumanized. The already hominized world of the "South" was devoid of imagination (*CP* 27), since he did not have to imagine much there, thus disallowing him to become "introspective" in order to study and/or evolve "mythology of self" (*CP* 29, 28).

For Stevens as for Crispin, a clear perception of the mythology of self was of great importance. For this, however, even the "unspectacular" Connecticut is not sufficient (Doreski 152), since it is more familiarized and humanized — hence more beautiful — as compared with the "North." Obviously, he must imagine or seek a more "primitive" or a nonhumanized landscape, where cultural impositions like the farms, barns, orchards, and houses have yet to make their mark. Stevens does this in "— But if we had —"; this is even reflected in the bits of images presented in the last two lines of the poem. For this reason alone the speaker of "Farewell to Florida" dislikes the flourishing South, which is seen as confining, and then is able to reach the North, which he associates with unconscious mental violence (*CP* 118). For, after all, "the specific nature of a setting," Doreski rightly observes, "determines ... the action possible within it, the undulation of the resultant meditation" (153). Thus, when he comments that the "houses thrive in this unadorned landscape much as Stevens' imagination does" (153), Doreski should also have taken into account the fact that the "little fastidious houses," as symbolic of the hominization and culturization and familiarization of the world, leave little scope for the imagination to thrive or for one's becoming "introspective" and evolving the "mythology of self," the reason why Crispin left the abundant "South." This alone would justify why Stevens bothered to write "— But if we had —."

As far as "A Mythology" is concerned, the issue is not one of the pressure of reality, nor of making it pleasant or bearable (though that is very much a possibility in Stevens as a result of its hominization), but rather of creating an atmosphere where the study of self (mythology) will become possible. It is therefore necessary to travel toward, as Crispin and the speaker of "Farewell to Florida" do, or to imagine, as Stevens does in "A Mythology," a terrain that is not familiar and/or not humanized — like the Connecticut of Stevens' past. One of the best examples of such a landscape, which essentially has to be strange, is in "Farewell to Florida" itself; Stevens characterizes it as Northern, wintry, and slimy (*CP* 118). Even in *The Comedian as the Letter C*, Crispin moves from South to North; America, which is his North, is more or less equally invidious (see *CP* 34). The North of "Farewell to Florida" is both "within" and "without" the men; it at once part of and apart from them. This suggests that Stevens' study of the self is both individual and collective. The men-minds move with their conscious. The water with its fluidity and formlessness suggests the consciousness, which is divided by the corporeal world, the other[17]; one's body is distinguished from the other, which could be both the pressure of reality and the approach of the "real" (or Stevens' "unreal") of that reality: while the reality shoves in and divides, the "real" seems to approach but escapes accurate perception — thus shattering the mind or consciousness that, in the process of perceiving the "real," rapidly creates ephemeral fictions in the form of images.

This is a demonstration of how the imagination "thrives" in a place that is "strange" or "primitive," enabling the study, observation, or (re)evolution of the mental processes. And without doubt, "The Snow Man" remains unparalleled in Stevens' canon as far as the issue of the "North" is concerned; it is the "North" of both the mind and place. In "A Mythology," it is not clear whether Stevens is referring to the mythology of the self or region. That this question should remain unanswered suggests that it is impossible to separate the two. One has to think in terms of both simultaneously. Indeed, if images are comprised of the mind and the outside world, one cannot really separate them from either. However, one must believe in the reality or truth of images, and "change" is Stevens' mode of attesting to it, and of progress (*OP* 157). A change from "South" to "North" alters the images; similarly, a change from one's "North" to another's "North" changes them, since it is *he*, the perceiver, who, as Stevens claims in "A Mythology," inhabits the place in which he lives. Like the word "mythology," the poet also seems to use "region" with all its possible connotations. It might suggest the external world as well as the internal. Further, "region" is derived from the Latin *regio*, meaning "direction": if "direction" suggests "way," Ragland-Sullivan's comment, which has already been quoted, might be recalled: she says that the study of one's imaginary reveals "the *way* identity was composed as a 'self' text [mythology]" (emphasis mine; ERS 142). Thus, "region" could also signify the process of the evolution of "mythology."

And again Stevens' use of "must" is ambiguous, as in "The Snow Man." In the light of the implications of the first part of the poem, his use of it in line 5 of "A Mythology" suggests the obviousness of the fact that the image does incorporate the nature of its maker; he consolidates this obviousness and turns into a truth through the repeated use of "is" in the following lines, thus eradicating the slightest possible doubt that might have filtered through the "must." His "must" is a certainty seeming—but only seeming—to traverse, in a flitter, the border of uncertainty.[18] With each image recorded as memory in the Other, the nature of its maker is quantitatively and qualitatively enriched, for images give rise to what we call "personality" or "self" (ERS 145), which is ultimately responsible for one's "sense of the world" (*NA* 118), where the world is not an object but an interiorized image (*NA* 151). This is the true mythology of human existence. The imaginary is as important as reality in our lives, and in Stevens' poetry. In fact, one could even say that all the major issues that Stevens' writing is concerned with were, for him, of great value. Man is one such value to which he keeps returning—or rather, which is always present in his writing. Considering the importance of the imaginary in our life, it is not surprising that images occupied Stevens much as the imagination and reality did (if not more so), since images are the mode of the function of the imaginary. He found images to be the best means of studying man, as is clearly stated in a late poem, "Study of Images I" (463–64). The two poems, "Study of Images I" and "Study of Images II" (464–65), imagistic in a different way, are placed much later in *Collected Poems*, just before the long and difficult *An Ordinary Evening in New Haven* (*CP* 465–88). This placement itself gives a hint of their depth and of the complexity of thought therein.

The difficulty begins with the image of the "bush" presented in the opening lines of "Study of Images I." The level of difficulty increases as Stevens further qualifies it by using the descriptors that associate it with the South, Italy and Satyr/Saturn. A lot depends, as William Carlos Williams would say, on the understanding of this image. The connection with the South immediately evokes the "North-South" dialectic in Stevens. As discussed earlier, the "North" and "South" correspond respectively to the unfamiliar (nonhumanized) and the familiar (humanized). The difference between them is crucial, as between living in a world *without* and *with* its preconceptions (*OP* 164), or between the earliest original form of something and its belated, plural nature (*CP* 382), or between the zero level of existence as in "Snow Man" and the highest level of existence as in the summertime Oley valley in Pennsylvania of *Credences of Summer* (*CP* 374), or between the initial "primitive difficulties" and the feeling of homecoming in Connecticut (*OP* 295–96). Thus, as Hoshang Merchant rightly observes, one can see how cogent and expansive the "North-South" issue is in Stevens (81).

From the beginning of *Collected Poems* to this point Stevens has continued his meditation on the structure and modes of functioning of the human mind. He has had glimpses of the all-pervasiveness of the Other, who is essentially bestial, as in "A Dish of Peaches" (*CP* 224). The primitiveness, animality (nonhuman-ness), and alien-ness (nonfamiliarity) of the Other make it the "North" of human mind. These qualities enabled Stevens to assimilate to the Other the satyr (who may be regarded as the mythological "North" owing to its ancient-ness and radical otherness) by way of appropriating the satyr's bestiality, primitiveness, and remoteness. Moreover, both the Other and satyr are "exiled" from the present in both literal and figurative senses (it is difficult to tell the literal from the figurative, though): literally speaking, the satyr belongs to the outdated past (Greek mythology) and the Other's otherness and veiled-ness remove it from the conscious; figuratively, satyr, the principle of "bestial desire and behavior," has been sophisticated to the point of being forgotten through generations of human civilization, and the *moi*-other circuit is unaware (or rather tries to be unaware) of the Other's existence. (Recall that Freud characterized the unconscious as containing the repressed desires that seek pleasures which are asocial and bestial). However, the satyr/Other erupts occasionally and makes its presence felt. This "North" of the human psyche is its earliest original form.

The incessant drive of human desire is to seek (the knowledge of) the Other (*É* 301). In the beginning of life, the preconscious imagistic world is the mode of the realization of this desire, and later the *moi* and *je* are formed, which strive for that realization. The *moi* and *je* are the belated plural of human mind, its "South." They function, especially the *moi*, to seek the sense of oneness or *jouissance* by means of imaginary unification with the other. Thus, if the Other is the "North Pole," *jouissance* of/or identification is the "South Pole"; these are the two extreme points between which is spanned human behavior (*CP* 382).

If bestiality is the principle of the "North," the imaginary identification is the principle of the "South." The desire links them inextricably with each other. That is why, although the satyr belongs to Greek mythology, Stevens must connect it with Italy, which, for him, represents imagination (*NA* 9). In other words, Greece is "North" as Italy is "South." In connecting them, Stevens' Oxford English Dictionary or some encyclopedia might have helped. The *OED* tells us that the Roman sculptors assimilated the satyr in some degree into the faun of their native mythology. Likewise, the "desire for the Other" is responsible for the imaginary function that seeks *jouissance* through identification with the other. Or, simply stated, it is in the small other that the subject seeks the big Other. Hence, it follows that the Other figures in what are generally referred to as conscious acts—albeit not very heavily in the normal subject, yet to some degree like the satyr in the faun. If, thus, the "South" assimilates the "North" into itself, one can say that the "South" seeks the "North." Lacan's *jouissance*, therefore, is also oneness with the Other; this is even reflected in the idea that the "desire of the Other" is also the "desire for the Other" (see *É* 312). This makes it possible to say that the "North" and the "South" are each a corroborative function of the other. This is why Stevens could speak of their oneness (*CP* 392).

Our normal conscious life exists between the "North Pole" (the Other) and the "South Pole" (ego-other). It is, however, governed directly by imaginary identifications; thus, it is more a Southern phenomenon. *Jouissance* being the ultimate principle on which the conscious functions, Stevens appropriately connects it with Saturn—the principle of unrestrained merry-making. However, like the imaginary, the conscious is motivated by desire, which is closely associated with the Other since Lacan's thought indicates that there is no desire without the Other (*É* 312). This suggests that the conscious life partakes of both the Other and *jouissance.* Though the word "day" in many instances can be replaced with "desire" in Stevens' poetry, it also points to the words forming from the root "wake" that represent the consciousness. Just as the image cannot be separated from the object, so the conscious cannot be separated from the unconscious; the conscious exists as a result of the coming into being of the unconscious, just as there is an image because there is an object. If the unconscious and the Other make up the "North" of human mind, the conscious life (consisting of ego-other) and *jouissance* (of imaginary identification) make up the "South."

As indicated earlier, there is a finer distinction between the imaginary and the desire. Though both participate in the conscious as well as unconscious processes, desire belongs more properly to the unconscious and imaginary to the conscious. Since the imaginary is largely responsible for the conscious phenomena, Stevens appropriately associates the conscious life with Italy. We know Stevens connects Italy with imagination; we also know that in the poetry of some powerful modern poets the symbol has become extremely complex and obscure, and has a wide range of associations. The conscious life is no less so; after all, persons like Freud and Lacan could become powerful only through keen observations of the conscious life. And because the imaginary is its mast, the poet elevates it to the status of a symbol. Thus, considering the expansiveness of the conscious domain, the bush is big; it is blue due the important role of the imaginary and, most importantly, it is associated with "day" owing to the genetic significance of desire in its functioning.

Stevens devotes nearly four lines to "catch" or describe this symbol. The fact that he describes the symbol at once aligns him with Mallarmé, especially with his earlier works. For the French poet, symbolism was the art of "evoking an object little by little so as to reveal a mood or, conversely, the art of choosing an object and extracting from it an 'etat d'âmè,'" and he believed that this mood should be extracted "by a series of decipherings" (Chadwick 1). The Stevens passage also evokes the symbol of the bush little by little through a series of what Mallarmé calls decipherings. That they are decipherings is very clear, since it would be virtually impossible to know without them what Stevens' "bush" symbolizes. Later Mallarmé is reluctant to even decipher the symbols or use the words "as" and "like" (Chadwick 2), while Stevens does decipher his symbols and does use those two words quite often in his poetry. Yet perhaps he found some worth in the practice of later Mallarmé since, though he describes his symbol of bush and uses the words "as" and "like" in the poem, he begins by showing a reluctance to describe them. Perhaps his unwillingness stems from the notion that such "speaking" is killing the object, stripping it of its life (*CP* 166). Stevens, therefore, prefers the enjoyment of the conscious phenomena, from whatever he has so far experienced of it, to knowing the truth (*CP* 166); the cause of this decision could be the painfulness of the obsessive, almost pathological, experiences that much of his poetry reflects. However, the fact remains that Stevens' experiences of the activities of the mind themselves have a great depth. Hence, he could talk about the mind, but in such a way that it does not become uninteresting; his reluctance to turning his experiences true, to speaking of them directly like a philosopher (he enmeshes them into the poetic), and his preference to be always tentative in making assertions about them, keep the interest in the psychic phenomena alive instead of killing it. With such a proposition in mind, he begins to narrate his experiences or/and observations in the rest of the poem.

Images are the produce of a conflation of the actual world and the imaginary. This makes up our conscious life, of which perception and cognition are both the inevitable means and side effects or precipitates without which the human psyche would perpetuate through a "life-in-death"—a deep sleep perhaps, or better, an unconsciousness. The conscious is not a state or something static, but a flux, a process; hence Stevens' choice of the gerund form of "wake." There would be no images, no perception, no cognition, and hence no consciousness without the object, which in the poem represents the actual world; we are conscious *in* images, which depend on the objects from the external world. In fact, we thus participate in the object's being just as the object participates in our conscious, which is ultimately responsible for our *sense* of being. It might be noted that Stevens does not say that we lend being to the object; instead, he says we participate in the object's being, but the concerned clause is without that "we." His use of inflections, phrases, or subjectless and verbless clauses instead of clauses or complete sentences is another way of qualifying his assertions; here he uses it to assert the "anima" of the objective world.[19]

The two short sentences that follow seem difficult to the point of obscurity. The "it" seems to point to the "object," since Stevens has been talking about it, but it could also be a reference to the bush, since the whole poem speaks of it despite the initial reluctance or since we have the sense of being or existence due to the conscious. However, the conscious depends upon the imaginary, which, in turn, depends upon the object, and as the conscious could be said to have been included in the "we," the "it" is more likely to signify the object. Thus, it is possible to read the first of the two sentences as follows: the object is, and therefore we are. However, as the second of the two sentences says, we owe our sense of being or existence not only to the object but also to "Him." Who is this "He"? There is nothing in the poem, no noun, for which this personal pronoun could have been used, except the noun "man" of line 3. But he is very much there in the "we," thus precluding that possibility. What complicates the problem further is Stevens' emphasis on "His" existence; the poet not only repeats the fact of "His" existence but is also most happy to know it.

Here, the sentence that follows the exclamation gives a hint—not without recourse to Lacan. The second comma in that sentence, at the end of that line, is important in this regard. It makes the sentence ambiguous, but this ambiguity helps. The sentence could be read in at least three ways by retaining the same predicate occurring after that second comma: (i) with "He" as the subject, (ii) with "we" as the subject, and (iii) "He is and therefore we are." The first two readings, however, suggest that the "therefore" in the third reading is not necessary. In fact, Stevens has not used either "therefore" or "because" even in the two short sentences discussed above. He is happy to simply realize the existence of the "it" and "He" and some vaguely understood relation of them with the "we." Therefore, one would do better without the logic of "therefore" or "because."[20] "He" and "we" are not only within the conscious but also within its shade, which could be either the rest of the imaginary domain or the unconscious; in the sequel, "Study of Images II," the word "shade" undoubtedly connotes the imaginary domain, but one cannot be very sure that it does not also represent the unconscious. Since the unconscious is also the consciously perceived discourse of the Other, "He" (as the Other) does exist in the conscious as an-other for the "we." Stevens' surprise-cum-happiness at the realization of "His" existence could be equated with Schreber's experience of "Him"; Schreber elevates the Other to the level of God. The Other being the subject of the unconscious, "He" is very much within the unconscious, but "He" is within the conscious too; the unconscious influencing or interrupting the conscious acts is a phenomenon accepted since Freud. If the unconscious is the Other's discourse (*É* 172), it follows that "He" is—as discourse—within the conscious; after all, the Other leaves nothing outside its domain. Similarly, the "we" also exists within both the bush and its shade. What is important here is the realization of "we" within the shade. Stevens is certainly also thinking of the conscious influencing the unconscious. If we exist within the conscious, we exist within the unconscious as well: If I think, something thinks of me too; if I am *here*, I am *there* as well. This is an addition to Descartes's gloss of *cogito*: "I think, therefore I am; something happens to me (or thinks of me), therefore I am." Indeed, the unconscious eruptions give a feeling that something is happening or speaking to us, hence thinking of or occupied by us.

Thus, both the world of objects or the real world outside and the Other within are important in relation to our being and for us to realize that we *are*. It is a question of both "being" and the knowledge that we are. In short, being is realized within the other-Other circuit or, said differently, the *moi*-Other circuit to which desire provides the necessary impetus; nevertheless, within that circuit there is also the desire for knowledge (*É* 301). The knowledge that one *is*—that is, one's sense of being a (unified) "self"—is the importance of the other and the Other. This between-ness of our existence was probably understood by Descartes when he wrote, "*Je suis comme un milieu entre Dieu et le néant*" (qtd. in Kelkar 165); Stevens, though, situates Descartes' *je* between "He" and the "object." However, as Lacan would say, Descartes' God is nondeceiving; under the name of Descartes and Einstein, Lacan attacks the religious projection of God as a guarantee of the truth, as something extraordinary and therefore supernatural, hence as nondeceiving (S III 64–66). Stevens does the same with the too-human God of religious faith (*CP* 315). Almost all scholars of Stevens know Stevens' enmity with such a God; at the same time, though, he dislikes Nietzsche's macabre killing of Him.[21] Stevens' belief in the death of God and His replacement with the Other as the external guarantee of our being is therefore remarkable; it is being more humanistic (though not too much) on Stevens' part.

All this discussion of the poem, however, is very much what Stevens had rejected at the outset. Has this analysis done any good? Speaking of the conscious has reached the Other and being. There is nothing beyond. It is almost as if Stevens has reached the truth by ticking and tocking it, so that even the role of desire is over. Hence, the question pops up again: Does it do any good to thus lay the mind bare (*CP* 166)? If the answer is implicit in the ironic tone of section III of "The Blue Guitar," it is explicit here; the answer is in the negative since this kind of analysis, this attempt to "rationalize" (Carrier 167), strips life of its delight, which lies in imperfection (*CP* 194), in incompleteness. Besides, it is a question of being, which cannot be answered when one is speaking or even thinking, for what is thinking if not the internal speech or discourse (*É* 299)? The answer to the question can come only when there is no speech or thought (*É* 166). This is precisely the function of Stevens' dislike for describing or speaking of the symbol of the bush. Note that it is only after he stops speaking of it (in lines 7 and 8, where "is" and "are" are repeatedly and emphatically used) that any thought of being becomes possible. However, he starts thinking as soon as line 9 begins, and the being escapes, *jouissance* is over; indeed, it was no good.

Ultimately, Stevens returns to the repetitive game of conscious life; there, to believe in it, to find a cause to believe in it. The imagery of musical instruments in Stevens refers most often to the imaginary. Mandolin is of the lute family. If "lute" symbolizes the imaginary, as in section XIX of "The Blue Guitar" (see *L* 790), then the "mandolins," being of the lute family, could be said to represent the imaginary processes. Stevens is adjuring the meditation not to exceed the level of the imaginary processes because, as he has experienced, beyond that it becomes a battering of the mind to make it seem true. Besides, it is worth stopping "here" since this is where the delight of imperfection can always be experienced. Therefore, instead of making deliberate efforts to reach the truth of things (*L* 602), one must stop at the points of conflation (mandolins are terraces just as emperor of ice cream is ice cream as emperor) of the "within" and "without," where images are cultivated.[22] The poet doubts the truth or originality of imaginary processes since they evade the object and create deviations in its perception. Yet one cannot evade them; being the central reference processes for object perception, they provide the basis for reality perception. Accepting human alienation and belatedness, Stevens uses a thermal-gustatory image for the body, suggesting that it either has become cold or is still cooling. The heat seems to assimilate the pre–Fall human existence, or the pre–Oedipal, even pre-natal, stage. However, imaginary processes are what help us preserve that heat as they mediate between it and the coldness or belatedness. How can they be fake when they are truly there, functioning as they do? The onus of falseness lies with images. If the image of an object is not the object as such, the image might be untrue. The image is a form of a realization of desire, and imaginary processes are the means; since desire is destined to remain unsated, the object cannot be perceived except in images that are not the object itself. How can the imaginary processes be falsified when it is what they achieve that is faulty? They cannot even be stale because they are our only possession. Thus, they are up to their task. If they *are* stale (Stevens now accepts that they "must be"), then they may only be as stale as ourselves — we became stale, and have been staling, as we Fell. Thus the same ancient demand refreshes — with each new generation — the desire for the mythical paradise, where the object did not evade us in images or symbols.

The desire will keep refreshing and getting staler since we possess nothing except images. If this is so, it is imperative for a poet like Stevens to stop there, to ponder over this, to accept the only nature we have and find possibilities of *jouissance* right here on the earth, so that it will destroy nihilism (*L* 602), thus creating *here* that mythical paradise which Stevens thought of as early as in *Sunday Morning*. The sequel to the poem just discussed, "Study of Images II," is a part of this project. In the prequel, Stevens stopped at the imaginary processes as they come into contact with the outside world. Being the sequel, this poem is likely to go further and deeper. Considering the rigor of the project, it is not surprising to see him meditate about the basics of images and emotions; after all, his competition is with the "ancient world" where the people (or the first couple) dwelled in the "fundamentals" (*NA* 145).

Thus, the moon is the imaginary and the heaven is the *jouissance* that we seek. It is in this seeking that images are begotten and through which we reach that heaven. Images are described as "heavenly"; however, they are neither wholly that heaven nor wholly the mind. They rather inhabit the thin and difficult atmosphere between the two. (This is quite similar to Stevens' treatment of reality in "Apostrophe to Vincentine" [*CP* 52–53], where the reality belongs neither to the earth nor to the sky, but between them.) They certainly exist, but have no concrete physicality; therefore, they are ethereal. Their significance cannot be underestimated; they are superior to reality and imagination, from which they come. Witch-like, they appear and disappear.

All this is a "Southern" phenomenon, however. It immediately reminds Stevens of its "Northern" counterpart: dreams. Dreams are comparatively rare. If images are of the imaginary, dreams are of the Other. The ice-bear represents the Other; his color is one of the colors of reality in Stevens, but ice is also a metaphor for reality—as in "Emperor of Ice-Cream" (*CP* 64). Besides, "brown" here stands in the difficulty of being adjective or noun or adverb, possibly all, but, more likely, none of them. This is because it is not a word from the symbolic order of cultural language—it is a Word. Considering "brown" as a noun gives an equation, which longer noun-phrases usually create, that befits Lacanian thought: brown = ice-bear = Real/Truth/Absolute = the Other. The word "dismiss" may also be applied in interpreting "Two Tales of Liadoff" (*CP* 346–47), since "Liadoff," which is yet another secret reference to the Other, is an anagram for "laid off," literally meaning "dismissed." However, the present poem's dialectic makes it clear that Stevens does not wish to speak of the Other, but of images; therefore, he does not spend much time coming back to them. Yet some things must be noted, as does Stevens, on the way back: dreams, the unconscious, and the Other all are real; dreams keep their otherness much as the unconscious or the Other do. Hence, they lack congeniality to the self. This is the point where images have an edge over dreams. Images are stylized on imagination and reality. Although the two are opposite in nature, they depend upon each other, are jointly favorable to each other in the image-making process. And since this process is aimed at identification with the other, it is pleasurable. Thus, they are favorable to us as well, as if they are ever ready to seek *for us* the *jouissance* we crave.

Images are treated as if they have life in them, as if they have their own beings. However, imagination without reality has no life, no significance; images are formed as the imagination comes in contact with reality, the manifold external world composed of other things and beings. The self-other dialectic is observed here as well. The relevant line encompasses almost the whole field of images, and therefore is a description of the individual's imaginary domain itself. However, thus far the poem has left out the imaginary processes; therefore, Stevens abruptly shifts to the next stanza in order to arrive at a complete description of this domain. It has been noted that images recorded in the Other's memory function as the frame of reference for reality perception. In this connection, Stevens' use of the past tense with reference to images is noteworthy (lines 5, 7, 14; note that Stevens also characterizes the Other as the product of one's past [*CP* 388]). The imaginary domain is almost equal to this frame. That is why Stevens equates, as in a noun-phrase, the imaginary domain with the images within that frame. The image of "women with other lives in their hair" is compact; just as a lock of a child helps imagine the child itself (*NA* 75), so Stevens approaches images metonymically, by way of the imaginary processes, the description of which should remind us of "live wire": a "touch" of reality, and these processes create the "spark" of perception and image formation that is always with reference to the earlier recorded images. Further, the image of the women is also suggestive of lice, the parasites (the other or reality) that inhabit hair. The lice enter their refuge through the hair and prosper on women. Stevens is clearly suggesting that reality thrives on the imaginary. This might be viewed as part of his humanism, of his project of "recovery of [human] immanence" (Miller, "Wallace Stevens' Poetry of Being" 161), rather than imputing it to his so-called anthropocentricism.

Stevens associates "women" with roses, one of their shadows, as in "Common Life" (*CP* 221). And women without shadows altogether lack voluptuousness. Thus, "rose" suggests the ability to evoke feelings and desire. The description of the imaginary domain seems to be complete here. Yet there is also a sense of incompleteness — the imaginary giving rise to feelings is not sufficient. It may be true that feelings thus roused give a sense of reality, but images do not become complete beings; they are still half-beings for all the real shine they might give. In order to become "complete women," they must get betrothed to their spouse in order to become true or real ("betrothal" is derived from "be" and "truth"). And the "spouse" comes from the symbolic order of culture and language. Stevens appreciates the role of language since it alone legalizes images — lends them a sort of permanence, lends them the sanction of being "true" and "complete." Here, the poet is opening the imaginary into the symbolic. However, images are composed of the imaginary and the real; thus, he is also opening the reality into the symbolic. In fact, Stevens is showing the imbrication and interdependency of the imaginary, symbolic, and real; Lacan did the same through using the Borromean knot (see S XX 123–36). Thus, Stevens suggests that even though reality is viewed as complete without human intervention, it is incomplete without its marriage with the imaginary and the symbolic. In the early years of life, certain sounds also have been recorded or "inscribed" in the Other's memory along with images (see ERS 145). The sound that a man makes later, like the images he conceives in later life, refer to the images and sounds inscribed earlier. Thus, it is in relation to these recordings that man later finds the right sounds, from which spring thoughts and ideas. In order to evoke feelings and emotions so as to fulfill desire, these recordings always remain awake, keep the cycle of desire in motion (notice Stevens' use of "-ing" in the final tercet), and are responsible for establishing man's relation with the whole world — this is the ultimate relation, as it is, after all, the relation with reality. They establish man's relation not only with the world but also among manifold things of the world. This must lead to the sense of Oneness with and of the world. This feeling is extremely satisfying; its anticipation makes human birth harmonious.

We have nothing except the imagination at our disposal. Though Stevens knew that the imagination has its limitations, yet he kept on inventing ways of transcending them. "Note on Moonlight" (*CP* 531–32) is an illustration of such transcendence. Even if imagination illumines things, the self-other dialectic is one of its limits. Thus, our mind and the universe make up a mundane circle where the imagination illumines only the objective nature of the universe (*CP* 531). Stevens transforms this activity into a virile one by extending the limits of the world of objects to include "being," which is in the field of the Other. The mundane routine of existence can be transcended for the better if "being" could be seen like an object or if, instead of merely seeing, one understands that the purpose behind seeing is "to be seen" (*CP* 531). Lacan maintains that one likes being under the gaze just as women like to be looked at (S XI 75). Thus, the poet also extends the limit of imagination by treating "being" as an Other, by creating an Other that sees us. To create an object is a very important characteristic of the imagination; it then evokes feelings with reference to that object and thereby reduces its objectiveness. Or, conversely, the imagination may find its objective in an insignificant object by transforming it into something that could evoke feelings. This is how one's inner world can be charged with power despite the external world's objectiveness; this ultimately helps bring about a positive change in the mundane circle of the mind and universe. This would give us a sense of certainty and a fresh purpose.

The poems discussed here bring out Stevens' preoccupation with the psychical phenomena. He meditated, brooded, very deeply on the possible ways of establishing a harmonious relationship with the world without and the world within. It was not only the other that his self sought; he could not stop there in his search of happiness; his desire urged him toward annihilation of the difference between self and other in order to transcend subjectivity, toward the Other and the Other kind of *jouissance*. This is the "subject" of the next chapter.

Chapter 4

Jouissance

All happiness lies in one's self. (*L* 81)

The highest pursuit is the pursuit of happiness on earth. (*OP* 157)

Things were all right in the Stevens family until 1907–1908, before the start of the tension over Wallace's relationship and possible marriage with Elsie. According to Lacan's formulae of sexuation that he introduced in Seminar XX, Wallace was a fit "man." The psychoanalyst characterizes masculine structure in two ways. According to one of these formulaic relations, *the whole of Wallace fell under the phallic function.*[1] The phallic function is asserted or grounded by the *Name-of-the-Father*. Wallace's life before 1907, as we know it from the available sources, especially the correspondence between Wallace and Garrett, bears witness to this fact. Also notice that this son of Garrett, like the other two, had decided to be lawyer like his father. In short, Garrett served as a perfect delimiting boundary, which the *Name-of-the-Father* or the phallus represents, for the sons. However, Lacan also describes "men" with yet another relation, which means that *there is some part of the subject or "man" that denies the phallic function* or *for which the phallic function is foreclosed.* The *Name-of-the-Father*, being the delimiting boundary, is both part of the subject and part of the Other; it functions to suppress, neutralize, or alleviate the subject's pathological desire for the (m)Other.[2] In other words, the *Name-of-the-Father*, in representing the (m)Other's desire, saves the subject from being absorbed by the (m)Other's desire. The absence of this protection is precisely what is designated by the foreclosure of the phallic function. And yet, it is a necessary function, the function of foreclosure, *but* only for a very short time, in which the subject can establish his relation with Lacan's object of unattainable desire, or object(a), *and* return into the protective circle. In the complete absence of the *Name-of-the-Father*, the subject fails to see that the object(a) is the cause of desire and mistakes it for the (m)Other, and even the (m)Other's desire is then centered upon the subject. In short, the *Name-*

of-the-Father is a directive for the desire pent up in the Oedipal triad, thus helping the subject resolve his Oedipal complex.

By discouraging Wallace from marrying Elsie, Garrett made the delimiting boundary abnormally thicker. What can happen in a case where the subject, having already established his relation with object(a), having become a desiring being, suddenly finds himself overcome by the sense of oppression by the symbolic order, without any avenue of "escape" even for that short time which is necessary if the subject is to develop a relation with the object(a)? Either he traces a retrograde path to be trapped within the Oedipal triad, or he revolts, with his desire, to overthrow the shackles of the symbolic that delimit him. Either way can produce abnormal effects in the subject, especially in the case of a sensitive subject, for the natural resolution of the Oedipal complex should be a smooth and imperceptible process. Therefore, in the former case the symbolic might become the Other, and in the latter it is the (m)Other that could be waiting for him unless, as discussed in chapter 2, the son develops a relation of rivalry with the father, thereby excluding him from the imaginary plane. Wallace preferred the latter way out, but without developing rivalry with the father; he revolted against his father's wish, and married Elsie. In this sense, Wallace's overthrowing of the shackles of the symbolic can be looked upon as overthrowing the *Name-of-the-Father* from the triangular dialectic (repression) and returning to the pre-symbolic time, to the pre–Oedipal time of the sense of unity with the (m)Other.

Lacan says that the obsessional neurotic is keen on confronting "the impossible as object of desire" ("Desire" 36). Lacan's object(a) is the rem(a)inder of the (m)Other-child unity. It is also the object that the subject *refinds* later in the world without the mother, and this experience parallels the (m)Other-child unity. Thus, the time of the (m)Other is not actually the pre-symbolic time, but an emphasis gained by that sense *in the outside world* and corresponding to the subject's unconscious memory of the pre-symbolic or pre–Oedipal time or his encystic unity with the (m)Other.[3] If Ophelia is the object that Hamlet substitutes for the (m)Other, Elsie became that for Wallace.[4] In both cases we find that it is when one comes to the impossibility of reaching the object of desire — and this impossibility itself makes the object correspond with that impossible (m)Other-child unity — that the subjects behave in a careless manner, with no regard for the symbolic order of culture and language: while Wallace quarreled with his father, Hamlet comes out of hiding, revealing his disobedience of his stepfather's orders prohibiting his stay in Denmark. These are acts aimed at overthrowing the delimitation imposed upon them, revealing the catastrophic power of desire. This happens in a normal subject as well, but for a brief moment only, and he then (i.e., upon returning to the domain of the symbolic) cherishes the memory of that moment. However, the neurotic remains implicated in the moment until his neurosis is over. The phallus, being repressed, can also become the Other of desire in neurosis. Therefore, such subjects are likely to exhibit both identification with the feminine and desire for the phallus. Hamlet does not show feminine traits, at least not strongly enough, as he is almost always in the vicinity of the phallus, unlike Stevens.

Since all this is a play of desire, and since Lacan formalizes sexual structuration on the basis of desire, one cannot lose sight of the subject's psychic restructuring with respect to the reorientation (even disorientation) of desire. While the normal subject returns to the symbolic order, the neurotic remains in "the time of the Other." The crossing over of the delimiting boundary is nothing but an opening to the Other's desire. The expression "Other's desire" (*desire de l'Autre*) is essentially ambiguous; from the normal subject's point of view it is the Other's desire for something else, which he takes upon himself and becomes a desiring being, while for the neurotic it is the desire for the Other as such (*É* 312). Thus, Lacan's second formulaic relation for masculinity, designating the foreclosure of the phallic function, has different meanings for the normal subject and the neurotic. And this is the difference between the object(a) and the signifier of the Other's desire, S(Ⱥ).

This is useful in showing the changes that may take place when something similar to what happened in the case of Wallace occurs. The subject's relation with the object(a) is problematized; instead, the relation with S(Ⱥ) is established as the subject believes the (m)Other to be that object. His relation of nonforeclosure to the phallic function changes into that of foreclosure. In other words, the second of Lacan's formulaic relations gains emphasis, allowing us to read it as *not for the whole of man does the phallic function exist*, which in fact is one of the formulaic relations that characterizes the feminine structure. Lacan's use of the negative here suggests that a very small part of the subject, if any part at all, falls under the phallic function; conversely, almost the whole, or a very large part of him, denies the phallic function. This is how the second relation gains emphasis in the masculine structure. However, it must be remembered that even that part which denies the phallic function, that part which rejoices with S(Ⱥ), is effected by the phallus itself—that is, by its absence or repression. So it clearly means that there is now *not some* part of the subject for which the phallic function does not exist or is foreclosed; this is another formulaic relation that characterizes the feminine structure. Even if—rather, because—the subject thus escapes the symbolic phallus, he remains tied to the imaginary phallus; here, he takes the phallus to be an actual object that he must become or retrieve.[5]

The signifier S(Ⱥ) is both at once—the signifier of the Other's lack or desire and the signifier of the desire for the Other. The desire for the Other implies the desire to recover the lost (m)Other-child unity, the "first loss" (Fink 114). Fink suggests that the signifier of the desire for the Other or of the "first loss" may be written as S(a). However, he does not seem to be sure whether to equate S(Ⱥ) with the phallus or with the lost (m)Other-child unity (see Fink 195n36). This confusion may be overcome if the "first loss" and the (m)Other's lack are distinguished. The former clearly implicates only the subject while the latter implicates the (m)Other. The latter, of course, indirectly implicates the subject as well, but for the neurotic what matters is the recovery of the "first loss," which in itself denecessitates the fulfillment of the (m)Other's lack since S(Ⱥ)—now reduced to S(a), that is to say, the (m)Other as the object of desire—is itself his *jouissance*. The (m)Other's lack or desire is not in question here since S(a) also means the (m)Other as phallic—that is to say, complete. Thus, S(a) is a signifier of both the "first loss" and the phallus; here the phallus is essentially a real thing in the neurotic's imaginary. Therefore, S(Ⱥ) is both the signifier of the (m)Other's desire or lack (desire and lack coexist) and the signifier of the phallus; here the phallus could be symbolic or imaginary depending upon the subject's normative or neurotic desire. However, even if the neurotic imagines the (m)Other to be phallic, it is still the ultimate human truth that no one is whole, that the (m)Other is also a barred, divided, lacking or desiring subject; thus, even S(a) is in reality the S(Ⱥ). This could be the reason why Lacan did not coin some signifier, like Fink's S(a), to convey the idea of the phallic (m)Other. The neurotic desire fails to distinguish between the object(a) and the phallic (m)Other, and therefore confuses them, whereas the normative desire can differentiate the two, allowing the phallus to be symbolic.

For this reason, upon the repression of the phallic signifier, the neurotic desire revolves around the (m)Other, precluding the possibility of becoming a desiring being. And because this is essentially a *re*finding of the lost unity, it is displaced into the "outside" world (i.e., the actual (m)Other is replaced by an[y]-other woman the subject thinks he loves). Herein comes the role of Elsie as the S(Ⱥ) in Wallace's life. One might think of all this as stretching things too far. But how, otherwise, are we going to vindicate the figurations of the phallic female and the joining of the mother and beloved in the poetry? The poet's obsession with death can also be accounted for with the help of the present discussion; after all, the desire to be one with the (m)Other is the desire for that pre-natal state of unity, or even for the pre-pre-natal state, which is almost the desire of/for death. Stevens kept consuming himself in his desire for the (m)Other, and the last two lines from "Madame la Fleurie" boldly suggest that he knew, or had realized, the root and cause of his consumption (*CP* 507). His unconscious desire for the (m)Other had an undesirable effect on himself and on his perception of the world around him, since it was the desire for the (m)Other-having-the-phallus (her masculinity is obvious in the relevant lines), the death instinct itself.[6] Without such interpretation it is simply impossible to account for the psychical energy exhibited by a man who was, properly speaking, neither a philosopher nor a psychoanalyst. In all its honesty, his poetry is a manifestation of the experience of something that lies outside the human sphere that Lacan calls the "symbolic beyond" (S II 76). This is why any study of Stevens' poetry with reference to his person requires an interpellation of Lacan's signifiers-in-the-real.

If Stevens had rediscovered the $S(\not{A})$, it was at the cost of his relation to the object(a), which I take as an indication of his restructuration as feminine. This stance might explain why he felt more affinity with his mother than his father (*L* 213–14) or why there is an unusual dominance and treatment of the feminine in his poetry. At the same time, there is the phallocentric nature of the "central mind" in the poetry since femininity and masculinity must be inextricably related to each other. This is the reason of my insistence in chapter 2 on treating the "I" of "Re-statement" as feminine. Lacan insists that "woman does not exist" because woman is closer to the (m)Other-as-object(a) in comparison with man. And since this relation decides Lacan's view of "existence," of the sense that one *is* or *is not*, it raises the question of "being." It is not surprising, therefore, that Stevens often leads us to this question, which was his own question, as will be seen after a while.

From this viewpoint, what is important is to see in Stevens' poetry "the time of the Other" and what may be called "the time of being." First, "the time of the Other." There are many poems in the *Collected Poems* in which we find the mention of the unconscious and the Other under different names and guises; Stevens' desire for the Other, manifest in numerous poems, is a very strong indication of his restructuration as feminine even as the Other is portrayed as essentially phallic. It begins as early as page 5, when Stevens' desire begins its "journey" of the unconscious (the sea is an image for the unconscious in Stevens). Out of the obsession with or observations of the unconscious, Stevens introduces new experiences and brings them into the domain of language. These moments in his poetry bring into our grasp an-Other reality that is essentially alien and gives his experience a certain sublimity, even exoticness. This is like Stevens translating a Russian poet into the French language (*CP* 234); this is the Other as *jouissance.*

Stevens' mind was always eager for the sound from and glimpse of the sea of unconscious (*CP* 5). So he tells a Fernando, in "Hibiscus on the Sleeping Shores" (*CP* 22), that on a particular day his mind-as-moth (the *moi*) went beyond the conscious domain, into the interior of the psyche. The noise of the movements deep within the psyche were not audible (as it was in "A Dish of Peaches," prompting the question "Who speaks?") because the mind had become one with those movements. The mind, then, did not remain *as* moth but became the moth itself; in fact, due to the effect of partaking of the movements, it became monster-like. Before its monsteration, the mind had been engulfed in the imaginary (Lacan's *méconnaissance*) and was nincompated by it; it was allowed only a "colored" or unclear perception of the unconscious. Therefore, for the mind, the "sea" (the real) was unmoving, dark. As the dominance of the imagination had obscured the "red" (Stevens' color for reality), the mind was lazily drowsing since it was denied access to the interior and was tied to the corporeal world.

However, the monsteration was extremely energizing, for the mind then saw, in a flash as it were, the bright, fiery reality that *was* beyond the corporeality, and perceived it more clearly (the "red" as "dabbled" with the "yellow" pollen), as clearly as it perceived the corporeal world. However, Stevens does not use the word "perceive" but rather the past-tense form of "seek." It would not be a great mistake if one hears it as "shot," for symbolization of the real is to introduce holes into it, to kill it (see Fink 24, 182n1). The symbol has the power to bring the real or ineffable into the domain of the symbolic, into the domain of language and culture; the illustration is to be found in the poem itself—"flag." It is difficult to see or say all that it refers to and represents—what it brings, as symbol, into the symbolic order, into use. Thus, though the poet says that the mind perceived the real as real, yet he doubts that it can do so; hence he immediately qualifies the perception by comparing it with the perception of the flag, thereby not only introducing a metaphor for the perception of the "real as real" but also simultaneously moving away from or abstracting the "real" real. Yet, as powerful a poet as Stevens was, he adapts his tool for the real, fertilizes his language with the "pollen" of this experience, by generating a powerful symbol for "the Other above man" or for "the real above the human," which is comparable to the image of the aureole in "The Well Dressed Man with a Beard" (*CP* 247). This is how he brings the "Hibiscus" to where his mind was. It is difficult, however, to suggest what Stevens designates by using the pronoun "there" in the final line. Where exactly? In the real, with the Other? Or on the shore to which the mind has brought the "Hibiscus"? Here, Stevens does not seem to care much about the place. What matters is "the time of the Other." It was afternoon when the poet's mind was with the unconscious reality.

At times, afternoon shifts to moonlight and Stevens shows concern for place as well. In "Anecdote of the Prince of Peacocks" (*CP* 57–58), he emphasizes the importance of moonlight, since it allows him to "place" the Other. Here, he meets the Other that he sought in the "Hibiscus" poem. The opening sentence is not as simple as it looks. Besides the ambiguity of the moonlight, there is the mention of the meeting place as time-bound ("moonlight" as night), which is the domain of the conscious[7]; the moonlight could mean "night," "sleep," "dream," or, as usual, the imaginary. There is no problem if the moonlight in this sentence is meant to evoke the imaginary. However, references to "sleep" and "dream" later in the poem raise a paradox: How can the consciousness and dream be integrated, as Stevens does in the poem? The poet's reading of Freud could have been at the base of their integration. According to Freud, says Lacan, the disturbing phenomena like dreams begin from the unconscious and, via the preconscious, reach the consciousness (S II 139). M. Valabrega, one of the participants in Lacan's Seminar II, calls this "a retrograde path ... regression" (141). However, even the imaginary, one of whose mainstays is the past (images recorded earlier), has the dimension of time and traces a retrograde path, especially in the process of projection. After all, what is the existence of the imaginary if not always in reference to what has already happened? Otherwise, it would be impossible to distinguish it from perception, but even perception without the imaginary is inconceivable. In this way, the problem posed by the "moonlight" may be resolved by suggesting that the imaginary does also participate in the unconscious processes, and that the "I" may be asleep or dreaming. Thus, the uncontrollable Berserk is "met with" by bringing it into the conscious. "He" was awake since the unconscious does not sleep but keeps talking without stopping. It is the poem's speaker that sleeps; it is we who sleep. Sleep, generally taken to be a loss of contact with reality, is in fact the time of access to an-Other reality. Sleep does not induce the unreal as dream but the real as real. This realization must have prompted the question that Stevens does not ask but rather says in the poem.

The question of dream led Freud to the unconscious manifestation. Why in dreams does the unconscious manifest itself so clearly? The answer Stevens' Berserk gives demands explanation. In Lacan's thought, the perception of the external world gains meaning with the help of the imaginary, thus constituting a meaningful world, which is the mark of the ego's supposed mastery of the world. Once the external object becomes meaningful, the desire renews, a search for a new object begins, and the previous object or symbol may be forgotten — the word "forget" is there in the poem. However, there are symbols that are perceived but do not gain, or are not given, any meaning or else have lost it through the forgetting. Freud calls these symbols the *Tagesreste* (the day residues), which are unimportant for desire but are stored in the preconscious nonetheless (S I 245). They exist there until the unconscious desire of recognition ignites and seizes them, and the unconscious expresses itself with their help; this is what we call a dream (S I 247). Thus, the unconscious "traps" the subject, as Stevens says, in dreams. The phrase "to set trap" is ambiguous. "Set," among all its meanings, means to "impose or present," and also to "fix";

"trap" is a "trick or device to betray or to reveal a secret," and it is also a slang term for "mouth." The phrase thus has at least two meanings: that the Other imposes or presents his discourse ("trap" = mouth) in the dream, and that he fixes or determines his trick to betray (to) the subject or to reveal the secret to the subject in the dream. What secret, what kind of betrayal is involved here? Before coming to an answer to the question, it is necessary to see the "why" side of the question. Why reveal or betray the secret?

The Other is also the Law. As long as the subject (the ego) obeys the Law, there will be an order to the subject's life. Nevertheless, *jouissance* lies beyond the Law, in violating it. The subject (the ego) violates the Law to deny the supremacy of the Other-as-Law and be the master of the world in which he lives. Lacan says that the subject does this out of his need for recognition (S I 247); which subject does Lacan speak of here? The ego or the Other? It could be either or both at once. The ego tries to gain or preserve its mastery by engaging in a search for the truth, whereby it may come to the conclusion that the Other-as-Law is idiotic (S II 128–29), while the Other comes down through the dream to the conscious — through this "retrograde path" — to prove that he is untouchable, that he is the master. The Other proves it through the navel of the dream, as Freud would say. The navel is that part or point in the dream which is absolutely incomprehensible, extremely obscure, belonging to the domain of the unknown. The ego has no clue to what this point is or even why it is there. This is the essence of the Law; it must remain incomprehensible to the extent of looking idiotic (S II 129). The navel of the dream painfully cuts short the ego's desire for recognition and mastery. The incomprehensibility of the navel of the dream creates doubt in the subject. He cannot forget it, the ego cannot forget its failure, and it is within this failure of the ego, or within this idiocy of the Law (from the ego's point of view), that the Law asserts itself, that the Other proves its untouchability, His High-ness. There are other modes, like slips of tongue, jokes, and symptoms, through which the unconscious discourse manifests itself. As Stevens' Berserk says, the ego normally tends to forget this interruption, but it cannot forget it when it happens in the dream. That is why the Berserk traps the ego's complacent "self"-ness in dreams.

We now come to the "what" side of the secret — in fact, it has already been answered in the preceding paragraph, but may be extended a little further. The secret is nothing but the reality that the subject-as-the-ego has failed to recognize in the waking state. The reality is that the subject is not unified but fragmented (S II 54), that there is something or someone within and outside him who hears, speaks, and refers to himself as "I." This realization reveals the intersubjective dimension or dialectic that is constitutive of the subject — in spite of himself. This revelation shatters the complacency of the ego's supposed wholeness. The resultant disintegration is the fear of the conscious domain. The dream was educational insofar as it yielded the knowledge that, in the way of one's knowing the landscape of the mind or the whole of psyche, there were still a lot of obstacles blocking that knowledge. However, the poet-speaker does not seem to harbor a negative attitude toward this disturbing revelation. Although it has curtailed the ego's aspirations, he still finds it beautiful. For one who celebrates death as the mother of beauty, the loss of the ego's innocence has to be a revelation of the Other beauty.

Due to the continual irruptions of the Other, Stevens feels committed to thinking of it as part of the "I." Section XII of "The Blue Guitar" announces this with élan in the opening line. What follows this announcement is a comprehensive description of the human subject. The imaginary is responsible for the ego's sense of wholeness or oneness (as "I"); in fact, the ego itself is a function of the imaginary (S II 36). This is given in the poem from the ego's point of view, which declares its unity with the imagination. However, that is not all. The "orchestra" is not yet complete. This lack is what creates the melody that rises, filling the unconscious with other people. These people are the audience to the "orchestra"; that they are restless (due to "lack") suggests that they desire something that would satisfy their desire, fill their lack. This audience, this other, this "listener" is constitutive of the *moi*; this is what "The Snow Man," "A Dish of Peaches," and "Of Modern Poetry" show. In Lacan's words, a formula that he derived from Rimbaud, "I (*moi*) is an other" (S II 7) or "Thou art that" (*É* 7); Lee presumes the psychoanalyst borrowed this from the *Chhandogya Upanishad* ("*Tat-tvam-asi*") (see Lee 217n54). It is possible that Stevens' image of the orchestra is directly borrowed from Rimbaud's famous "Lettre du Voyant," quoting the relevant passage from which Alan Williamson comments, "The conscious ego is at best something like the conductor of an orchestra" (4). In the very first few sections of "The Blue Guitar" we see that the guitarist sees his desire in his audience's desire, in the other's desire, which is present before the guitarist begins to play. From a Lacanian perspective, this is a precondition for one's entry into the world. One can see the guitarist's pose, bent over the guitar (*CP* 165); the pose is reminiscent of the foetus. Patke's opinion that the guitarist is "improvising" is enlightening (81); indeed, like the foetus, he lacks foresight and is trying to foresee — that is, to make his way into the world (the roots *in* + *pro* + *videre*, from which "improvise" is derived, yield this meaning). The guitarist has no means except his guitar to accomplish this goal. It is the other that helps him make his way. It is not a chance event that Stevens had his guitarist pose like this, nor is it a coincidence that the other speaks first in the poem. It is the audience's desire that is instrumental in shaping the "music" of the guitarist. In Lacan's view, one's desire is the other's desire. He also relates — or rather integrates — the other into the unconscious. The unconscious, in his thought, is full of the desires, talk, conversations, goals, aspirations, and fantasies of the other people around the subject (*É* 55, 172; S III 112; Fink 9–10). And this is brought about by the imaginary. Hence the "orchestra" fills the unconscious with the other men, and since the unconscious is made up in large part by these men, they are equal to the unconscious itself. All this is precisely what Stevens says as he writes that the noise made by the people becomes the speech of the unconscious (the Other), who does not sleep. The speech of the people (the other) becomes the speech of the Other. Stevens recognizes the Other's discourse, which shies at the presence of the other or at the other's speech. Lacan believes that one (the ego) speaks to "screen out the Other" (ERS 197); conversely, "the less we speak, the more it speaks to us" (S III 138).

In the question that Stevens asks regarding the beginning and end of the "I," he is trying to specify or fix the human subject within some system, like Descartes. However, the Other cannot be formulated like this; it retains its Otherness. Obviously, Stevens has gone beyond Descartes to be able to express the knowledge that the Other — even though it keeps its Otherness — cannot be anything but his own "I." Insofar as the imaginary is concerned, what this poem emphasizes is that the formation of the Other and the knowledge of its existence — or, similarly, the knowledge of one's own ex-istence (with reference to the Other)[8] — is the role of the imaginary; that it is the "orchestra" of the imagination and the "I" (the ego, which is the function of the imagination) that fills the unconscious with the other people; that it is the functioning of the imaginary that makes one realize the "I"-ness of/in the Other.

The Other is like a politician who is completely "absorbed" among people, existing within them, and who has no existence or personality without them (*L* 526); yet he manages to keep himself aloof from the people. His politics, deceptive nature, supremacy, indispensability and inevitability easily match the nature of the Other. Therefore, Stevens sketches the Other as the "ultimate politician" in "Sketch of the Ultimate Politician" (*CP* 335–36). Here, the building and dream represent human body and its psychical world respectively. (We know that the poet uses architectural images like cell, cabin, room, chamber, house, and so on for the self; the "building" seems to be another variant of the same image.) Since the physical and psychical cannot be separated, Stevens declares their oneness. And yet he is forced to separate them in the second stanza. Why do we all feel, as we live our daily lives, the otherness of our own psyche? This is the problematic of human existence, this gap between psyche and soma, each of which cannot be separated from the other, yet must be; they are really two-in-one. The universality of this problematic is particularized in each individual. One more gap is to be noted, complementary to the one mentioned above: between the Me and the Not-

Me world. This Not-Me world, the other, is extremely important from the viewpoint of the formation of the unconscious—of the whole psyche, in fact.

In the times before language, in the times before the Disobedience, man was one with his environment, the reality around him. Now reality evades him. This gap between him and the reality, this "linguistic damage attendant upon the Fall" (Morrison 81), is perhaps reflected in the divide between psyche and soma. The rise of language is simultaneous with this division and man's separation from his environment. Thus our "words" are essentially embedded in the storm of desire that seeks to bridge the gap between the structures that, once, were one. Therefore, the "storm" is compared with the wind's cry. Stevens often uses the image of "wind" to depict the movement of thoughts and emotions in the mind; "The Wind Shifts" (*CP* 83–84) is perhaps the best example of this. While the wind image appropriately assimilates the transient nature of the movements within the mind, it may be interesting to note that literally or physically inverting the first letter of "wind" creates "mind." The wind's crying, then, would not be far from suggesting the mind's crying or craving. In fact, in "To the Roaring Wind" (*CP* 113), Stevens adjures his crying mind to speak out the lost signifier, which has become the Other of his desire. For what does the mind cry or crave? For the Other, as the rest of "Sketch of the Ultimate Politician" seems to confirm. There is certainly this sense of the "desire for the Other," characteristic of psychoses. Something or someone speaking within himself fascinates the psychotic; however, this discourse of the Other also "rankles" its hearer's life without making any (audible) sound as such. The last three stanzas of the poem show that Stevens' poetry becomes arcane due to the symbolism of extremely private nature, originating as it does from the symptom that remains hidden. Anika Lemaire writes, "Pathology ... stresses the private nature of associations at the expense of their universality by introducing 'secret motivations'" (44). Stevens' genius, however, is evident as we see him universalize his most "private associations" and "secret motivations."

The fourth stanza is a continuation of the thought presented in the preceding stanza in that it speaks of the Other's activity in relation to him who hears its speech. Stevens says in line 10 that the Other hears too. We know from Lacan that the Other only speaks, speaks all the time, and therefore cannot listen. That the Other listens is a fantasy of the neurotic, who is free to imagine or doubt—like the poem's speaker—that the people in the photographs on walls may listen to his speech; this is clearly symptomatic of neurosis (Stevens' own), whereby the speaking subject always suspects that someone is listening to him even though he has not spoken. Freud's observation that the unconscious discourse intervenes in the conscious discourse in the form of jokes, witticisms, and slips of tongue is important in this poem.

In restating this idea, Stevens says that the Other's speech runs in the subject's speech; Lacan calls it an "interruption" or "interpellation." The louder the unconscious discourse, the greater the failure of the subject's speech, which suffers from its own suppression[9]; similarly, the disappearance of the Other—which is same as the disappearance of its speech—is equally frustrating for the psychotic subject since it alone "maintains" him or her "at the level of discourse" (S III 205). Lacan also believed that this discourse is the only thing that sustains the subject at the level of being. This is precisely what is implied when Stevens writes that the fall of Other's speech fails the subject. The discourse of the Other may be unsettling, even "rankling," for the life of the subject, but its disappearance is annihilation. The "storm" of the "desire for the Other" is equally destructive. Since the Other is structured through the subject's past life, it interrupts from the past; what it interrupts is a "dream," as Stevens prefers to write (life is a dream?). By "dream" the poet could also be suggesting the subject's complacent sense of unity, his happiness thereof. Though our past is our own and is as near to us as the unconscious memory, though this Other is so close to us, unity with it is an impossibility; it is as impossible as to actually live our own past. The last line of the poem insinuates, painfully, the desire for the Other and the impossibility of attaining it.

The poem lends the Other qualities that are generally attributed to fate, wielding control over human life. "He" decides the fate of the human; "he" is like a politician whose policies or decisions can make or destroy the structure of a nation, and who still manages to remain outside the nation's interests or ruins. As one might suspect, Stevens is not far from elevating the Other to the level of God. The suspicion is not baseless, as section XXI of "The Blue Guitar" proves. There, the Other has replaced all the gods. This replacement was dreamed of long before in *Sunday Morning*, one project of which was to find or found divinity within the self (*CP* 67). This is not an instance of egocentrism in the least. The ego is not the center of this divination, but the Other, which is continuous with the other—even in *Sunday Morning*, where the woman protagonist seeks heaven in the immediate world around her. The thought of heaven and gods was thus disinvested from our desire much earlier. Against the heaven and gods, Stevens weighs the human "within," which he finds most beautiful in its lack (*CP* 317). Referring to Nietzsche, Riddel writes, "The return of God to the self is ... the imperative reflex of 'man stripped of myth, [who] stands famished among all his pasts and must dig frantically for roots'" (152). Stripped of all myths, Stevens finds in the Other qualities inherent exclusively in God. If this idea is not yet acceptable, he is certain that in time it will be. This future is made the present in section XXI of "The Blue Guitar"; and yet, Stevens does not forget this lord's relation with the world in which we live (*CP* 176). In Stevens' poetry as in Cézanne's painting, the mountain figures as the grandest form of the other, as the epitome of the real world, the immensest form of the environment. Or one could say that the mountain in their works is the symbol of the external world, a symbol having supreme importance, since both artists realized the significance of the world in which we live (*CP* 86). Thus, both artists' search for God is centered on the *here and now*, on the real world, since it is *here* that they find man's "roots." Section XXI of "The Blue Guitar" ends by suggesting that the real world is composed of the most ordinary things — the quotidian "roots" from which we spring — in which Stevens believes and which the religious belief spurns. The Other, being the "shadow" of the real world (i.e., of the other), may then be compared with the "holy ghost."

Even the ordinary reality that we inhabit is not easily comprehensible, as reflected in the thinking of the people who spurned it, believing it to be unworthy, as if they had understood it. Well, they may have understood it, but the past and the myth that sustained it have vanished (*CP* 143). They are not useful in the modern world and society (*CP* 153). Having realized the problems of modern reality, Stevens could not yearn for the hymnal way (*CP* 471). The modern reality kept evading him, though. If reality can be so unreal as to evade the human and remain nonhumanized, what would its "shadow," the Other, be like? Obviously, less human (*CP* 327); this is what the poet finds fascinating about the Other. This is why he substitutes it for all the gods; after all, it is the essence of the concept of God that he remain nonhuman (even inhuman). The pagan gods were projections of the human within into the outer world; in this sense, their world was self-centric, more so than even the Cartesian worldview. It must have been the people after the pagans, or the people before the dawn of Christianity, who imposed on themselves gods from the outer world and also vested their desire with these gods. One would be wrong to find fault with Christianity, for it introduces the element of humanity, in the form of Jesus, into this outer world; Christianity may be praised for projecting the "within" into the "without," although it retains the face of the "holy ghost," God's unknowable, unfathomable aspect. This is not an attempt to defend the religion, but to get to its roots. In this sense Stevens is in line with Christianity — if not perfectly, then at least by analogy. Whatever faults one would find with Christianity must be really with the additions that were made by various people through different ages and generations. There could be no better example of such unsolicited and unwarranted additions than in the Hindu mythology, which, with so many hands contributing to the original myths, especially in the period called *uttar vaidic kaal* (post–Vedic period), now appears to be more false than true. The difference is clearly perceivable: in order to make people believe in God and Jesus, the "contributors" made Christianity exceedingly human; and in order to make people revere (or fear?) God, they made Hindu mythology—with the respectable exception of a few things like the four Samhitas and the *Bhagavad Gita*—exceedingly unreal, almost inhuman.

Insofar as the Christian tradition in which Stevens was brought up is concerned, the exceedingly human God cannot be different from man, because through too much "pity" he "weakens" us by ending almost all evil and pain in life (*CP* 315). However, for Stevens, life consists within the oppositions, since the continual play of balance and imbalance between two opposite things constitutes the "change," enabling the desire engaged in its cycle of destitution and fulfillment to save our lives from perpetual ennui (*CP* 392). Therefore, our fate must be strong to bring about unexpected changes in our lives: for this, God must not be too human, like Jesus as we see him now. Yet Stevens does not prefer a totally inhuman God either; thus, a compromise is sought in "Montrachet le-Jardin" (*CP* 260–64) by hopefully introducing the element of mercy, enabling one to speak of God in human voice (*CP* 262). However, this does not distinguish between the ordinary man and the hero (*CP* 262). So the poet comes down to the ordinary man, to himself, who dreams of the humanized reality as the paradisiacal Other (*CP* 263), since even this reality is not wholly and fully humanized. This compromise between the human and the inhuman realities is essential to Stevens' conception of God. And what he experiences is that the Other-as-cat is only momentarily seen, and vanishes as quickly (*CP* 264). There is a definite positivism in these lines; the Other is seen at midnight and his speech has become audible (*CP* 261). This is the moment of an experience of the Other as *jouissance* since hearing the Other speak is an experience of freedom, of another world beyond oneself, who, aided by imagination, sings its praises (*CP* 261).

Hence Stevens' God, being neither over-human nor inhuman, is simply "less human." While the poem's title, "Less and Less Human, O Savage Spirit" (*CP* 327–28), grieves over the less human aspect of "god," the poem's body justifies it. This is not only one more opposition that one can find in Stevens' poetry but it also marks the origin of desire. The poem employs a repetition of "Let him..." and "he must..." syntaxes, a rhetorical move depicting wistfulness. There is something of what Campbell and Dolan call a "praeteritic antithesis," in which "'the rejected thing, the thing denied' ... ends up becoming the focus of attention, with the ostensibly endorsed term fading into the background" (120); in this rhetorical device, the rejected thing or term becomes dominant as the author "talks about something while promising not to talk about it." Although the poem seems to vindicate the less human nature of God, the repetition of the above syntaxes praeteritically hints at the speaker's anxiety over God's less human character. Thus, the truth of the Other is revealed in the rhetorical move itself.

"He" moves silently, dwells quietly, and shows his excellence or superior rank — that is, his alienness — through the signs of stars. Although the poet writes that "he" must not be able to speak, he knows that "he" speaks. It is only that "his" speech cannot be understood, since it remains undeciphered; it is a closed system in the sense in which "light," "color," and "shape" are closed systems (we cannot literally touch them — we "touch" them only through the emotion they produce in us or through the way they affect us). Stevens knows this, yet has an embittered feeling that the Other does not respond to our desire as other humans do. The poet is aggravated by the Other's indifference, by its radical otherness, by its unsociable quality. The word "stick," apart from meaning "unsociable person," might suggest a "support." Similarly, "mass" could mean people (recall that "the unconscious is full of other people" [Fink 9–10]); in fact, just three lines before, the poet writes that the "mass" cannot be communicated to or addressed, thus pointing to the unconscious. While the Other is characterized as unsociable, the relevant phrase in the penultimate line also seems to gloss it as the support of people — in the sense that *because* there is the Other's radical otherness, there is the human subject and the "desire for the Other," in much the same way as God's otherness makes him desirable. Stevens wished the Other to replace God in the hope that it would, like God, be the support of people, enabling them to live their lives as human subjects. Hence the longing expressed through the poem's last line that reveals the poet's wish to reduce that "apart-"ness. However, it is not possible for the human subject to identify with the crass inhuman; this impossibility characterizes Lacan's "real." The whole poem being a rendition of the Other as impossible (and this is precisely what generates the very concept of God), the word "stick" may seem to gloss the Other as "fate," the utterly unsociable or nonhumanizable reality that controls us even as it supports our existence as human subjects, thus making us part of it. Everything in the poem seems to suggest the poet-speaker's desire to be one with what he ambiguously calls the mass. In this poem as in Lacan, the real is complete, full, and does not require human intervention; it is the human that is alienated and desires the Other to respond (ERS 93), craving a union with it or the real, desiring an eradication of the distance between the place we inhabit (*CP* 326) and the place we wish to inhabit (*CP* 336). This is a question of being and existence; the two expressions of Stevens, one at the end of *Esthétique du Mal* and the other at the end of "Sketch of the Ultimate Politician," recall Lacan's notions of "existence" and "ex-sistence," and also the desire "to be there where *it* was" as laid out in Freud's "*Wo Es war, soll Ich werden.*"

All the poems discussed so far in this chapter reflect Stevens' meditations on the Other that are closely analogous with Lacan's glosses of it. *Collected*

Poems is full of references to the Other in various guises, beginning with "Paltry Nude" (*CP* 5–6), which initiates desire on the path of the Other, up to the final poem, "Not Ideas about the Thing but the Thing Itself" (*CP* 534), which depicts the otherness, in relation to the subject, of the continuity between "inside" and "outside," where "the Thing" that is referred to could easily be what Lacan calls "the Freudian Thing" (*É* 114) or the Other. Stevens' figures of nobility and heroes could also be assimilated into Lacan's Other. I will not discuss all of them here since Grosvenor Powell has already done something similar. However, I would like to elaborate on the hero-figure. One of the best examples is provided in *Examination of the Hero in a Time of War* (*CP* 273–81). Between sections V and IX, the common man as hero undergoes a gradual transformation through the classical hero to become an inhuman, beast-like figure. Whether this is a future projection of the common man as hero or not, the movement certainly depicts a projection of the human "within" into the "without." Here, Stevens' idea of God as a little human but largely inhuman is realized. Yet Stevens would not be content with a God who can be thus outlined or statued for fear that "he" might be desecrated by those who will not believe in his God; therefore God must be "saved" (*CP* 277). Thus, in section XIII, the new God of the poet's faith is presented as a closed system, needing no reference, in this way abstracted beyond any humanly possible outline or design.

In "Two or Three Ideas," Stevens says that the gods are stylized on the model of human beings (*OP* 213); still he believed that God must not be too human. The Other-as-god is thus created out of Stevens himself, but as more pure and more grand (*OP* 212). Now the poet is free to worship him, to try to be in the presence of him or his images. Thus, section XIV of *Examination of the Hero* proposes composition of hymns to apprehend the Other in anticipation of more satisfying perceptions (*CP* 279–80). What is most striking in section XV is that the Other as the composite of man and hero is able to compose poetry on "the syllable *fa*" (*CP* 280). It is as if the Other knows the meaning of this syllable, which I take to be another disguised reference to the signifier *father*, or *Name-of-the-Father*. In this sense, the central figure of the poem's meditation is undoubtedly a bearer of the phallus. The same can be said of the "major man" in the *Notes*; he is described as one who remains unweaned (*CP* 388), free from the threat of castration — for him there is no question of the loss of phallus. The description is ambiguous; Powell prefers to dwell on his own question: "Whose breast?" (745). I think the lines would be better read as "the major man remains unweaned *forever*" and that "he is (forever) precious to Stevens *for his touch with the breast*." With such a reading, "touch" acquires the meaning of the mother-child unity.

However, it is important to also observe that while some works in the

Collected Poems, especially the first few poems, and notably the "Snow Man" and "Re-statement of Romance," show Stevens as a patient, the later poems, like "A Dish of Peaches," are mostly written in the spirit of an analyst or observer. One can always object to accepting Stevens as an analyst, owing to the fact that he could not wipe out his fascination for the Other. Nevertheless, that may be part of the memories of his earlier experiences. Besides, fascination itself is what the ego psychologists call the "health" of the ego. Lacan also observes fascination essential in constituting the ego (S II 50), even though, in his view, fascination must be discouraged in order for the desire to remain normal. Let it be said that this fascination for the Other was never discouraged, was never moderated enough in Stevens, such that his experience of or encounter with the Other was part of his existence (S II 177, 178). This is opposed to the ego's disintegration into several parts on encountering the ultimate real. This is obvious in "The Snow Man" and "A Dish of Peaches"; however, most of his remaining poetry reflects what the ego psychologists would wrongly call (in Lacan's view) the ego's "health." If this health has any meaning for Lacan's body of thought, it is that the ego is in radical otherness with itself *and* in a dyadic relationship with the Other of its desire. That is, the ego is an-other to itself and is also a patient trapped in a dyadic closure with the Other; the former implies the ego's alienation from itself, as in the Lacanian model of the relation between a patient and his analyst as an other, whereas the latter evokes identification between a patient and the analyst, as if the analyst-other were an Other. Stevens' poetry shows both traits; sometimes we see him alienated from himself, trying to gather himself through the dyadic relationship with the Other, but he often appears to be a patient analyzing himself, as if he were an analyst-Other to himself. His poetry, therefore, appears to be a commingling of the strange experience of a patient and the analysis thereof. In this way, as Brogan seems to believe, it will not be totally out of context to say that Stevens sought to treat himself, although the fascination and obsession inherent in the earlier experiences are sensed to have been remembered from time to time even in the later poems.

If Stevens attempted to recover from his illness (Brogan 15), it would be interesting to see if and how he did it. This obviously means a freedom from the "time of the Other" by allowing "traversing of the fantasy" and becoming a desiring being oneself or assuming one's own "being." Let us first try to understand what this important stage of "traversing of the fantasy" means in Lacan's thought, since *how* one comes to "be" is important from the analytic point of view.

Prior to the sense of being a "self" or to the sense that one *is*, one is almost nonexistent; to use Lacan's term, one "ex-ists." Later, the processes of alienation and separation take place, effecting one's "existence." One more important process that Lacan describes is the "traversing of fantasy," which may be seen in some detail. Before the traversing of fantasy, the subject is tied in a dyadic relation with the (m)Other. Fink distinguishes a castrated subject (who has successfully entered the symbolic order) from the "insufficiently" castrated subject (who is not successfully alienated from the m(O)ther) (72). The latter confuses the Other's demand with object(a)—with the Other's desire—and hates his castration as the cause of the Other's *jouissance*. The properly castrated subject has learned that the acceptance of castration is essential if he or she has to breach the limits ordained by it; it is in this acceptance that the subject stands a chance of experiencing the traversing of fantasy, which further alienates him or her from the Other, enabling one to establish the "utopian" relationship with object(a).

Now, before the start of the tension in his family over his marriage with Elsie, Wallace was a properly castrated subject (as opposed to what Fink refers to as insufficient castration); he had undergone the further separation. In short, he was a normal subject before his father started resisting his access to manhood. When the quarrel between father and son took place over the marriage and the son broke his relationship with the father, Wallace lost his relation with object(a) and mistook the Other's demand for the Other's desire. It is interesting indeed to see what or who this Other is in this particular case. The father as paternal Other is clearly one possibility: Stevens knew too well that this Other was making a demand that he could not fulfill; in this sense, he in fact renounced castration and went ahead with his decision of marrying Elsie. This should have naturally led him to establish the relation with object(a).

Let us pause here a moment to ask a question: Is the "traversing of fantasy" possible for a properly castrated subject or for an insufficiently castrated subject? On the one hand, castration—the subject's entry into the symbolic order—is necessary if the traversing of fantasy is to take place, if he is to cross the barrier of the Other's demand in order to establish the relation with object(a); on the other hand, as Fink says, castration must be renounced (72). If castration is welcome, why renounce it? It would seem as if there is a contradiction, since the insufficiently castrated subject is almost the same as the subject who has breached the limits ordained by castration, for both are closer to the real-as-(m)Other as object(a). Fink is not wrong, however; he only needs to add that castration must be given up *for the time that would be sufficient for the traversing of fantasy* in order for the subject to subjectify the object(a), "the cause." This is because, after all, the subjectification of object(a) is a momentary affair, though its effects are long lasting for the subject, and also because the subject does return to the order that castrates him after the moment of subjectification is over. The point is that it is from within castration that the subject breaks through to the real, thereby abandoning castration for that moment. One more important point is to see when the subject is likely to renounce castration. Something radical must happen for the subject to switch over to the other extreme, to object(a). This "something radical" is nothing but the subject's sense of his own castration by the Other—he must feel burdened by it; castration must reach its peak, for the stronger the sense of this burden, the better for the subjectification of object(a) (by "peak" and "stronger" I do not suggest excessive castration, which leads to abnormality, but rather adequate or sufficient castration). In this way, the subjectification of object(a) depends on castration.

Wallace's castration by the paternal Other—even parental Other, since his mother cannot be altogether excluded from his father's resistance to his marriage with Elsie—his sense of castration or its "fullness," and Wallace's overthrowing of it are all obvious. Yet it confounds our imagination as to how this period (1907–1908) should be the prologue to a great literary "career," the beginning of which shows a psycho-pathological character. Why is it that Wallace, instead of writing joyful songs, wrote poems of a pathological character at the beginning of his career, since in overthrowing his castration by the parental Other he must have established the relation with object(a)? To this end, there is little proof. Nevertheless, this should not be a hindrance. Though we have no proof, it is not impossible to see that Wallace's love had something to do with this. What is not obvious is the demand of his love for Elsie, without which Wallace would have either achieved object(a) or would have respected his father's—or rather his parents'—demand, thereby retaining his castration by the parental Other. However, neither of these was to be. Wallace revolted against his father's demand, but at the same time he was entering, fulfilling, tying himself—despite himself—to an Other, the pivot of which was Elsie. Stevens' situation is very much comparable to that of Hamlet in the sense that both were deprived of the phallic signifier and in both cases the beloved became for them the object of fantasy that replaced the phallus.[10] What must have happened is that Wallace separated himself from the parental Other and got engaged with an-Other (Elsie), believing the latter's demand that the marriage take place to be the latter's desire. We know that Stevens was postponing the marriage since he had to be sure of his ability "to provide" (*SP* 247), and Elsie was concerned about "moving past the age when she should have been married" (Richardson, *Early Years* 176). Even though the demand is not explicitly made, yet the subject in love, which is really his "wish to be loved" (S XI 253), makes him the object of the Other's (here, the beloved's) gaze; this is a form of the demand the beloved-as-the-Other makes. Deserting her would mean falling in one's own estimation, jeopardizing the wish to be loved. This is the Other's gaze, where the subject desires to see himself as he would "like to be seen" by the Other (S XI 268). For this, the subject in love might prefer to make any sacrifice. Freud, therefore, says that love means that the object attains impossibility or is sublimated in such a way that the ego is completely at the mercy of the object and whose "self-sacrifice," which could take the form of "self-injury," is "a natural consequence" ("Group Psychology" 113). Thus, Wallace sacrificed his phallus, his masculinity. This is how, even after revolting against the parental Other's demand, he remained subjected to the demand of Elsie-as-Other. Yet even that revolt was not a complete revolt since he still had a lot of respect for his parents. This situation was dangerous, for, on the one hand, he sacrificed his phallus to show his love for the parental Other and, on the other, he could not disrespect Elsie's demand that the marriage take place. Unconsciously, he was trying to fulfill only the Other's demand on both fronts. Remaining thus tied to the Other's demand is what Fink means by "insufficient" castration.

Chronologically speaking, the real as the mother-child unity is cancelled out (as it precipitates into the unconscious) due to the child's entry into the symbolic order. This is what constitutes alienation and separation from the (m)Other. The *Name-of-the-Father* plays a crucial role in these processes. However, the subject can refind "some modicum" of that unity later in fantasy, which is capable of supplying that utopian sense of wholeness or "being" (Fink 60–61). Lacan refers to this fantasy object as object(a).

In adult life, some traumatic event can transport the subject back into the Oedipal situation, or to what Lacan refers to in the seminar on *Hamlet* as the "time of the Other" ("Desire" 17). The quarrel between Stevens and his father was just such a traumatic event; it changed Stevens' relations, including his relation with his being. He was thrown back to the phase of castration-threat and lost the sense of being, of "self," of his "wholeness" or "completeness"; this situation is, however, conducive to the formation of that dangerous dyadic relation. In short, his relation with object(a) was problematized. This anticipates the loss of the *Name-of-the-Father*; to aggravate the situation, this situation was further followed by his father's death in 1911. If we denote the object(a)—which is both the object responsible for the subject's sense of being and the signifier thereof in Lacan—as S1, and the *Name-of-the-Father* as S2, it could be realized that the loss of S2 strips S1 of any meaning at all. This retroactive effect that S2 has over S1 is important, since S1 cannot mean anything without the appearance of S2 (see Fink 64). The child's unity with the mother, comparable to the subject's being-as-object(a), is reduced to a signifier (S1) by the institution of the symbolic order, the pivot of which is the *Name-of-the-Father* (S2), and this precipitates the subject (S). If, after this, S2 disappears ... what will happen? This is our concern. The subject's status as subject or his sense of "self" will be problematized. The S2 now becomes the

S1. Unless this S1 is brought into relation with other signifier(s) (a relation of opposition or difference as between two signifiers), the subject's relation with object(a) cannot be (re)established, thus preventing the subject from attaining fuller subjectivity, the sense of the "self." A little careful observation of Stevens' poetry reveals that he has often used what he calls "reality" as a binary signifier or signifiers (S2) that lead to the apprehension of the "real" real, to the object(a). Perhaps he unconsciously hoped that this way he would not need the phallus (S1). (Of course, as we will see in the next chapter, there is ambivalence in Stevens' view of reality.) That is why there is a realization in him that the reality one sees is not the end in itself; it is the beyond—where one's being resides—and the sense that it is capable of bringing, which ends the subject's search of himself, of his being; the fifth stanza of "Sailing after Lunch" says as much (*CP* 120).

It is this essentially happy or comic end that the whole of Stevens' work strives to reach. Eliot's motto was to be holy, but for Stevens happiness was holier (*CP* 185). Thus, while most of Stevens' readers find his *The Comedian as the Letter C* (*CP* 27–46) comic, even as a "comic debacle of Crispin,"[11] their sense of the "comic" falls utterly short of the essential comedy—which is Crispin's serious quest for the objective he finally attains—that is deliberately masked. Stevens was not a poet who would indulge in the comic without serious reasons; poems like "A High-Toned Old Christian Woman" (*CP* 59), "Of Heaven Considered as a Tomb" (*CP* 56), and "Nudity at the Capital" (*CP* 145) are proof of this. The central theme of *Le Monocle de Mon Oncle* (*CP* 13–18) is laid out in the fourth line from section VI, where "substance" can be interpreted comically as amorous tendency or seriously as imagination; even in Stevens' life he was reservedly serious. Most readers of *The Comedian* do not seem to see the serious intention of the poem. Daniel Fuchs even goes to the extent of calling it a mock-heroic poem (32). Bloom is close to calling it a bad attempt by the poet and to rejecting "intentionality to some manifest poetic blots" like "Crispin's four grotesque daughters" (82). Beneath all the "zany brood of disgruntlement" consisting of "burlesque, farce, satire, parody and travesty" (Patke 34), *The Comedian*'s search for self-aggrandizement remains masked. If "From the Journal of Crispin," from which *The Comedian* was expanded, incorporates "the saintly inheritance in Crispin's name" better (Patke 25), it is because Stevens was serious about the theme; otherwise, he either would not have written the poem or at least would not have bothered to submit it in a competition on hope of winning the prize (*L* 224). R. P. Blackmur, however, understands this (see his "Examples of Wallace Stevens"); Vendler says that Blackmur considers the poem's subject as serious and the poem as "conveying a sort of heroism" (*On Extended Wings* 38). However, one can see the seriousness of "The Journal" and the happiness of *The Come-*

dian. Even the former is full of the comic element, but what needs be discerned is that Stevens, from the germ of the theme onward, kept mitigating the degree of seriousness and made its final form look more comic. It was deliberate. Stevens daubed *The Comedian* with almost everything that could evoke the reader's mirth, and turned it into an anecdote so that it would amuse even those who could have derided the theme in the face of the then ruling world-view represented by *The Waste Land.* However, the choice of "anecdote" instead of "fable" for describing the story of Crispin suggests the poet's desire for credibility and acceptance of the theme: it is not a fable because Stevens did not want it to be taken as "not based on fact," and, though anecdotes do not require a moral, the poem *ex professo* entails a moral that one has to "score" (*CP* 45). The style of this anecdote may not seem prescriptive, but its structure is. Therefore, the whole poem could be ascribed intentionality.

The first section is wholly devoted to embark Crispin on the introspective voyage (*CP* 29). The purpose is to rediscover the self and establish a new world order, since the glorious human past is no longer useful in the present where the contingent reality that surrounds modern man is essentially inhuman (*CP* 30). Thus, the old notion of man's centrality to the world must be rejected. This is achieved by disbelief in the idea of acquiring sainthood through hardship, as St. Crispin did; such miracles cannot happen in the present circumstances. At the same time, since every post–Adamic man is removed from the "C-Natural" (*L* 393),[12] the once natural position of man's superiority over the world in which he lived, he is alone—without help from the heavens. Thus, Stevens breaks human attachment with God and the Adamic world order by "dissolving" Crispin's ancient namesake (*CP* 29). Here, the use of "an" instead of "the" in relation to the protagonist's name evokes the "every-day man" (*L* 778), and the allusion to the saint evokes man's relationship with God; this suggests that although man now stands alone, he still has the power that saints had and need not succumb to the satanic pressure of reality. Yet, being human, man still needs help, as if from some present equivalent of the old god. So Crispin hears a heavenly trumpet against his insignificant voice (*CP* 29). This brisk and decisive sound, this "crisp" that is "in"-side, is what he must seek. Thus, the voyage to the inner world has already started on an auspicious note. The crux of Stevens' organization of the world is that God must be inherent in man (*CP* 67).[13] At this point begins Stevens-Crispin's odyssey—which Miller appropriately refers to as the "recovery of [human] immanence" ("Wallace Stevens' Poetry of Being" 161)—his search for the "mythology of self" (*CP* 28), which is not without its psychical import. This is the central concern not only of *The Comedian* but also of Stevens' poetic career, toward which most of his writing is incident.

This kind of Husserlian reduction to a naked self allows Crispin a perception of the reality within himself. The whole of the final passage of section I is a description of the unconscious, the *here and now* equivalent of God. On becoming introspective, Crispin stands confronting *it*, which is the ultimate real.[14] It speaks from the dark recesses of the mind and is both audible and visible,[15] but it is not Crispin's other (*CP* 29), the external reality as Crispin's *alter ego* that his ego-as-imaginary function can manipulate.[16] This suggests the radical otherness of the unconscious in relation to oneself. This is precisely the reason for that rift between Crispin's ego (*moi*) and his unconscious (the Other). Although the romance in the form of "speech" does exist between the two, yet it is a (strange) romance that encourages the feeling of otherness in the ego instead of the sense of their oneness, thus deserting Crispin the egotist.[17] The reality Crispin confronts here is beyond his (ego's) control. The imaginary *méconnaissance* has finally given way to a realization of the godlike indifference of the unconscious. Yet this is a renewing experience for Crispin in that it is, after all, a new knowledge of reality. While Crispin is spellbound by the unconscious reality (Stevens' descriptor of it can be divided as "pan-o-ply"; "Pan" was the god of the natives of Arcadia inhabiting mountains, caves, and lonely places—this easily aligns it with the unconscious, which "plied" Crispin-Stevens with its speech and questions, hence his awe—signified by the "o" in the descriptor), he wonders—rather, is wonder-fully sure—that it originated when the Adamic (egocentric) world order came to its end. The unconscious reality is further glossed as something that renders wholeness as well as shatters the imaginary perception of reality. Nevertheless, the experience yields a new knowledge of reality and revives Crispin's spirits.

In section II, Crispin seeks to express, like a poet, this new experience and the knowledge thereof. The unconscious and its discourse must be clarified. However, bringing the real into the domain of the symbolic is a difficult part of an artist's life, for his language must be adequate, must come to terms with the grandeur and novelty of the experience. Hence, Crispin tries, in the spirit of *avant-gardism*, various forms and techniques of expression, "rebelling against conventions, experimenting with poetic forms" (Simons 456). Crispin's experience of reality has also refreshed and revived his desires. This is also the cause of his "heat," which is well expressed by William Carlos Williams as he wrote about the years around the early 1920s: "There was heat in us ... a drive ... of a rediscovery of a primary impetus, the elementary principle of art, in the local conditions" (qtd. in Martz 10). Well, Crispin has found that impetus, but he lacks the mode of expression. He eventually realizes that the lack will not be fulfilled from the outside, that there is no ready-made help and that, in fact, the satisfaction of his desire can come only through his own indigenous language and style enriched by a totally new aesthetic (*CP* 31), different from the aesthetic(s) cherished by the litterateurs walking under Eliotian influence and the movement of the object-ridden poetry. The newfound aesthetic has given Crispin a new vision that will lead him to things not yet known to humanity but wherein lies its fate. He has only sensed this promise at this point in his voyage; however, he does realize that the unconscious or the Other speaks of a reality that keeps augmenting in what would be Lacan's real (*CP* 32), which is productive since it keeps eluding its interpretations and yet makes the real world more desirable, more beautiful, and more opulent. The poem's reader is likely to be confused here: If Stevens is speaking about the unconscious or the Other, how does he suddenly shift to the outside world? It is because the Other or the unconscious is a continuity between inside and outside; his awareness of this continuity is reflected in the final poem in *Collected Poems*, "Not Ideas about the Thing but the Thing Itself" (*CP* 534), in which the bird's "cry" comes both from outside and inside simultaneously.

Crispin proceeds with these "notes." However, he does not know that the productive principle can also be destructive. Lacan reveals the (m)Other's threat in a shocking way by comparing her with a crocodile that devours her child (see Fink 56–57). Thus, Crispin experiences this harsh reality in the form of the thunderstorm. He realizes that the reality he desires is not very gregarious — it is fearsome. From Lacanian viewpoint, the thunderstorm is the "master" (or "master signifier") and Crispin a "slave" or subject. Lacan says that the first function of language is "imperative" (Fink 198); perhaps it is the basic function since the primary-process thinking operates as an imperative function for its subject. Hence, the master's speech is harsh. It is through such speech that the master wields his authority, making the slave envy that discourse (*CP* 33). Nevertheless, the slave must obey him, must bend to his command, and so Crispin kneels in the cathedral. It may be noted that he does not kneel out of reverence for God but because of the threat of the harsh reality as master. And all the while, the slave awaits his master's death like an obsessional; however, he does not know that by the master's death, he will come (psychically) closer to his own death — this is the slave's substitution at the master's place and awaiting the same fate. The master's death provokes anxiety; this is particularly evident in the father-dreamer son relationship that Freud describes ("Formulations" 225–26). There comes about a destruction of the structure of which the slave/son is a part and in which he has an identity. Perhaps the loss of identity is one of the meanings of "death" for Lacan here: he says that the slave's waiting for the master's death is an intermediary between the slave and his own death (S I 286). What is happening in the poem is that the *Thanatos* principle has become operative — Crispin's desire for the Other, to symbolize it, is proving fatal. He does not know that there is no *jouissance* in seeking the Other (*É* 323). Like every man, he desires to conquer death; like a slave, he desires to own the master's power through acquiring his speech (*CP* 33) or seeks to symbolize the master (to symbolize is to "kill" in Lacan). Fortunately, the "master" does not die and thus Crispin remains alive: the thunderstorm, the master's speech, is still heard on the cathedral's roof. However, something has surely happened here. The harsh sound of reality has dwindled to droning. Has Crispin succeeded in "symbolizing" the "master" to some extent? In any case, like the adventurer (Odysseus? Columbus?) who has seen death closely and faced and survived it, Crispin emerges feeling energized and rejuvenated; his limits have extended — he has gained in experience and knowledge as a slave does while slaving (Fink 131). For the adventurer, after this experience, death does not matter; he almost feels equal and opposite in relation to it. Thus, it is *while* the torrent is still heard that Crispin feels the Andean anima. Both Cézanne and Stevens associate primal power and force with the mountain image. In feeling the Andean anima, Crispin feels like or becomes the Andes; he feels the mountain's strength as his own being, or at least part of it. This is how he matches himself with the thunderstorm and its harshness, though only when it is in its lesser potential form. Though Crispin is not equal and opposite to the thunderstorm in its most potential form, he has at least gained some knowledge of it, which has transformed him. However, the thunderstorm has retained its mastery; death is still the master signifier against which Crispin struggles. He can think of speaking only after the thunderstorm has subsided.

There is another dimension to this episode. It is not the cathedral where the thunderstorm stalls and abates but rather beyond where Crispin is (the cathedral) and beyond his reach. While the sound of the thunderstorm may be interpreted as a perception of the ineffable, the primal, the absolute, it is still beyond Crispin's understanding, or returns to what is beyond human reach. This may also be interpreted as the insufficiency of religious belief and faith since it is not the faith that helps him — it is the Andean anima, which *he feels*, that really helps him; it is his own transformation into a different self that comes to his aid. Was there no cathedral in the town from which he began his voyage? The descriptor "crusty" suggests there must have been (*CP* 33). When it did not help him there — and it is one of the reasons why he embarked on his "voyage" — how could it help him here? He is a man who would neither borrow the desired assistance nor see through someone else's eye (the available religious perspective); he would rather see with his own eye/I (*CP* 35). Thus, whatever he will speak hereafter will be indigenous, from his own experience, knowledge, and imagination. Hence the claim for a room for Crispin in the book of imagination.

The justification for this claim obviously comes from the originality of his experiences of the unconscious in which he hears its discourse. In the last passage of section II, Stevens avoided a direct confrontation with religion; here in section III, aware of Crispin's unique ambition (it might be Stevens' own), he hides his "voyage" behind the name of "pilgrimage" (*CP* 33, 37), lest it should raise the eyebrows of the contemporary litterateurs. For the same reason, he also gives the impression that Crispin's desire for the ultimate religious experience — which would be nothing short of a direct experience of or confrontation with God — has come true in an unforgettable twilight zone between consciousness and unconsciousness (*CP* 33); this is why the discourse of the unconscious is juxtaposed with the religious imagination/meditation/faith that Crispin seriously thought of earlier. However, the whole argument is ambiguated by the mention of an unspecified continent. Is he referring to his erstwhile place of living? The sarcastic tone of these lines certainly supports this reading. Besides, America is mentioned in the very next line, suggesting a change of place. And the rest of the passage describes America in a manner not too promising. However, this is precisely what must suffice; Stevens very much preferred to inhabit such a land. He portrays America in this way because he wanted himself to overcome the initial "primitive difficulties" so as to create a mythology not only of the region but also of the self as is stated in the poem's first section, so that he would feel the joy of his own origin in what he has "endured and mastered" (*OP* 295).[18] Thus, Crispin returns — has returned — from the ancient imagination and that vague continent to the continent that may comparatively be raw but, for the same reason, is desirable (*CP* 37), and begins "progressing" toward the North.

The "Arctic" imagination replaces the ancient one, and Crispin writes poems. Though neither religious nor mythological in the traditional senses of these terms, Crispin's writing has for an object something that is no less than the object of great poetry. The ancient imagination could also be the Romantic imagination; in any case, since Crispin no longer espouses it, he also denies its insignificant creations. With this, Stevens is free to compare Crispin's poetry to religious or mythological writings in the sense that great writing aims to be an object of great magnitude.[19] He works to establish his liaison with the environment — both of which are real, not two transcendental entities, nor a transcendental entity and a real entity, nor a transcendental entity and the human being, as generally happens in religious and mythological writings. This liaison is the primary aim and the source of ultimate happiness of Crispin-Stevens' enterprise. It will yield that happiness not for Crispin or Stevens alone but for every other person as well. Herein lies the root of why Crispin will later abandon the project of a colony; there is no need of the colony if each individual can find the aim and happiness in life. From the Lacanian perspective, the liaison between oneself and the environment would be the goal of identification between self and other, and the happiness thereof would be the *jouissance* of the unity or wholeness of self accomplished through that identification. Once this is accomplished, there would be no sense or feeling of otherness; the "colony" then would be unnecessary.

Thus far, Crispin has been wavering between his desire for the real and his imaginary indulgences or, as Patke would say, between the solar and the lunar (or, in Lacanian terms, between the real and the imaginary). The real, insofar as it is religious (God), and the imagination, whether it be religious or mythological or Romantic, both are part of the ancient world order. However, Crispin is determined to rid himself of anything that might take him backward. He has realized that it is the solar, the real, which is untouched yet closer, that he requires; the real in its raw originality, this "North" is what he needs for his refreshment or recovery.

Crispin abandons the highly fantastic creations of the past, as they are dating him back to the past. This is his rebirth as a poetic hero who has very high regard for the quotidian. Creativity is a search for an august reality, which Crispin seeks in the quotidian; it makes him see in it much that he had never seen before at all. It is a purifying experience since it has given him new vision and a new knowledge of the real world in which he is living, of the world that was misrepresented by the contemporary scholars who either remonstrated against the world and went in search of "Shantih" or thought that "so much" of the external world "depends upon" the perceiver for understanding. None of them ever allowed the introjection of the outside world into themselves; they either forsook it or forced themselves onto it. By becoming introspective, Crispin sees something that the falsifiers could not: being. Here, one might think of Lacan's object(a). However, it is more probable that he sees the phallus here since, in Lacan's thought, being-as-object(a) is not something that can ever be seen or said as such. The poet seems to be using "being" in the sense of "existence," in the sense of the feeling of being a "self," as having a separate identity that the phallus is responsible for; for the moment, Crispin does not approve of the change or lack of an identity, as will soon become clear. However, one should first see how Stevens has used the words "prose" and "poem": his lines suggest that if the prose wears the guise of poem, then the discovery of being will come to an end; that is, if this happens, one will discover the being and there will be nothing to search for. The reason is that by "prose" and "poem" Stevens seems to be speaking of the two levels of the experience of being — namely, "being on the level of the object" and "being on the level of the subject." In Lacan's thought, the experience of being is always subjective; what one sees on the level of the object is the phallus ("Desire" 48). It is becoming the phallus oneself, or having it, that is capable of yielding the sense of being[20] — this is the relation that Lacan pays attention to.[21] Therefore, "being" as prose is the phallus, and its becoming the subject's own is called its wearing the guise of a poem. "Poem," because the experience is intensely personal, and "guise," because "being" is evasive, such that the accomplishment of being is never really an accomplishment but simply a feeling or sense of it; the subject shares only some modicum or portion of it, *momentarily*, in his fantasy. Thus, he always tries to "grip"—the word is used by Stevens in connection with reality (*CP* 376)—the phallus; his question is whether "to have it or not to have it" ["Desire" 48]) or, said differently, whether to embrace masculinity or femininity, as opposed to the neurotic, who is "a negative object" in the sense that he is "at the level of privation," which forbids him to be or have the phallus ("Desire" 48–49). This must be the reason that did not allow Stevens, before this period of about 1920, to experience "the traversing of fantasy," thus deferring the achievement of (the sense of) being; he was at "the level of privation" in his *Harmonium* years, which prevented a change of identity. It is clearly from this poem, or from this part of the poem's third section, onward that Stevens' poetry acquires a distinctive panache as against the pathological and death-ridden character of the earlier poetry. It is from here that the "recovery of immanence" really begins.

On realizing the significance and importance of the real world in relation to the self, Crispin changes his earlier "note" to make the soil (or reality) superior to man (*CP* 36). The world that is falsified by the so-called scholars is still new for Crispin, where he can live a fruitful life. With this, he is free of the influence of the past. The exit of the past was necessary since the purpose of his voyage is to establish a new order, knowledge, or intelligence, which will lend primacy to reality as the pivot of human existence. However, his notion of reality, of life, is not without "men," and this is the trouble. Though aware of the sovereignty of the "soil," Crispin is still thinking of the world in terms of anthropocentrism. He still seems a democratic-minded European, even a socialist—hence, still caught up in the past. This is why he projects a colony. Though renewed, he still has old dreams (capricious indeed). This is the reason why his prolegomena to the new knowledge is a commingling of both past and future. Nevertheless, what is commendable about his conception is the necessity of a harmonious relationship that he envisions between the men of colony and the world they inhabit. The application of this concept, however, anticipates a change of place for the "men," and hence a change of identity, since, for Stevens, identity is determined by the place. Thus, there is a distrust regarding the idea of a colony, perhaps due to dislike for a change of identity (*CP* 38), since it is determined by the real world one inhabits. At the same time, he also does not approve of the lack of the awareness of identity. Both the instance of the señors and that of the Brazilians illustrate these views. The señors are not happy, as they lack desire for the world they have "colonized"; the Brazilians perhaps lack the imagination, since they do not realize the importance of their language and hence are not inspired to write. In both the cases, what is suppressed is the human potential, but it remains latent; its recovery is, therefore, important. This is the reason why Crispin will later give up the idea of "colony" and embrace the "recovery of immanence" as his object.

The "colony" is essentially a dream at the end of a democratic or socialistic line of thought. How blindly Crispin was lured into it! In George Orwell's words, these thinkers believe that "all men are equal," and are ultimately forced to practice the law of nature that "some men are more equal than others."[22] They turn a blind eye to the fact that each is not equal, or is only more or less equal, to every other; this difference is what constitutes life. Why do those thinkers unnecessarily believe otherwise (*CP* 39)? Every man has a different nature and has to devise his own way of living; this is, more or less, what Stevens understood by "up-to-date capitalism" (*L* 292). The socialist dream cheats by glossing over the text of life; their dream remains a dream, however grand and promising. Crispin realizes this. He does not want to confine his desire like them. Therefore, instead of depending upon dreams that depend on us, he prefers to depend on fate, a strange line of thought but true to life, since we do not preordain the future. This may make Crispin look like a comic character—as most critics have made him since they do not see that human life itself is, in Santayana's words, "comic in its existence" ("Carnival" 45)—but an aspiring one, like Auden's Icarus.[23] The socialistic or democratic cozeners intend to defy diversity as the reality of human nature. Hence Crispin vows to let the reality go unconfined, to let life go on as it does, to let things be as they are. Instead of flaunting false thought and theory, Crispin prefers to stick to reality in order to be true to the true texture of life.

In section V, Crispin has abandoned the project of a "colony." He has instead turned to his own self. The movement from the outer to the inner brought about by desire is characteristic of the formation of the unconscious. Without (noticing) this movement, Crispin would be no different from the realist of the movement called Realism who forbids desire in spite of his desire. Crispin sees the limitation of this realism: reality survives its descriptions (*CP* 41). The real cannot be grasped in its entirety. How can one grasp more of it? Not without the desire for it, of course. Therefore, he concludes that what is real is what we desire; the use of "should" in the relevant line introduces the dimension of the subject's desire in the perception of the real; it is not as stubborn for Crispin as those "shall" and "ought." It is true that the real can be perceived or described—though never fully, yet a little better—only in terms of possibility. Nevertheless, even the possibility tends to go in two different directions: one that produces objective structures without human interventions as such, and another that produces structures of which the very cause is the human imagination or desire. If we consider Stevens' remark seriously, that our imagination can only use nature but cannot create a new one (*NA* 74), then we can realize that both kinds of structures mentioned above are not without human intervention, and that the claim that the objective structures erected by the so-called realists are without human intervention—or their theory of objectivity itself—is a big lie, an illusion, unless we refer to the whole of the real as objective. We have concrete examples at our disposal from the field where objectivity dominates: physics. Did not Archimedes apply his imagination to make his personal experience of the hydrostatic law the instance of all such phenomena, which had evaded human perception until his time? Did not Newton's experience of things falling on the earth prove a boon for later generations in the same way? Has not Stephen Hawking used his imagination, which he applied to what was known already, in order to (fore)see the beginning and end of time? Can we say their revolutionary thoughts have arisen without any subjective involvement? If yes, why could not the common people see these things? It was these scientists' imaginations, the roots of which are in the desire for the real, that ultimately succeeded in approaching the real, and we know to what extent and with what precision. The cause of other people's failure in seeing these things lies in their immanence remaining suppressed.

Crispin is an ordinary man like those common people but, unlike them, he is an aspiring human being like those scientists, attempting his own leonine rise before the lion of reality (*CP* 175). This is neither a digression nor a minor point in discussing the poem, for here one must observe a synthesis of the two notes, "man as superior to the reality" and "the reality as superior to man," a synthesis for which Cook is desperate and unnecessarily suggests that another set of three sections, devoted to the synthesis, would bring the poem to a better denouement, so that Crispin's career does not become what she calls "one long diminuendo" ("'The Comedian as the Letter C'" 192–93). One must notice that in section V Crispin has arrived at a point where neither man nor reality is superior: overcome by the reality, man does not remain superior, but reality has not retained its sovereignty either; instead, the reality has become "suzerain," which "humbles" but "attaches" as well (*CP* 40). "Suzerain" literally means someone controlling the other while granting the other internal autonomy. This is where Stevens allows the subjective element implied in that "should" discussed a moment ago. Subjectivity may be repugnant to the so-called realist, but it befits Stevensian realism, the aim of which is not to balk before reality but to rise before it.

"But how to produce this leonine imagination?" asks Cook ("'The Comedian as the Letter C'" 197), and the rest of the poem responds positively. Crispin's questions in the second passage of section V are not all negatively answered. He seriously ponders those questions; here he is seriously thinking about whether it is possible to make himself an exemplar for all other people (*CP* 41), like those scientists. He realizes that it is possible if he avoids the peculiarly personal. In other words, he seeks to make the personal the universal. Within himself, he searches for what is in every man that needs to be recovered or revived. And he does find it, as will be seen in the discussion of the final section of the poem. This is why, despite being a hardcore realist (*CP* 40), he sticks to his own thought and opinion (*CP* 41). Thus, he becomes a representative of the human race, his single head representing all people; by sticking to his opinion, he will represent the opinion of the whole of humanity. He opines that it is only what we desire that exists, that is real, or that is permanent. Having introduced desire in perceiving reality, his inner world is completely refreshed (*CP* 42).

And the real gives in to him, though not fully. It can never be perceived fully; instead, it comes in the form of its representative, the prismy blonde. The word "prism" is derived from Greek *prisma,* meaning a thing cut short, removed, or reduced by sawing. If "prismy" also suggests "many meanings of domestic felicity" (Sukenick 58), then she represents all the subjective interpretations of the real as its reduced or removed versions, each revealing a different aspect. Sukenick uses the expression with more or less the same meaning in believing that the blonde breaks up the "'one, vast, subjugating, final tone' of the reality" (58). With this understanding, Crispin "latches up" (and latches on to) the "night," which is "man's interior world" (*CP* 333). What happens in his mind is given next in lines that are highly unparaphrasable — Crispin experiences that "shantih" in which truth is revealed. It is here that he achieves the leonine rise as he becomes the master of his inner world; it is a sign of the internal autonomy given by the suzerain reality.

This is a very important movement that the critical attention has preferred not to take note of despite Blackmur's attempt; while this wise critic observed the decline in the "sovereignty" of reality, others could "make nothing better of [Crispin's] world" (74). Realism, objectivity — the then cherished literary or even philosophical views — and the absolute subjectivity of the earlier periods are combined in an effort to comprehend the maximum of the real, and thus to effect self-upraisal. The need here is to elevate, qualitatively, the subjective view of the real, without which *The Comedian* would have been a complete failure due to lack of ambition. It might be true that in the unknown past man was superior to reality. What is true now is that man has lost that seat of superiority and reality is superior to him. Crispin's effort is directed not toward regaining that seat — that would be a false ideal — but toward becoming equal to reality, toward closing, as much as possible, the abyss between the two "notas." To this end, what is essential is the recovery of human potential. Hence, Crispin's sticking to his opinion and returning to domesticity is worthy of the cause.

Thus, it is a new morning. Crispin's journey becomes walking in a circle; it is immaterial whether he is in Carolina or elsewhere since even the quotidian "saps." His new way of looking at reality has made that walk less difficult but more intent and, more importantly, there is a promise that it will be fruitful (*CP* 42). He owes all this to the newfound relationship with reality, which has become his "duenna." He realizes that the quotidian, being part of reality, survives its "poems" too. Like the sun, it "saps" laymen and philosophers alike. It may be suspected that "sap" is used as both verb proper and noun made into verb—the former usage suggests that it exhausts, as opposed to the latter, meaning it invigorates (both like the sun). Men like Crispin appreciate the philosophers' intention since they do not overlook the quotidian; the only problem is that they have no desire for it. The sexual connotation in the "humped return" is useful in understanding the "birth" of Crispin's four daughters and his enrichment: Here, one must see the mutation of the reality that was superior to man; first it becomes "suzerain" and then "duenna," and now it is his sexual partner, his equal. This does not mean that the reality has succumbed; rather, it is Crispin's upraisal that makes him feel equal to it.

Critics have not been able to agree among themselves on the significance of the four daughters.[24] They are neither the four seasons nor literal daughters or progeny, nor does each daughter stand for a century, each representing an age in the history of the American imagination. Taking stock of all these views, Patke unnecessarily doubts whether "the poem can sustain this type of allegorical interpretation" simply because "such an elaborate degree of continuous allegory is not discovered elsewhere in the poem" (30), a view that supports a similar opinion earlier expressed by Cook ("'The Comedian as the Letter C'" 203). Is not the whole poem an allegory? Is not Crispin himself an alter ego of Stevens? Is not his "voyage" allegorical? Is not the poem an allegorical (hence disguised) pronunciamento of Stevens' situation and his attempt to define—to quote Martha Storm—"his place in the American literary milieu" (259)? I think Stevens presents his daydream, as Freud would say ("Creative Writing and Day-Dreaming" 153), through the poem. In fact, the poem easily reminds one of Jonathan Swift's *Gulliver's Travels*, where Gulliver is the alter ego of the author's own daydreams and whose travels and travails both may be compared with those involved in Crispin's enterprise. Crispin is a hero of a quest at the end of which he accomplishes something, like the hero of the traditional quest. Northrop Frye argues, "[T]he hero of a quest first of all goes 'away': that is, there must be some direction for his movement ... If the quest is successful, he normally returns home" (213).

Crispin certainly goes away from Bordeaux to Yucatan, then to Havana, and then to Carolina (*CP* 29), but the return journey is deliberately problematized by the poet: even though there is a reference to Crispin's "Nice Shady Home" toward the end of his journey (*CP* 40), yet there is something more to the journey since "home" in the literal or usual sense is not the end of his quest—the "Daughters with Curls" are where his journey comes to an end. Since the voyage is not literal, as in non-allegorical romances, but introspective, the "home" and "daughters with curls" are allegorical, perfectly disguised.

Stevens gives enough clues to decipher the significance of the "daughters." The five children of a 1919 poem, "Piano Practice at the Academy of Holy Angels" (*OP* 21–22), provide an added support. Patke notices the resemblance between the first four children and the four daughters of Crispin. It is also important to take note of the absence of Crispin of "Piano Practice" in *The Comedian*. Her absence is fulfilled by Crispin himself, whose liking for thought (*CP* 42), dissatisfaction with the old masters' philosophy (*CP* 40), and desire for truth (*CP* 40) all match Crispin's description. *Ex uno disce omnes*. The description of Crispin's four daughters is analogous with that of the first four children of "Piano Practice," and the two poems need to be read simultaneously for a better understanding of the "daughters": The first cannot see things as they are because things are changed when she looks at them; this change itself illumines the "room" as it beautifies reality.[25] She is imagination and, being an attendant maid of reality, her mistress, she focuses her attention on her mistress's beauty that is not seen by the physical eye but is unique. The second is a dreamer, having less contact with the outside world or reality than the imagination, but still very close to the imagination. She is desire, not "passion" as Guereschi suggests (80). Though not yet awakened (desire as unconscious), she is responsive to whatever feeds or satisfies her (does the reference to mother here suggest desire for the (m)Other?), since she hates emptiness or "lack." Her wondering at any disturbance of sleep may be interpreted as conscious desire wondering at the unconscious desire's fantasy.[26] Her description in *The Comedian* is also important here. Her works would be dreams, which are like a rebus. What is not revealed in the dream is what Freud calls the navel, which remains with or in the field of the Other. Thus, the Other restrains itself from yielding to the subject ("to pinion" is "to restrain"). The desire remains unfulfilled due to the Other's restraint or otherness; in this sense, she shies away from her goal. Yet she is full of passion and insists on achieving the Other all the same. The third one is inspiration, who, admiring the poetic, enables the writing of poetry. Poetic art, terse as it is, requires Aristotelian mimetic vision that allows selection and arrangement of only the necessary while discarding the unnecessary, under which the inspiration keeps creeping before elevating herself above it. The fourth is pleasure and happiness ("Marie" is close to "merry"). She cannot remain hidden and always "blusters"; she is blasphemous because she may bluster irrespective of the gravity of a given situation. Cheap things will do for her, as she can be very undemanding most of the times. She soon becomes quiet, but also restless, since she is always curious, always alert to bluster. She is inactive now because inspiration is at work, for Stevens is in the midst of writing his poem. By this, Stevens might have wanted to comment on his own life at the time: it was a time when Stevens had started feeling uneasy about his reception as poet—not only was he not well received by readers but after the publication of the 1923 edition of *Harmonium* he also almost stopped writing until 1931. In short, he was in need of a recovery through the "revelations of ... [his] powers" in order to overcome the reality that had almost "decreated" him (*NA* 174–75).

Though different, these daughters are very similar in spreading their light and enlightening the mind. Each and every man knows them even though their habitat, the mind, is extremely complex. Apart from the subject or his person, they are four additional personages living within him. They question for him what will suffice, and they themselves answer it since they have the power to manipulate the world in which they live in order to satisfy themselves and the subject (*OP* 21).

This is Crispin's most valuable discovery.[27] It has helped him prepare a body of thought that is to be taught. This is why his social involvement must not be underestimated (*CP* 43). The foundation of his discovery or doctrine is that the world, even the inner world, was congenial in ancient—perhaps Adamic—time (*CP* 45), but time has obscured and alienated it from us (*OP* 21). Crispin has merely recovered or reproduced it, but for that alone his value is much greater. The contemporary scholars might think that he has done nothing special, because they have no idea that we have been alienated from our own "family." However, Crispin is prepared to swallow his humiliation at their slanderous remarks without complaint. If gravity grips him here, it is not because he is defeated (as is commonly thought), but because his work/anecdote is finished. Now the narrator's voice will be heard ever more clearly, and he, by the end of the poem, will not only completely separate himself from Crispin but will also be his critic, albeit a qualified one: Has Crispin concluded without achieving anything? Is what he proves nothing (*CP* 46)? Does he remain profitless in the end (*CP* 45–46)? The final two lines provide an answer, though not uncharacteristic of an ambiguity the source of which is Stevens' ambitious swim against the contemporary literary current. Not confident of the acceptance of his theme, he hands-offs Crispin's enterprise in the manner of a raconteur who comes to the end of his incredible story and looks satisfied that he has told his entertaining story successfully.

Here, the poet uses the words "relation" and "end" with multiple meanings in mind. This also enables the suggestion that Crispin, through the relationship with the daughters, has achieved his objective, which was to establish a happy relation with the surrounding world, as stated in section III, where he was not sure whether it would be possible. This further allows reinterpreting the word "clip" in the final line as "achieve." The etymology of "clip" suggests that it originally meant "to draw tightly together."[28] Moreover, the final line's syntax indicates the manner of a blessing, a good wish; Stevens is thus wishing for each man to have a harmonious relationship with the world within and the world without.

Apart from Blackmur, Patke, and Cook, who are not willing to show much of disapproval of Crispin's enterprise,[29] most other critics wrongly interpret the poem as a failure or as Crispin's comic debacle. In reality, it is Crispin's attempt at self-aggrandizement right from the beginning (*CP* 31), which he accomplishes through the "recovery" of his own "immanence" (Miller, "Poetry of Being" 161). It would be a mistake to believe that he is selfish in not thinking of others since he rejects the idea of a colony. As a condign poet, on the contrary, he recognizes his duty and returns to the social sphere; his poetry almost becomes the light of gospel for others (*CP* 43). If this aspect is not emphasized more than one might expect, it is because the individual and his spiritual growth were fundamentally important for Stevens in the sense that they were for Mohandas Gandhi, who did not look upon people as masses but as individuals. The poet believed that each man in a society is equal to the society (*CP* 206); he even criticizes Marx for going against nature (*CP* 134). And what right, morally speaking, would Crispin have to teach others without having achieved his own spiritual growth? In this sense, he is both an everyman and an individual; ordinary as an everyman and exemplary as an individual, he shows the ordinary man a way toward spiritual growth. If Crispin becomes fatalistic (*CP* 44), it is because what counts in the individual's growth is the upliftment of the *fatas*, the human faculties represented by the four daughters; one can easily establish the Italian connection by tracing the root of "fate." In Italian medieval romance, the *fatas* were fairies and worshippers of Demogorgon, who controlled them. There is more than one avatar of Demogorgon in English literature, but the one Stevens might have considered here is Shelley's gloss of him as the eternal principle that ousts false gods; this is very much in line with Stevens' thought: Crispin's pilgrimage is intended to get rid of the staleness of the past and establish a new world order. Crispin plays Demogorgon to the four vital sisters (not the "three fatal sisters" as in Spenser). He is Shelley's Demogorgon, ousting the faith and beliefs of the past, for they have become outdated and useless; he is also, as a human being, Shelley's Prometheus, who achieves a mental equilibrium by resuscitating the human faculties or potential or immanence as it matches "the difficult and unbending realities of actual life" (Webb 196).

However, Crispin's relationship with the "daughters" and the world, interior as well as exterior, is not the end; it is just the preliminary minutiae, the *prolego* with which to initiate the search for being (*CP* 36). Stevens-Crispin's voyage has yet to reach that destination. Human life, from its origins, has been going through the same insipid circular movement of birth and death. "Sailing after Lunch" (*CP* 120–21) seeks to transcend this cycle in order to attain that destination. The poem renders human existence altogether false until that transcendence happens. In Lacanian thought, too, the subject is merely a supposition (Fink 204). This seems to correspond with Plato's view of our world as mimesis or with the concept of "Māyā" in Hindu philosophy, but Stevens will not partake of such a hopelessly grim view of human existence; he will not resign his "boat" to the insipid to-and-fro movement in the portage formed by birth and death or allow it to sink in the deep waters of illusion. The subject as *supposé* in Lacan is the result of the subject's entry into the symbolic order. Stevens imputes it to the staleness of the creations of our imagination ("musty" suggests a preestablished order, and hence is very close to Lacan's symbolic order into which the subject is "submerged" [Fink 52]). Stevens speaks of the inseparability of image and sound in "Study of Images I" as he mentions the betrothal of image to the right sound, which he has already glossed elsewhere as casting imagination in sound (*CP* 345–46). The preexisting order in "Sailing after Lunch" involves both the symbolic and the imaginary, the knot between the imaginary and symbolic orders.

However, in a propitious moment of desire the subject can — and this is what matters most in Stevens — shed the web of the prevailing order, allowing the "traversing of fantasy." Desire helps escape the treacherous fate (*CP* 17) when it seeks to transcend the mundane cycle of birth and death. In the poem's last stanza, the poet literally refers to people and suggests that it is only after expunging the order established by them that one can be a "pupil." This obviously anticipates a relation between the self and people. The way the people implicate the subject is very obvious in Lacan's formulation of the Other as language, law, and culture. The subject's very entry into the world sees him encrusted with and encroached upon by other people through language. The subject inevitably assimilates their activities, a "forced choice" as it is, which is the essence of the unconscious structuration.

How can one be a pupil by expunging people or the Other, by going beyond the sphere of the symbolic? In fact, the poet seems to be playing with the word "pupil," which could mean the "ephebe," who sees with an "ignorant eye" (or "I") (*CP* 380)[30]; that part of the eye which allows "light" to enter or the center of the cycle/wheel of birth and death. Whether this wheel is one of birth and death or one of Fortune, Stevens looks forward to transcend its mundane routine with the concentration of the ephebe, since perhaps only one who studies its motion can think of escaping it and thus partake of "being" as the cause of existence. If by "pupil" Stevens means that of the eye, combining it with ephebe vindicates the concentrated attention of the beholder, who must be all eye(s) to study the wheel's motion in order to see the transcendental beyond as its central organizing principle. In Stevens, the act of looking is very important, for it allows the beholder to *be* what is looked upon or to make the looked-upon part of him; here the vision and desire cannot be separated (*CP* 466). This is caused by the lack that is felt more acutely in the scopic drive; however, the feeling of lack also means the invigoration of desire, promising ever more the desire's fulfillment. What is this fulfillment if not the "symbolization" of what is looked upon?[31] Thus, by becoming "all eye," the ephebe can "symbolize" that wheel. Further, upon "symbolization" of the wheel, the ephebe become all eye, or the pupil of the eye attains a centrality in relation to the wheel. Just as the pupil is to the eye, so the ephebe is to the wheel. Hence, like the pupil of the eye, he transcends the wheel using light, allowing the lack to be fulfilled. This is analogous to the "subjectification of cause," or "subjectification of being." Stevens, however, does not forget the momentary nature of this "subjectification"; besides using the image of bright flashy light, he deliberately follows it with a suggestion that the moment is over. However, after that, it is not darkness; instead, the subject cherishes the memory of that moment, allowing him to traverse the reality with a rejuvenated spirit—that moment serving as a "rem(a)inder" of (the sense of) his being.

Stevens celebrates this moment of *jouissance* in "Of Bright & Blue Birds & the Gala Sun" (*CP* 248). The opening stanza might shock the reader with its reference to human beings as "things." It recalls the two outstanding instances of the word's use in English literature; one is in Wordsworth's "A Slumber" (136) and the other in Shakespeare's *Hamlet*. In both instances, "thing" and death are closely juxtaposed. In *Hamlet*, however, the process of relating death with "thing" takes a convoluted path: First it is Polonius who (literally) dies, and everyone then refers to him (his corpse) as the "body." When in Act IV, Scene ii, Rosencrantz asks Hamlet the whereabouts of the "body," Hamlet strangely uses the word "body" with such ambiguity that it means both the "body" of Polonius and the "body" of Claudius; or rather, he shifts the context of the word and refers to Claudius alone, and by the same token he brings about Claudius' (metaphorical) death, which enables him to discern the "King." Lacan advises one to read "phallus" in place of "King" ("Desire" 51–52). Without Claudius' "death" on Hamlet's psychic plane, he would not have discerned the "King." When Lacan said that "the letter kills," he meant the process of symbolization, of signifierizing the real. Claudius' metaphorical death is nothing but Hamlet's use of Claudius-as-signifier (S2) to see the "King" or phallus (S1). This is called the process of dialectization. Dialectization is similar — not identical — to symbolization. We symbolize the real, but we do not symbolize the symbol or signifier. In repression, a symbol or signifier, already part of the symbolic system, can lose its meaning and defy the role of signification allotted to it (Fink 119). The subject, thereafter, constantly "butts up" against the signifier (Fink 77), which thus exists in a radical otherness to the subject and resists signification or meaning-making. Such a signifier needs to be dialectized, to be brought into the analysand's own discourse, so that it will mean something *to him*. In this way, the signifier that masters the subject (S1) is brought in relation with the other signifiers (S2) that mean something to him. This process, which analysis effects through talking, is called the "dialectization of a master signifier."

Thus, in saying that "The King is a thing — " Hamlet tries to "dialectize" the "King." Here, we come across the word "thing" (S2) as an important material in the dialectization, for what comes after its occurrence is a revelation of the meaning of the "King" to Hamlet; this is what the cut in his speech suggests. However, he fails in the attempt; he can only say "Of nothing," since no meaning emerges; this is probably because he is still "at the level of privation" ("Desire" 48–49), which precludes the revelation of meaning. This is helpful in understanding that it is immaterial whether Wordsworth's "she" dies a biological or metaphorical death. While "she" may have actually died, there is no question of grief for Wordsworth's speaker, absolutely no question of fears or feelings; this is precisely what is suggested by his "slumber." Geoffrey Hartman in vain makes him shed "tears" (420–21) since in that case the "I" should have seen the "nocturnal course," evoking human fears and feelings. In fact, the conflict or tension that is characteristic of poetry lies in the fact that "she" has died but the "I" does not accept it. The woman's (dead) "body," which has now become a "thing" or signifier,[32] allows him to discern that which causes life on the earth eternally ("eternally" because, according to the *OED*, "course" [derived from Latin *currere*] means a "continuous process" in terms of its constancy or regularity).[33]

Stevens also treats human beings as signifiers in reducing them to "things," like Shakespeare and Wordsworth. His speaker himself becomes a signifier and relates, in both senses of the word, his experience to that of other human being(s). It is only the signifier that allows any reference to the real. The subject's becoming a signifier is nothing but becoming a pure desirousness himself, his object or signified being object(a), which is never really an object but rather a signifier (S1). And subjectivity precipitates, or the subject attains a greater degree of the sense of "self" as the primordial or the master signifier is brought into some relation with the other signifier or signifiers. The sense of "self" will be greatest if the subject himself becomes the other (i.e., a binary) signifier (S2) and establishes for him or her a new position with respect to the master or primordial, the unary, signifier (S1). This is because, for Lacan, "everyone's desire is somehow different and their own — lack is nevertheless my lack" (Easthope 94). Hamlet and the speaker of Wordsworth's poem do not become the S2 themselves; this is the reason, I suppose, why they do not strike as exultant a note as does the speaker of Stevens' "Of Bright & Blue Birds & the Gala Sun." The moment of transition from desirousness (or the relationship of desirousness) to "being" is well caught in this poem. It is also, Stevens implies, becoming part of another sphere, the real of Lacan. It is the moment of *jouissance.*

Nevertheless, on returning from this moment, the ego/subject feels invigorated, at peace with himself, and happy; Stevens has tried to catch this feeling in the epigraphical set of lines placed before the *Notes* as he recalls that moment of "trans-appearance," derived from *trans* + *parere*, "appear" (see *CP* 380). The moment is over no sooner than *it* occurs; the "it" is the *Es* in Freud's "*Wo Es war, soll Ich werden.*" In the passage from the *Notes* it becomes "you" since the ego (*Ich*) has again been left with the humdrum reality without, where he knows himself in or through the "you." However, during that instant of *assomption*, the ego does not remain an object but subjectifies his "being," merges with it, and after returning (or being returned) to the human reality, attains a greater sense of being that it cherishes from then on. Yet that moment is what he constantly desires and is denied, this *jouissance*; hence that wistful feeling at the end of the first stanza.

CHAPTER 5

Rubbings of Reality

> Everything which is imaginary, everything which is properly speaking illusory, isn't for all that subjective. (S II 49)
>
> It is she that he wants, to look at directly. (*CP* 232)

Insofar as literary criticism is concerned, the thinking of "reality" goes at least as far back as Plato. And the objectivity of what is "real" has been cherished since its origin in formal human thought. Various thinkers in different ages have tried to describe reality with different means and from different points of view. However, not only have none of them succeeded—success is an illusion here—in verbally catching it among other ineffables, but it is also impossible for us to say or see that someone's description is better than someone else's. There has always been the invariable feeling of total evasion by "reality." Yet it is impossible for us to forget the thought of it. It pervades and engages human imagination and life so forcefully that an objective approach to it seems utterly futile. This is precisely why reality is more a poetic subject than a philosophic one. The subject of all great poetry is that which is elusive; of course, the philosophic discourse also aims at the ineffable and the elusive, but the greatest blunder it commits—and this is where it parts with poetry—is that philosophy tries to tame it, to systematize and formalize it instead of merely touching and feeling it in a chance event that comes as it comes, and subsequently returning—inevitably—from it with whatever satisfaction the experience offers or the desire deserves.

While it is difficult or impossible to define and thus confine reality, it is no less so to segregate it from the human. The so-called realist proposes to present what he sees of and as the real with minimal intervention or comments. Minimal, because he cannot altogether put aside the human faculties, senses, emotions, and feelings. The early realists of the modern Realism were aware of this truth. At the hands of people like Alain Robbe-Grillet, however, nature or reality is being dehumanized. While the idea of the dehumanization of reality so as to depict it verbatim is intellectually sound, reading such literature—a sample of which from Robbe-Grillet is provided in Ellmann and Feidelson—or even writing it would become intolerable.[1] The fact is that the physical eye is very much present, and it is human. It responds to the human desire of survival: the eye, which is required to do nothing but see, nevertheless blinks or widens without conscious efforts, for example, in response to the changes in the intensity of light. In this sense, it is impossible to dehumanize the eye's vision. To see the way Robbe-Grillet proposes and seeks is not simply dehumanization of reality but dehumanization of the human being as well. A dangerous proposition, obviously. Another problem of recording verbatim what the eye sees is that it can see more than one thing at the same time. The spoken or written record of this activity would present those things one after another as opposed to their simultaneous visibility to the eye. This gap will never be bridged. However, if the eye's automatic response to the changes in the intensity of light is *therefore* called nonhuman, then the automatic responses of our senses and feelings to what the eye sees are nonhuman as well. Why not record them? In this way, the categories of human and nonhuman seem absurd, and everything then becomes real and we come to where we had begun in our efforts to perceive reality. The truth is that reality is independent of the human as such; it does not require its humanization or dehumanization—it is complete without our mental conceptions of it. It is we who desire to see it, whether by humanizing or dehumanizing it. Insofar as this desire is present, it is a humanization of reality; it betrays the desire for recognition: Stevens emphasizes getting into focus, not out of it like Nietzsche and the radical dehumanists (*L* 431–32). The dehumanizers argue that "The new sensibility ... is dominated by a distaste for human elements in art" (y Gasset 29); they give examples of the grave-looking statues at Madame Tussauds or blank expressions on the faces of fashion models. However, this blankness or nothingness in modern art, it seems to me, is a rem(a)inder, or an effect, of the ineffable void that, perhaps, has its origin in the death of God, which, in turn, has effaced the human. Thus, in modern literature, the speaker is effaced by the speaking voice; in modern music, the singer's voice is swallowed by music; in painting, the human face—if there is any—does not seem human. Unless that void is filled up with another "supreme fiction," there will be no place for the human face.

Even though seeing reality is most important, the ages have cherished, surprisingly enough, the habit of priding over their respective view of the real. Stevens has no pretensions of this sort; one finds in him what may simply be called his efforts at seeing reality. What he speaks of it may find its roots in the thoughts of other thinkers, but all of it nevertheless comes from his own experience of reality. His views of the real may not be fixed into one particular line of thought, for the real itself is a flux that cannot be staged (*CP* 471); it is evasive and cannot be caged (*CP* 264). This is the reason why he once wrote that Realism—the "-ism" suggesting a kind of staging, formalization, or systematization of the real—corrupts reality (*OP* 166). In other words, Realism does see the real the way it *wants* or *desires* to, be it through the eyes of the earliest realist or the latest, or any humanizer or dehumanizer of it. In a way, Stevens does admit that the real is apart from the human as does Lacan, in whose view it is "inhuman or mechanical" (ERS 188). And yet Stevens was the one poet in an age in which Realism was on the verge of eliminating the human role in the perception of the real who boldly upheld Ernst Cassirer's view of imagination as "the only clue to reality" (*NA* 136, 137, 139). There being no other practical way of perceiving it, he asserted the human role in doing so. Here he comes close to Lacan, who believed that perceiving the real objectively was impossible (ERS 188), that the real is available or knowable only in its effects or in one's feeling of it (ERS 189). It is in this sense that Stevens' language struggles, often successfully, to convey his knowledge of reality; unless one elaborates on the effects the real has created in Stevens' poetry, it is futile to see or say what he meant by "reality." Any discussion of Stevens' conception of reality is therefore trash unless it sees and elaborates upon the role of the imaginary, of the human, in it.

The real does depend upon the imaginary, as in Manichean binaries (*CP* 392). In the title of a poem Stevens clearly says that reality is the activity of imagination (*OP* 110), and describes parts of reality as real *because* the "I" grants them "reality" (*CP* 313), where the "I" could be replaced by the "imaginary" of Lacan,[2] thus asserting the principle of interdependency between the real and the imaginary, the two opposites. The real depends on the imaginary for coming into (our) being and for the significance it has for humans.[3] Here Stevens may be aligned with Johann Fitche for making the imagination or "I" the Cartesian center of all reality; however, he would not hold on to this proposition forever. Yet the role of the imaginary is so crucial in the poet's thought that he could not resist the temptation to almost deify it in the well-known and often anthologized "Anecdote of the Jar" (*CP* 76), where the animal of reality is tamed by the ringmaster of the imaginary, which then achieves a kind of godlike supremacy and indifference in relation to the real world.[4] Here Stevens might have segregated the imaginary from the real in an ecstatic mood—one may even think of that deification as a reaction against Realism, to which reality was no less than God—but he was well aware that it was impossible, that the imaginary has to keep, to use his own words, weaving its fictions around the illusive, godlike real (*CP* 396).[5] Lacan finds the roots of the imaginary in desire when he describes the ego as the metonymy of desire (the ego is an imaginary function, or the subject of the imaginary; *É* 274). If the imaginary has its origin in desire, it will never stop that "weaving," since desire itself remains always unsated. And, as the poet writes in "Of the Surface of Things" (*CP* 57), the incessant contact of the imaginary with the real is necessary for an understanding of both the interior and exterior worlds and for whatever satisfaction the experience can offer. The acts of walking and seeing in the poem suggest the complex intermutative activity between the imaginary and the real. The hills and clouds are by no means full knowledge of the real; nevertheless, the poet's acts let him know the surrounding world. Stevens deliberately avoids saying explicitly which world he is speaking of; he is probably referring to both the internal and external worlds. That is to say, it is necessary to believe in both as real.

The so-called realist's dislike of imagination speaks of his disbelief in the imaginary perception of reality. It is the same as not believing in what goes on within oneself; this makes one's position very precarious. For the same reason, the realist-disbeliever in "Palace of the Babies" (*CP* 77) is advised to drive out his doubts or disbelief regarding the inner reality—not merely in order to make him believe in the imagination but also to free him from the travails of loneliness so that he may feel closer to the real world, since the truth of reality is seen only in the light of imagination. The disbeliever's objective approach to looking at the palace (another architectural image for the self and its interior) is obvious. He is inadvertent to its reality, which is very close to him; instead of seeing and experiencing it, he imagines things that will lead him to sleep. Then he becomes a moonlight walker, walking without any "-ism" with him; as he looks into the palace windows, his disbelief and loneliness vanish (stanzas 3 and 6). In his assertion of the role of the imaginary in the perception of reality or in one's love of the actual world, Stevens would rather be a child than a "square hatted rationalist" (*CP* 75; *NA* 133). In fact, he believes that the innocent belief in the imaginary is one of the foundations of civilization. He says this in the not-so-innocent fourth stanza of "Palace of the Babies." Here, Stevens obviously recognizes the importance of the narcissistic circuit constituted between the imaginary and the real world, a very important aspect of the "night-as-the-interior-world." The above stanza has its resonance in Lacanian reflections on the imaginary. Each of the babies recognizes the otherness of the others (they needed to be brought close); this is essential to the *moi*, for without this recognition the O/other will cease to have anything to do with the *moi*, and this will result in an extremely complex psychosis. Thus, the real as O/other must be brought into contact with the imaginary, forming the *moi*-O/other circuit. It is this imaginary circuit that brings the babies close—though they are not perfectly identified with each other[6]; they are thus served with the nursling care. This is the importance of Lacan's concept of the "mirror stage" in the child. The import of the Stevens poem lies in the contrast between the innocent belief in the imaginary world and the intellectual disbelief in it, for which the poet brings "babies" and a "disbeliever" together; they represent the innocent and the learned (i.e., realist) worldviews, respectively. The result is that the babies get close while the disbeliever — from his disbelief he must be an adult, learned human being — experiences loneliness. The disbeliever thinks that the imaginary does not allow access to the real. However, since there is no reality except what one imagines of it, he has no access to it, and since it is "the base" (*OP* 160), the disbeliever's failure to approach it makes his life lonely and tormentful.

Toward the end of the mirror stage, the identification process builds up the *moi*, which has its supposed sense of self, and thus begins the child's interaction with the world. It begins to "walk" (*CP* 57), to construct its own reality, to create an order in its pre-mirror and mirror stage existence as chaos. The *moi*'s growing sense of its reality, or of "self," is very much the essence of "The Idea of Order at Key West" (*CP* 128–30). Brooke Baeten suggests that the "she" in this poem is Stevens' own mirror image (31–32), which is rightly rejected by Wallace Martin. Martin's proposal that the mirror stage, when subjectivity is yet to be attained, must be anchored in the symbolic to avoid psychosis is quite correct (93). However, both Baeten and Martin have not paid attention to the middle ground between the mirror stage (imaginary) and the symbolic. In psychoses, a subject already fully anchored in the symbolic often ends up in this middle ground — this is where Stevens was for most of his life. Owing to the poet's psychical restructuration as feminine (discussed in the previous chapter), there is no harm in suggesting that the "she" in the poem is the poet's own (poetic) projection (not mirror image); it is feminine, and seeks to "sing," to (re)anchor itself in the symbolic and the real world. Besides, the identification process never comes to an end, even in a normal subject. Martin admits that "the [female] figure in the poem appears ... to entail ... mechanisms [of] identification and introjection" (97). There is one more mechanism involved in the poem: imaginary symbolization, implied in mastering the night and the sea's portioning out (*CP* 130). Thus, while Martin is justified in discarding Baeten's assumption of the female figure as the poet's mirror image, "she" may be looked upon as his imaginary personified, betraying his desire to order the reality (*CP* 130). Both the reality as "sea" and the imaginary as "she" are supposed to be real. The rest of the second stanza confirms that the poet is speaking of identification between the two. The sound of the sea and the voice of the singer have become one, and what she hears could be both her song and the sounds of the sea and wind. Yet Stevens retains the difference between the "song" and the "sounds" as he resolves the confusion of the two by maintaining their identification with and otherness to each other at the same time by qualifying his argument using the modal "may" (*CP* 129).

The two persons who are witness to the event, nevertheless, give an Aristotelian preference to the singer's song since they believe in her creativity, to which the sea of reality merely provides an occasion. The two wonder about the impetus behind the singer's creative ability. Although they seem to acknowledge the debt of reality, they realize that credit must not go to the real alone, since without human creativity it would be monotonous, almost a "vacuum" (*OP* 168).[7] The real has no meaning, is nothing, unless anthropoeicized in the way of the imaginary. This is obviously against the basic tenets of Realism, but Stevens was fully convinced that "Things seen are [always] things as seen" (*OP* 162). Therefore, what they heard was not only the sound of reality, nor solely the singer's voice, but also a conflation of both the human voice and the nonhuman sound of reality. It was due to the importance of her voice that the real became more significant than it was. Stevens then emphasizes the human role in making the real more significant by saying that the woman's song granted a self to the sea. The listeners of the song realize that there is no world for a human being except the real that he covets *and*, out of that coveting, makes; Stevens thus acknowledges the importance of both the real and imaginary in the "reality" that the human being inhabits, both physically and psychically. This is perfectly in accordance with Lacan's thoughts on what he calls the "humanized, symbolized" reality (S I 87).

Though Stevens would not disagree with the view that the real does not need or depend on us, he still sides more with the human ability *to make*—perhaps not so much because he wanted to exalt the human role in the apperception of the real as because the Realists were forgetting the human side of it. In fact, he does concede that the real is independent of the human — it has a "self" of its own (*CP* 129)— that it undergoes a change with human intervention, that finally we do not see things as they are — they are always "things *as* seen" (*OP* 162). Nevertheless, he does not want to lose sight of the human ability to "make." This resolution of the Platonic and Aristotelian temperaments is essential to his conception of reality. This is why the speaker of the poem, who is also one of the two listeners of the "song," asks what almost becomes a rhetorical question of Ramon Fernandez, who is perhaps a Realist (for he is still grave, as opposed to the excited speaker), and answers himself by saying that it is the maker's desire for order that masters the real and makes it significant, beautiful, even romantic and sublime.

The "night" of the penultimate stanza could be understood better through the word "unknown," which captures much of Lacan's conception of the real; the psychoanalyst includes the unconscious in his real order (S XI vii), which assimilates Stevens' "night" as "man's interior world" (*CP* 333) since the human mind is real too. The night "descends" as the singing ends, suggesting that the time of the song or the song itself was like the light of day when one could "see" things clearly. Now that the song has ended, there is only its memory in the minds of the listeners. But even the memory is like the light of imagination that breaches and masters the reality.[8] This recalls Lacan's gloss of the real — that it is without gaps or divisions (S II 97) but the symbolic (the "song" in the poem) introduces them into it (Fink 24, 182n3). By introduction of gaps or holes into the real, Lacan means bringing part(s) of the real, or its "portions," into the symbolic order. This suggests that the experience of the song's listeners is a kind of breakthrough in the knowledge of the unknown or real. It does not mean full knowledge of it, but nonetheless they have been enabled to change the overall structure of the unknown, or of the real.

Stevens knew that the real cannot be known except in parts and patches, for he earlier admitted in section II of "The Blue Guitar" in a Whitmanesque note that he cannot sing a man, only parts of him (*CP* 165); "July Mountain" also rejects the idea of the singleness of the world we inhabit (*OP* 114). And human beings are a part of reality for him (*OP* 215).[9] He shows further in section II of "The Blue Guitar" that any knowledge of the real is but a subjective affair. Lacan likewise asserts that all knowledge is paranoiac in essence (*É* 17); here, Lacan also suggests that it is first of all identification that is necessary for there to be a possibility of knowledge, which emerges as knowledge only upon a critical examination of that identification, therein objectifying it. And identification, in Lacan, is the result of the fundamental gap (*béance*) introduced by the signifier between the self and the outside world of objects (including other human subjects) or the other. This "abyss" between the subject and object (*CP* 437) is constitutive of "new knowledge" (*CP* 534). Stevens attempts to fill it by "patching," as in section II of "The Blue Guitar." Disinterest or distrust in such "patching" could be the reason why Ramon Fernandez is grave while the other listener of the same song looks aggrandized toward the end of "The Idea of Order." Perhaps the anonymous listener is Stevens himself, who has, after the woman's song, "objectified" his "identification" with her and gained in knowledge, which is conveyed through the poem. Stevens advocates such objectification in "Of Modern Poetry" through changing the phrase "mind in the act" to "act of the mind."

While resisting Baeten's view of the female figure as Stevens' mirror image, it must be kept in mind that Wallace Martin's inconclusive problematization of the figure's identity is a knowing evasion of "triggeri[ing] explorations of [the poet's] psyche and the unconscious" (95). McCollough would say that the poem is a "desiring-production" that keeps finding "what will suffice" endlessly, restlessly.[10] However, this is a sign of an ailing desire since, as Martin might agree, the poem denies specificity or concreteness to the characters in it. Like the images in the poem, the characters are also "transabstractconcrete" (McCollough 104). Unless they swerve to become either fully concrete or fully abstract, this poem, in its attempt to find what will suffice, would not end even though the woman's song ends long before the poem itself. Broadly speaking, much of Stevens' work suggests that it is a "desiring-production." This includes his view of reality, since the poet never got tired of seeing it every time in a different light, thus evading codification of his desire of perceiving reality. Although we do not see things as they are—rather because this is so—we have in us the *desire* to see them as they are. In Stevens' case, this desire exhibits extraordinary power. He always saw reality like a voyeur; in fact, his view of reality is always "produced by desire"; it seems that his "desire and its revolutionary energy" has something to do with "repression" (McCollough 102). Therefore, desire is a very important aspect of Stevens' reality.

The audience of "The Blue Guitar" is not simply an audience but also the guitarist's desire objectified. It is difficult, a futile exercise, to separate the voice of the audience from that of the guitarist. This is precisely why, as Patke correctly observes, the two voices become one (inseparable) as the poem progresses and the quotation marks demarcating them vanish after the first few sections (82).[11] Lacan justifies or complements Stevens here when we see him repeating in Seminar I that desire is first grounded and recognized in the other, which functions as an agency or intermediary (147, 170, 177). Here the "other" means everything that is outside of the subject and with which he identifies himself. In relation to the alienation of desire, Lacan writes that before the subject's entry into the symbolic order, desire exists merely at the level of the specular stage (S I 170). The specular stage covers the pre-mirror and mirror stages that are the result of man's "prematurity at birth" or his "native insufficiency" (S III 95). After the specular stage, the subject enters the symbolic order, which includes the other people and their language. Now, for recognition of his desire, the subject needs active mediation by those people (S I 171). Thus, desire enters into the dual relation of *I* and *you* (S I 177). In this sense, the audience before the guitarist may be taken as a literal audience, as physically present; nevertheless, the desire of both is almost the same (see S I 177n2). The guitarist has the desire for the real, as is clearly stated. However, what is also clarified or sensed by him is that the desire is satisfied only in a metonymic way, for he can only perceive the real in patches. Lacan has also emphasized the insatiability of desire. Since the real is "always in the background ... excluded" (S I 206), the desire for it cannot be fulfilled. The real is excluded from the subject's perception or from his attempts at symbolizing it. Stevens' guitarist seeks to "patch" or "sing" it but never succeeds in doing so to perfection since the real evades its symbolization (S I 66).

Thus, the clear distinction of the two voices, suggested by the alternate presences and speeches of the audience and the guitarist, is indicative of the fundamental gap between desire and its fulfillment. The gap decreases, however, with the blurring of the distinction between the two voices as the poem progresses. Yet, since the guitarist realizes the impossibility of satisfying his desire for the real, he mitigates it to perceive it imaginarily (*CP* 167). The difference between sections III and VI is the difference between the stubborn attitude of the so-called Realist and the imaginative way, respectively, in perceiving the real. Desire prefers the imaginative way since it invigorates the real (so that the desire may be partially fulfilled), while reason destroys it. In fact, Stevens would rather keep the real not fully perceived, for he prefers the life of desire; the consistent invigoration, elevation, and abstraction of reality in his poetry is a way of keeping the desire for it alive — it betrays the desire *for* desire. Thus, all his words are embedded in a storm of desire or chosen out of it (*CP* 335, 441). The impossibility of the satisfaction of desire for the real and the desire's merciless renewal find a temporary resolution in section VI (*CP* 168). If it is impossible to place, as such, things as they are beyond further change, then the imaginary could itself become that place; there may come a moment in the life of the imaginary when things will seem to have revealed their final truth. This would be, of course, for a moment. Indeed, the knowledge of "reality" that Stevens sought comes, in his poetry, suddenly, in momentary flashes. This occurs precisely because the imagination can never be equal to or compatible with reality; yet it is what enables us to stand before the storm of reality. Therefore the poet must "play" upon his "guitar" (*CP* 169).

Even though Stevens kept eulogizing the imaginary, he was not unaware of the attendant *méconnaissance* principle; he knew that the reality perceived through the grid of imagination is a deviant form of reality. The identification process inherent in the first four lines from section XI of "The Blue Guitar" is false since, as the rest of the section highlights, the imaginary and the real are fundamentally discordant with each other. This discordance is brought in the dimension of time and desire. The desire is pregnant with the time that has separated us from the noumenal real. The "time" Stevens refers to here seems to anticipate the Fall myth, when man failed to respect God's first law (*CP* 17), and it does so in all its complexity, since the "rock" is not simply the symbol of the real but also has a certain psychical dimension to it, as will be seen in the discussion of *The Rock*. The loss of paradise and the loss or "exclusion" of the real in Lacanian sense are comparable. The time that has passed after the Fall is the time by which we are away from the real. Stevens' version of this loss is not strictly mythological, since he glosses it over with the loss of the female parent (*CP* 308). It is, more or less, psychoanalytic since he imputes it to one's birth, the very origin of dualism. Thus, in "To the One of Fictive Music," the poet refers to our present existence as the result of our birth, which separates us from the elemental reality (*CP* 87). Birth not only separates us from the elements, with which we were once united, but it also alienates us from the mother (*CP* 525). Stevens' love of reality is marked by the sense of alienation from the mother as the "rock." This is why, if at all one wishes to categorize Stevens' conception of reality, it may be called, following Lacan, "psychoanalytical realism" ("Structure" 194).

It is no wonder, then, to see section XI of "The Blue Guitar" followed by one that cannot be understood better without recourse to Lacan. Here, as in the poems discussed in chapter 2, the poet delineates a picture of the human subject. It presents the reality of the human subject while acknowledging the debt of the other. The opening sentence of this section is an announcement of a definition of the "I," the human subject. The very next sentence breaks it into two parts, the "guitar" and "I"; though it asserts their unity, there is still that unmistakable coordinating conjunction separating them. Nevertheless, they come together and form an "orchestra"; orchestration — that is, arranging or combining harmoniously or for maximum effect — is to be expected. Since the one who speaks is a problem in both Stevens and Lacan, one could say, following Lacan, that here the *moi* speaks *to himself with* the *je* (see S III 14). This completes one triangle of Lacan's *schema L* (S-other-*moi*), the one that may be called forming the imaginary circuit of the intra-subjective intersubjectivity. However, it remains incomplete without the mediation of the other. In Lacan, the ego himself is an other just as the other people are; the other people of line 3 in Stevens' poem are also the other since the *moi*, the poem's speaker, recognizes himself inextricably in the other men. It is at this point that Stevens' description enters the other — symbolic — triangle, that of the unconscious, implicating the Other. Stevens' image of the "hall" for the mind and his treatment of thought as someone else's voice is helpful here (*OP* 168). The unconscious is the "hall" filled with people, whose shuffling suggests their restlessness, thus indicating their desire, which can never be completely satisfied. Their language and the desire expressed through it go deep down, or high up, to the unconscious or the Other (S II 243), who is placed at the lower right corner in Lacan's *schema L*. This is how the other is assimilated into the unconscious; in fact, the unconscious is the discourse of the other in Lacan. The other triangle of Lacan's schema (other-*moi*-Other), or the symbolic circuit, is completed here. The Other, the subject of the unconscious, is the one who does not sleep, and the subject's knowledge of the existence of the Other within himself is an unsettling experience. Here begins the instance of "interpellation" in Stevens: the question of finding the coordinates of "I" (which is the same as asking "What am I?" or "Who am I?") shows that the "I" does not know himself in his totality. Stevens seeks to answer the question *for himself.* The poet is certainly dealing with the irrationality of human subjectivity, within which the Other radically proclaims its Otherness from time to time. Yet Stevens says that the Other is also the part of his "I." In fact, everything that the human being (or subject) comes in contact with becomes, with varying degrees, part of him, of his reality, however apart it may be from him. The "inside" and "outside" are not mutually exclusive. In reality, the "I" begins at the other and ends at the Other; this is almost as if the *moi* is excluded from the "I." This precariousness of its existence is perhaps the reason why normally the *moi* tends not to recognize its origin in the Other. However, Stevens recognizes this, which is indicative of his illness.

Stevens was indeed interested in the irrationality of things in general, and of the human mind in particular. He acknowledges Freud for granting it legitimacy (*OP* 219). By irrational he meant something that cannot be explained in a rational way (*OP* 218). His glosses on the human mind do erupt irrationally in his poetry and have that air about them, yet one can see a rational mind behind the writing. Of course, the irrational he speaks of here has nothing to do with particular cases in the pathological sense. It is what all human beings experience with varying degrees of intensity. This is why what he depicts as irrational is almost always the reality of the human mind. Owing to his sense of the irrational, one feels that Stevens might have read Freud's "The Uncanny," especially Freud's explication of the word *heimlich* (meaning "of the home," familiar, intimate), which finally arrives at a point where the word's meaning coincides with its antonym, *unheimlich* ("not of the home," unfamiliar, extimate) ("The Uncanny" 220–25). Stevens' experiences of the unconscious manifestations are often expressed with this double sense as it declares itself not to belong to him and yet precludes any other possibility.

One of the aspects of the inner reality was articulated by one of the two French poets that Stevens mentions along with Freud in "The Irrational Element in Poetry" (*OP* 216–29): Arthur Rimbaud, who wrote, "Je est un autre"; Lacan explains the truth behind this apparently irrational statement (S II 7). Stevens had also realized the significance of the statement and the truth behind it. His "On the Road Home" (*CP* 203–4), apart from other interests, depicts this drama of the human mind. The use of Aesopian fablatura at the poem's opening is not benign. There is that secrecy of reduction which needs unfolding. Aesop's fox comes out of the hole because he gets hungry *as* the sun begins to shine. The sun is thus the cause of the fox's desire. By implication, the poem's beginning suggests that the sun — which is Stevens' symbol for the real — had been eclipsed, most probably by the idea of a single truth dominating the world. However, it is when the "I" abandons this idea of a singular truth that the real or the actual gains significance and the desire finds its bearings. Such instances are often found in Stevens, since desire is an important aspect of his conception of reality. The last poem of the trilogy that includes "On the Road Home"—that is, "The Latest Freed Man" (*CP* 204–5)—also contains an illustration where desire and the real are juxtaposed through the image of the sun awakening the doctors' desire (for "bed" as desire, see stanza 4 of "The Men That are Falling" [*CP* 187]).

The actual world as the other is one of the themes that underlie "On the Road Home," much as the "sea" is the other for the "she" in "The Idea of Order at Key West." As part of that world, the "you" of "On the Road Home" is also an-other. And the identification between the "I" and the other takes place in the second stanza as both the "you" and the world yield to the "I." That the desire of the "I" has found the right path is ascertained by the "you," a real human being as the other, whose speech accords with that of the "I." However, why those dots between "You" and "you said"? The speech of the "I" certainly finds some hindrance there. Lacan regards such hindrances, abortive actions, and errors as successes (S I 265), since it is here that the Other—the real—becomes manifest. What one senses in the dots is the abortive character of the speech of the "I." Why is the speech interrupted? As Lacan would answer, it is the Other making its presence felt since, he says, when the subject's speech goes beyond the relationship between *moi* and the other, it encounters the Other, and the subject then must speak to the Other (S II 270); thus, the "you" in the poem could also be this Other, to whom the "I" resumes speaking from the place where his ego must have arrived in its desire for the Other (S II 270). It is in this sense also that the "I" is on the road home. What normally prevents the discourse between the ego and the Other is the resistance offered through the ego's imaginary function, but when the resistance vanishes, the two may strike an accord, establishing an "isochronism" or a "simultaneous positivation" (S II 325). This is precisely what happens in the poem, and the feeling of the "I" is one of homecoming, as may be observed in stanzas 3 and 6. This feeling immediately follows the speeches of the "I" and "you" as they strike an accord.

A seeker of *the* truth is like a man who does not believe himself to be the truth (*CP* 242). He rejects himself as the truth and is alienated from that which constitutes him. One of his constituents being the actual world in which he lives, he is alienated from it as well. The idols in the fifth stanza of "On the Road Home" probably represent such people who, in their search for *the* truth, have forgotten to believe in their own self as the truth. Thus, they never achieved, ironically enough, what they sought. However, the life of desire or, said differently, of senses and feelings, (re)instates one's self and one's love for the actual world, which the poet says must be looked at with the eye or "I," since he does not distinguish between vision and desire (*CP* 466).

Language (or philosophy of the truth, for that matter) fails to achieve its object since, being symbolic, it is a function of castration; the attempt fails since tropes are but deviations. This is why Stevens disapproves of such attempts and, instead of taking into account the past in order to modify the present and project the future, as in philosophy, he prefers the *carpe diem* attitude in order to see things as they are in the present and thus experiences a change, which yields a measure of the satisfaction of desire (*CP* 202). One desires to get closer to the actual plural world, believing in the truth of its parts. So the "eye," representative of the world of senses as a means of achieving desire, is summoned up to "measure" the world. The poem of "homecoming" thus must end with amassing sensuousness, as it indeed does.

Perhaps in an attempt to overcome "the linguistic damage attendant upon the Fall" (Morrison 81), Stevens strives to see reality as ignorantly as possible; he prefers seeing and experiencing over imaging and naming, at times even sense over senses. His preference for the life of desire as opposed to the life of knowledge (with its usual meaning) stems from his belief that desire alone provides a closer contact with "reality," and also fosters a closeness toward it, even in its harshest form. Of course, there is no desire or knowledge without ignorance; Lacan hails ignorance as a fundamental passion, for ignorance ignites the desire to know (S I 271). However, the knowledge Stevens seeks is that of the real and, what is more important, he does it through senses and feelings, as opposed to speculation, since what one senses or feels through their mediation is immediate, close, and therefore real, whereas what one merely speculates more often lacks that immediacy and reality. Thus, ignorance is a virtue (*CP* 222).

Stevens' insistence on knowing the immediate world is a result of the desire to know his world, the world in which he lived. He remarks through a rhetorical question at the end of "Waving Adieu, Adieu, Adieu" that we *are* because there is reality (*CP* 128). Here, the poet's use of the pronouns "there" and "here" is not benign; one may make an excuse and not take "there" is the dummy subject and say that what is out "there" is in "here." The "here" seems to point to the "being," which comes from outside—hence the poet's interest in the reality without and desire for a sensuous contact with it, which almost borders on sensuality. This is obvious in many of his poems and very clear in his choice of Mario Rossi as an epigraph to "Evening without Angels" (*CP* 136). A sensuous contact with the external reality is a hunger in Stevens that is never satisfied, and so he often returns in his poems to this reality (*CP* 128); the series of infinitives in "Waving Adieu, Adieu, Adieu" is indicative of the insatiability of that hunger. The cause of this insatiability is best expressed through the ill-matched conjunctives of the "as ... so" syntax of "Nomad Exquisite" (*CP* 95). There can be no better reason for not using the more acceptable "just as ... so" syntax. The single sentence that comprises this poem shows the inevitability of the relationship between the beholder and the beheld. The ill-matched conjunctives of the syntax do not prevent the intimacy in the relation between the external reality and the beholder because of the poem's impressionistic *bon*fusion of them. Perhaps the mismatched conjunctions speak of the primordial discord between the self and reality, of this abyss that gives rise to desire. Lines 5, 6, and 7 indicate the influence of reality on the "beholder." These influences provide the basis for an understanding of the debt of honor Stevens feels for reality as it ignites the desire in him. This dialectic of cause and effect, which might lead one to take the "as" in the sense of "because," is essential to the imaginative life, without which the human mind would perpetuate through a state of imbecility (*CP* 172).

Though Stevens regarded the external reality highly as the shaping spirit, he did occasionally try to compete with it, as in section III of "Six Significant Landscapes" (*CP* 74). The senses and the concomitant feelings may be responsible for such overdetermination or elevation of the human being, but the Whitmanian wonder at the least significant aspects of reality, like a leaf of grass or an ant, was not baseless either; man may think of reaching higher forms of reality, but what about the fact that he has neither mastered its least significant forms nor fully known them? Thus, Stevens is not sure of his supposed superiority and notices or feels "ants crawling beneath" (*CP* 74). Where Whitman merely wondered at the leaf's ability to confound us, Stevens dislikes it out of the realization that even the most minor form of reality affects him, has a sort of control over his emotions and feelings; one wonders whether Stevens did not have in mind the informal "to have ants in one's pants," owing to the ego's desecration (which breeds anxiety).

Like the external reality, "man's interior world" also remains obscure in spite of our desire to know it (*CP* 333). The second landscape describes the "night" as obscure yet desirable (*CP* 73). In landscape III, there is a little suspicion about the thought of man as the master of his world; however, when he cannot see even his interior world clearly, how can he feel pride in that thought? The internal reality's obscurity does in fact sustain or facilitate one's desire for it and, as in Frost's "For Once, Then, Something" (276), finally the veil of obscurity lifts for a moment and the internal reality, which has become the object of desire, comes shining out into a glade, as in section II. However, in reality, it is only a superficial aspect of the object that shines, which is not its own part; the object as such is far away. Stevens does not say this explicitly, yet goes a little further to speak of the effect of a momentary manifestation of the internal reality on the consciousness; this is the beauty of landscape II.

The first six lines of the landscape conceal an object of desire and also the desire itself, and the remaining three lines reveal the "response to desire" within the economy of the mind (*CP* 218).

In "Dezembrum" (*CP* 218), Stevens wrote that the reason cannot achieve what the desire can since the former believes in the objectivity of reality while desire—not remaining content with its objectivity—subjectifies it, which is the most natural phenomenon; it enables one to feel at the center of the world. There are many instances in Stevens where this feeling, of being at the center of the reality or world, is gaudily celebrated. In those instances, one may think of Stevens as reverting to the ancient belief of "man's superiority to his soil" that Crispin rejects and changes to assert "the soil's superiority to man." However, proposition making was never the poet's aim; what he constantly strove toward was happiness, not a pre-decided belief as such. Although one can point to his desire for establishing a final belief in a supreme fiction, it must still be noted that this is ultimately a desire for happiness. This desire is the most central feature of his poetry. He always craved the sense of being at the center of things or the world, where he could simply be joyous (*CP* 430). In his thought, this sense alone gives *jouis-sense* and *jouissance* (by the former term Lacan meant the joy of meaning), which make the world meaningful so that we enjoy living in it or feel we are at its center.

Now, this may be a purely subjective stance, suggesting the extreme idea that the world of imagination is "the only real world" (*L* 252); nevertheless, Stevens was clever enough to suggest elsewhere that if, ultimately, we do not see things as they are—which the effort of the whole school of Realism goes to prove—then the sole truth is that we can only experience, feel, and subjectify them (*CP* 219). This is how he returns to his major premise—that reality, in reality, is always a conflation of the objective and subjective realities. Direct access to the real being impossible, our senses employ metaphor(s) to comprehend it (*CP* 219). This is the result of what Lacan calls the *manque* (lack) in us, which is the mainspring of the eternal motive for our metaphorical combination of the subjective and the objective. For this reason, in "Crude Foyer" (*CP* 305), we see Stevens despise not only Realism but also philosophical and theological thinking in general for their belief in a false happiness and for their emphasis on the otherness of happiness. The first three stanzas of the poem, in a way, summarize (and reject) the ancient Grecian, philosophical, and theological ways of thinking: the ancient Grecian view that we can know the phenomena of the universe merely by thinking, the philosophical tradition's general belief that thinking ultimately opens up the door to the spirit, and the theological understanding that everything is the doing of God. All these views brood on the *thereness* of the real or truth, when in fact it is *here*. What is needed, therefore, is the capacity to create metaphors by conflating the subjective and objective realities if one is to find true happiness. Stevens' reality is thus composed of the actual things that rejuvenate the mind (*CP* 263).

In "Crude Foyer," Stevens echoes the Socratic experience that he has quoted from Valéry's *Eupalinos* in "Two Prefaces" (*OP* 268–86). Socrates said to Phaedrus that it is useless to seek God through thought, for it is only in our "acts" that His presence can be felt (*OP* 269–70). Why does Socrates, or anybody else, for that matter, desire this divine feeling if not in order to experience the *jouissance* of Lacan or the happiness of Stevens? Stevens and Lacan both created a special place for themselves in their own fields out of keen observations of and rigorous thinking on the relationship between the objective and subjective realities, between one nakedness and another. And that relationship is nothing but an "act," to use Socrates' word, that never stops—even when one is asleep, as Lacan and Stevens both would like to add, owing to the Other manifestations to which Socrates refers as the divine presence, since the Other is an objective reality in the works of both the psychoanalyst and the poet.

Happiness being the end that never ends, the sense of being at the middle of the world as in "The Ultimate Poem Is Abstract" (*CP* 429–30), or the feeling of being at the center of reality as in "The Latest Freed Man" (*CP* 204–5), it is cherished and desired to remain as the singular purpose (*CP* 264). However, the moments of such tremendous sense vanish (*CP* 430), and the desire returns afresh in its utter poverty. This leads Stevens to turn to writing analytical poetry of reality. One of the first poems among such works is "So-and-So Reclining on Her Couch" (*CP* 295–96), in which he examines reality, the invisible gestures it makes, and the perceiver-examiner poet's view of the gestures. The "she" of the poem is reality, and is perfectly discordant with the "she" of "The Idea of Order." The process of her cognition is divided into three "projections." In projection A, she is presented in her actuality as the eye falls on her. She has no ancestry, no language, and is born at the age of twenty-one; this suggests looking at reality in its full form but without its having entered into the symbolic order, unnamed as "she" is—it is very much like looking at a newborn infant, in its pristinity or, better perhaps, like looking at a young maiden who has not yet violated her "quaint Honour."[12] She has, however, the potential to affect the perceiver; her attractive figure and imaginative eyes are indicative of that potential. Though the perceiver seems unaffected as yet, there is a suggestion that he might soon be. Her eyes remind one of Lacan's concept of "gaze," which affects the subject under it; her voluptuous figure might make her the object of the perceiver's desire. In its medical context, the word "drip" suggests something that can be injected into the patient's vein. By implication, the blue that drips from her eyes could well mean her capacity to induce the imaginary domain of the perceiver into activity. If the poet has used the word "drip" with its medical nuance, then it is obvious that he is set to examine reality as clinically as possible, with a view to remaining unaffected by it; this is implied in the reference to learning. Learning as knowledge demands clinical objectivity; hence, her attractive figure does not move the perceiver.

However, one wonders how long the clinical attitude will survive. Projection B seems to belie that clinical resolve as the speaker muses on what Stevens would call the "unreal" or "infinite" of the real. Indeed, the imaginary domain of the perceiver seems to have been affected by the "drip," for there is no reason why he should think of the crown above her head. However, he is still conscious of the fact that to perceive a thing without being affected by any gesture it makes is to perceive it as an idea. It is, in other words, to get at the reality in its real. To see reality without any of the gestures it makes also means seeing it without any preconceptions of it; it is *not* to see it *as*. This is something that Stevens also advises the "ephebe" of the *Notes* to do. However, he also recognizes, like Lacan, the difficulty or even impossibility of such a view of reality. Therefore, he immediately adds that she exists as a flux and fluctuates between herself as idea and as thing (*CP* 295). The actual, visible, felt or sensed reality *and* the idea or the real of it — the *con*tention between these two projections — are what make it remain in "the difficulty of what it is to be" (*CP* 381). Thus, she is only half-made so far. This may be the final projection, C, but the C does not by any means suggest complete description of reality, for the remaining half is yet to be completed by the beholder. Herein enters the role of the symbol, which functions to "make" the other half of reality.

Despite Stevens' clinical assessment of reality — he seems to realize this — his three projections are nevertheless his attempts at "making" reality and therefore contain his desire; thus, fact cannot be perceived as fact (*OP* 237). And desire being insatiable, he is not happy with the role played by the "projector"-being, who is, ironically, himself. He realizes that, by way of the three projections, he has been the creator of reality; that they are *his* views of reality and not reality *as such*; that his attempts have found *a* language (though not *the* language) to describe reality, and an ancestry for her as well, since describing is "naming." This is nothing but symbolization of the real that *was*, was in the difficulty of *to be*. In the final stanza, Stevens is not merely referring to painting and sculpture as such; by them he also suggests our attempt to symbolize the real, as he has done through his language, and thus to render it static. Therefore, he decides to walk the uncreated shores and rejects the idea of confining reality.

The nature of desire is such that it seeks to symbolize the real and then gets dissatisfied with its *statikos* so as to renew itself and its search for that which has not been "created" or symbolized. To be within this loop is the very nature of desire. Thus, toward the poem's end, Stevens bids farewell to its symbolic form, Mrs. Pappadopoulos, which, being a name, belongs to the symbolic order. Stevens would rather leave reality unsymbolized despite his desire to restore his liaison with it. (Again, this is another mode of elevating reality through abstracting.) This is obvious in his aversion to naming the sun (*CP* 381). For the same reason, the poet also despises naming and imaging the major man, who is the exponent of the idea of man (*CP* 388); the major men are beyond the confines of reality but made of it nevertheless (*CP* 335). Similarly, the hero remains anonymous, in the difficulty of *to be*, in the idea of him, since the idea of his existence depends on the impossibility of his conception (*CP* 279). Yet Stevens thanks Mrs. Pappadopoulos for what she was and what she offered before she was symbolized by the poet's desire and language.

"Apostrophe to Vincentine" (*CP* 52–53) is a poem that enacts the same cycle of desire, but with a little variation — it also speaks of the polyvalence of the real and its capacity to invigorate the physical world. In section I, the real-as-Vincentine is assumed to exist in her essential nakedness between the earth and the sky, the purely subjective or humanized and the crass objective, respectively. "Subjective" is in the sense that the "earth" is the near, the visible, the humanized; in the sense of the lines from "Anatomy of Monotony," we owe our origin and nature to the earth (*CP* 107). "Objective" is in the sense that the "sky" is the far, the unknown, the nonhumanized. Apart as such from the two, she is at once without a name and *as if* from heaven (not exactly from heaven). Stevens does not place her in the sky, probably because he does not want to suggest that the real is totally unknowable, nor does he place her on the earth, since it might give the impression that the real is altogether a subjective phenomenon. Saving her from both the earth's monotony or familiarity and heaven's impossibility or radical otherness allows him in the second section to feel her warmth, which keeps his desire for her alive. This engenders her figurations, and the changes between the two sections may be noted: the assumption of her existence turns into a kind of certainty as the speaker "figures" (or fingers?) her, almost feels her. This makes her brunette, which is Stevens' color for reality as it comes in the domain of intuitive experience. Her heavenliness turns to greenness. The increasing degree of personification speaks for an anthropomorphization of the real; however, it is not fully realized or humanized as yet. In section III, this growing real-ization by anthropomorphization makes her part of humanity. The emphatic speech in this section reveals the speaker's happiness over this hominization of the real. In this process, though, her heavenliness seems to have vanished altogether, as no adjective precedes her mention here; she seems fully symbolized.

Yet there is a sense of total evasion by the real in the final section. The first sentence of this section is extremely involuted. The feeling that the speaker imputes to "you" can exist only with himself. The "you" has already been figured as a human other in the preceding section; it is indicative of the establishment of narcissistic bond between the "I" and "you." In an example of the child who beats another and comes complaining that "he beat me," Lacan sees imaginary transitivism — the child who beats the other identifies with the other child, thus making the other the "I" and himself the "other," and speaks *for* and *as* the other (*É* 19, 27; S III 39, 145). This identification is obvious in the Stevens poem: first he makes the real an "other" in section III, and then identifies himself with it (the past-tense form of "come," repeated thrice, cannot be all that benign), and subsequently speaks *for* it *to* himself as if the real-as-himself is speaking to himself-as-other. In reality, it is the "I" who feels. Therefore, knowledge — the question of knowledge is certainly involved here even though Stevens uses the past-tense form of "know" — belongs within the domain of the other, of the "you," or of the real. Hence, to read it anew, it is "what I felt you knew," which properly reinstates the feeling on the side of the "I" and the knowledge on that of the "other." Nevertheless, one cannot altogether dismiss the sharing of that knowledge by the "I," for otherwise the question of identification will remain unanswered. Besides, irrespective of how we read the sentence, the feeling and the knowledge seem almost equal, which is what the identification process is all about in the case of the poem's speaker, or even in the case of the two children in Lacan's example.

The remaining lines speak of the knowledge the "I" shared or felt. He saw the concrete, physical reality — which was uninteresting — transforming into charming plurality, and everything of it seemed to be a part of the real. "Sphere" means a field of action, influence, or existence; formerly, the *OED* suggests, it also meant "each of the revolving shells in which heavenly bodies were set." The speaker thus sees that the real operates and exists very much here on the earth and in everything that is related to the earth. This is how the reality became charmingly *poly*tonous. In an adage, Stevens affirms this plurality and suggests that it depends on the perceiving subject (*OP* 178), and Juliet Mitchell, with reference to object-relations theory in psychoanalysis, says, "It is never only an actual object but also always the fantasies of it, that shape it as an internal image for the subject" (*FS* 3). It was the importance of the real that the physical facts as reality came alive as if animated, ensouled. As suggested in the discussion of the poem's first section, Stevens believed that we owe our nature to the earth (*CP* 107). Hence, if the earth has become a limitless sphere of the real, so must the human body. The poet often uses the word "anima" for the noumenal essence and "animal" for the body in which it is grounded (Doggett 39); in this sense, the reference to the animal in the poem suggests the human body. However, the repeated mention of the change in the animal seems to implicate the ego as well, since that rejuvenating change is an imaginary effect, whose pivot is the ego. Thus, like the earth, the self (which does not exclude the body) has also become the dwelling of the celestial real. In fact, the repetition of the heavenliness in the final lines, especially in the last line, makes the heavenliness of the self exceed in degree when compared with its reference to the first section's Vincentine herself. One wonders whether it is an apotheosis of the real or of the "animal."

At times, however, Stevens had to admit that the real does not always respond to desire in the manner that it does in "Apostrophe to Vincentine." He was acutely aware of the impossibility of confining it within the walls of perception, yet he never got tired of seeking it even though he became miserable that he could not do so, except in uncertain "reflections." "Bouquet of Belle Scavoir" (*CP* 231–32) depicts these very thoughts through elaborating the desire for her, the feeling of misery, and the sense of total evasion by her (sections III, IV, V). And yet Stevens could foreground words that assert "her" significance, with which the poem begins. This shows that the mind may never be satisfied, but that the search for the real must or will never end, for "she" is the maker — to reverse the argument of "Idea of Order at Key West." The real as the object of desire brings only frustration, depriving its seeker of any possibility of satisfying his desire. The more this desire is elaborated, the greater the subject's sense of alienation from his *jouissance* (*É* 242); as Stevens puts it in "Bouquet of Belle Scavoir," the thought of the belle alienates her from the thinker.

The elusive nature of the real kept Stevens unsated and interested, in the hope that his relation with reality might be restored. However, there is more to it than simply its elusiveness; the poet viewed the real as an alienated part of himself. His nostalgic desire for the real is marked by the irreparable loss of the symbiotic unity with the mother; therefore, he often sees the real as a feminine figure — sometimes as the mother and sometimes as the beloved (Doggett 39) — without whom he feels incomplete and imperfect. His attempts to close in on the real, to embrace it, are really his struggle to complete himself (*CP* 431). His truth was that he had lost the phallus, out of which came an emphasis on the desire for that mythical, unrealizable unity with the mother where there was no loss, no incompleteness or imperfection, where he was like a Dane in his own country (*CP* 419), since the phallus was very much present within that unity. Now he must either demand the phallus from the lost mother who supposedly (in his unconscious) has it or desire that unity itself, an accomplishment that is impossible to achieve without returning to the point of birth (*CP* 321). Here, in the concerned passage from the "Esthétique," the mother is portrayed as phallic, as the Other of desire, because she is for him the ultimate real (*CP* 322). This phallic (m)Other often led the poet to write of her in terms of masculinity. His desire for the (m)Other is an essential part of his nostalgia for the noumenal real.

On the one hand, it is the phallic mother and, on the other, there are other figurations engendered by Stevens' desire for the phallus. In any case, the Other is phallic, and therefore real. For example, the hero in "Examination of the Hero" is described as an actor and his act, but undivided since he is real (*CP* 279). What is not divided: the hero and his act or the hero himself? Both ways depict his reality. For Stevens, the Other is certainly not divided, which is also the cause of his continued malady. The desire for the Other as the outcome of Stevens' problematic past remains alive through his creativity ("hand" as creativity), wielding authority over him while remaining a fascinating object, whose praises the poet must sing (*CP* 388). Had Stevens visualized the Other as divided — barred, like a human subject — he could have effected the "further separation" from it and might have (re)established a relation with the object(a). Perhaps this was not to be. Like the hero, who is anonymous (*CP* 279), the poet resists naming and imaging the major man. The major man's description as one who remains unweaned leaves him undivided (*CP* 388), hence in the real. Both figures are impervious to entering the symbolic sphere and remain imperious.

Throughout Stevens' poetry, the inner and outer realities are inextricably linked since the two are inseparable in his conception. *An Ordinary Evening in New Haven* (*CP* 465–89) is a poem about reality; nevertheless, unlike many other poems of reality, it is interesting in its juxtaposition of both inner and outer realities: the Other (as the Ruler of Reality that resides within) and the outside world (as Queen of Fact) form a couple here (*CP* 485). Hence the poem's title: "evening" is the time when the distinction between the inner and outer worlds becomes imperceptible; the city of New Haven, apart from symbolizing the external world, also suggests a "new" place that becomes the self's "haven," its newness being an effect of the complementary consortium of the two worlds or realities. Stevens begins this long poem with a promise to deal with a perception of the outer reality; appropriately, it starts with what the physical eye sees, the vision that is not yet interiorized. This would be a sort of official version of the eye's experience, supposed to be believed by all, similar to the Vulgate; perhaps this is in line with realists like Robbe-Grillet. Stevens decides to speak a few words about this but soon finds it difficult, hence the tag drawing him into the meditative aspect of the experience: in the repetition of "yet," there is a hint of the imagination or desire's intrusion here, an affirmation of the ever-meditating mind's role in reality perception; therefore the poet must also speak of the perceiving self. The "house" is Stevens' image for the self, the mind, the interior world. The sixth line of section I has a rhetorical question answered by the poet himself— that the house is composed of the sun alone. We know the sun is a giant in Stevens, but so is the "house," since its meditations are giant, never-ending. The poet must speak of it.

The "house" becomes "houses" owing to Stevens' mingling of particularity and universality, which will be discussed in the next chapter. Stevens suggests that the darkness of the self cannot be changed into light unless it becomes equal in strength to the first giant — the sun, the lion or violence without. While this conceptual adequacy was sufficient for the poet in "The Blue Guitar," he means to kill the first giant in this poem. This killing must be taken in the sense of its symbolization, of bringing something from its noumenal solipsistic presence into intuitive experience. Such perception of reality will allow the sun-like emergence of the self (*CP* 465). The self or mind is a great poem for Stevens (*CP* 238); Lacan takes a similar stance in Seminar XI in referring to the mind as a poem (Preface viii). Perhaps both Stevens and Lacan mean that the human subject is not an individual or a whole but rather a text being written and seeking that which will end its status as text and unite it permanently with the object it seeks (the Signified or that Other which it represents). However, it needs to overcome its inherent weaknesses and fragmentary nature, which alone can make existence an experience in symbolic *jouissance*. The infant, before entering the mirror stage, exists without any awareness of its body as a whole; it is a fragmentary body, which starts uniting in the infant's imaginary from the mirror stage on, when it is ready to experience moments of jubilation and to enter the symbolic order, making its existence festive. The poet seems intent on (re)enacting the same stage despite his age.

Section II is more direct in suggesting that the "house" is composed of oneself; however, since it is a poem, as has been previously suggested, it is not palpable. However, the image of the "house" takes on a more palpable form in this section as, unlike in the first section, it evokes the unconscious domain, which can be sensed only in the mental movements.[13] Stevens' conception of the unconscious, like that of Lacan, includes other men and sounds (including the particular language they speak), as in "Two Tales of Liadoff" (*CP* 346–47). The subject (*moi*) is literally suspended when the Other — the subject of the unconscious — begins speaking even as it loses the sense of time and place because the Other becomes the central reference point of the subject's never-ending meditation, such that the subject cannot isolate himself from the Other. This moment, for Stevens, is the cause of the subject's feeling of being himself, a feeling that section XII of "The Blue Guitar" should have arrived at.

The blurring of the distinction between the sun and mind, between the idea and its beholder, between the metaphysical and actual, is effected by the desire that is evoked at the moment of vision itself[14]; this is why what the physical eye sees cannot be separated from the mind's eye, or from the "I." This leads to affirming the unity of the moment of vision and desire in section III. And man's desire is always the desire of the Other in Lacan. The Other has supplanted God in Stevens; it is to this new God, who shows himself more clearly in the night, that we now pray in order to transform the ordinary reality into a mountain. The holiness of religious men has made God a sort of possession, for it made him too human. The Other is not that human; its recondite aspect still shines brightly on the newfound world of faith. Its obscurity may be a misery for us, but it ignites our desire for the Other nonetheless; this misery or poverty is therefore more important than holiness and also more important than the object of desire. Possessing the object of desire brings but frustration, for it then becomes disinteresting, incapable of igniting our desire. Our misery, poverty, or lack is our desire, which cannot attain its object. The desire is set in the unconscious and operates behind the physical eye as well as in the actual things seen. It always remains empty, but with the promise of fulfillment since its lack is its essence, which cannot be contained by refusing its fulfillment. Here Stevens asserts human life with its inherent poverty owing to his love of the life of desire; he transforms human native insufficiency into a potential asset. Section IV says that desire is stronger, more savage, without a specific object. This lends the self a leonine aspect deserving of equally primitive satisfaction. In the cry of desire, the self experiences reconciliation, integration, and harmony in its relation to the divine. This gives rise to the romance of life's seasons.

Thus, Stevens continues in section V, there is no space for disillusionment — like the disillusionment of the man in the preceding section — when reality is perceived by the mind's eye; instead, one embarks on the voyage of romance and dreams. The mind's eye may not see things exactly as they are, but it yields *jouissance* nevertheless since such perception affects the perception of the physical eye as well, thus leaving no division between the mind's eye and the physical eye. The physical eye is not exquisite: derived from the Latin *ex + quaerere*, "exquisite" literally means to search out or seek out. It is the mind's eye that searches or seeks out; the physical eye merely sees and therefore is not exquisite. The poet seems to suggest that the mind's eye makes the real unreal even in the physical eye — that the physical eye's vision does not remain plain when reality is seen by the mind, thus barring the division between the actual and the abstract, between the purely physical and the purely psychical. If this is so, then there is no reason why man should inquire into the division of the world and self when he has not divided them, especially when the divided self enables contact with both physical and metaphysical worlds. The mind, one of the two parts of the self (the body being the other part), aided by the body's roots in the ordinary reality, is able to search out the ultimate reality with its "exquisite" eye. This is a Stevensian attempt at human redemption from the dualism set deep in Western culture. However, it is not simply the poet's fanciful wish; he has already suggested toward the end of *The Comedian* that the recovery of human immanence is essential before one can dream of redemption.

Stevens now concentrates more on reality itself. The opening line of section VI confirms that the poet's quest for reality will never end. The section collects contrasting pairs of terms denoting the difference between beginning and end — naked : hierophant, Alpha : Omega, infant : polymathic, A : Z. The terms on the left represent beginning, freshness, innocence, simplicity, purity, and so on, while those on the right indicate fancifulness, maturity, wisdom, age, end, and so forth. Reality has no end; therefore Stevens puts it before its mature conceptions, which are detrimental to its pristinity. The Omega either destroys its pristinity or else its thoughts make man the intelligence of reality, so that the search for reality ends. Among the crowd of these men, there are also those for whom the search for reality does not end. Whether Alpha's men or Omega's, reality *is* since all hanker after it in order to interpret life as faultlessly as possible. But reality cannot be confined in this way; its search never ends. What ends is Omega; however, reality has the potential to refresh Omega's attitude, such that even Omega becomes Alpha and the search for reality continues. In this sense, reality in Stevens is a "desiring-production," which "outmaneuver[s]" all attempts at its confinement or codification by endless renewals (McCollough 100).

Stevens' derisive tone resounding throughout section VII indicates that he is looking down upon the institutions that try to confine reality.[15] Therefore he says that though the founders of these institutions seem to be rich, in reality they are very poor. When our own foundations are not stable, shaken by reality, how can we found or institutionalize reality? Reality is a flux, ever changing in our conception; we internalize each of these conceptions and "move" with it. However, it is a pity that we also move with objective representations of things made by realists who spurn desire or subjectivity. Men moving with these realists are lesser men. However, the lesser men must be there around us; they function as the Omega (Bloom 316), allowing the Alpha to begin again. Man's ability to hide is the ability to abstract and elevate reality. Realism has made man lose this ability. Yet Stevens looks at this positively since it is an arrival at the Omega, which is concurrent with the emergence of the Alpha; it is what makes the function of the Alpha possible, and the search for reality continues.

The next section begins from the actual and arrives at its "unreal." It evokes our carnal existence and desires. However, breath links us with the "real" real, or with the "unreal," as Stevens would have it. Breath is our anima, which fills our otherwise dead bodies; it is our being. It is also the origin of our mother tongue, which enables us to speak to the real; it is what makes us capable of expressing our desire for reality, as the poet shows in the second stanza; it is what enables us in this strange world to utter our desire for "recognition, avowal," to cry out our question of "What am I?" Bloom notices "how prevalent and central in Stevens such a cry is" (316).[16] The cry does not go answerless in this section, since its converse exists in itself. The cry is exhalation; its converse is inhalation — inhalation of being. The resultant sense, combining the seen and felt, is an answer in itself. Inhalation and exhalation are intrinsically related; the cry is modified through breathing in (as an echo of the cry) as soon as it issues. The love between our body and the "real" real, between the body and its real (breath-anima-being), is of an inexpressible essence.

In this way, Stevens would not leave the "body" behind in the act of seeking the "real" real. Section IX is written in the vein of Baudelaire in Paris, in the sense that it is in the immediate, physical, practical world that Stevens seeks the "real" real, which can transfix the beholder by being pure, itself, as it is.[17] This is possible when the eye (I) is cleared of its uncertainties borrowed from the preconceptions of reality, so that even the physical eye's vision, without meditation, would be enough. Here the physical eye's vision is different from that in the first stanza; it is seeing without an *effort* to see so that everything becomes real and the real everything. This sense of the real includes not merely the visible, the solid reality, but also the transient and evasive; this is the moment of divinity, of the *jouissance* that we seek. This divinity has nothing to do with the traditional heaven that has been emptied out. The moon of section X is not the usual imagination but represents the world of (religious) fantasy, which Stevens sees as disastrous. The immediate world of our experience is much better. The world of experience contains both the inner and outer worlds (their conflation), where each thing has a double and hence has an enigmatic appearance, such that there is no difference between real and "unreal." However, this is not like the dead man in section IV who fought against illusion because he had fixed his object.[18] The mind of such a man is determined; this constancy is detrimental, as it rots existence. The spirit of one who believes in the fluid, immediate world of experience dwells in a permanence of impermanence, which is a new faith — as opposed to the simple permanence of the imagination that fixes reality in images — that keeps the cycle of Alpha and Omega refreshing, renewing the quotidian things and the (metaphysical) hallucinations their physical existence creates.

As usual, in section XI, Stevens relates the metaphysical or mythological with the present, the immediate, the physical, and also with the self. Thus, the spirit becomes a lion and New Haven replaces Juda. If the new phrase, "the cat of New Haven," has to evoke the same things that the old phrase did in the past, the self must become strong in order to face the contemporary reality that has become strong. However, the mythological past still walks with the walker in the present. Since the walker, awakened, knows how new mythologies can be created, he destroys these old forms in such a way that they lose their majesty. Now they exist in the mind with the difficulty of *to be*. This kind of viewing of the ancient mythology is a device that helps in relating it to the present and also in creating new mythologies. This is how the spirit can become strong. This is when it can become a *voyant*. This is the truth of the great men. Standing potent in the contemporary harsh reality is a desire in Stevens. For such a poet of reality, he says in section XII, there is only the present, neither the past nor the future. Yet he knows that the present is gone as soon as it is lived (*OP* 190). Therefore, due credit must be given to the immediate past, which is a vital part of perception. And, since poetry depends largely on perceptive ability (*OP* 191), the poet's fiction must contain the subtle exchanges between the past and present. His fiction resembles thoughts; it recognizes the other, the Not-Me world, as equal to the self; it *makes* the world for us, and ours. Stevens did realize the significance of this process of symbolizing or grounding reality, of making it available to the self as if it belongs to the self. Stressing the importance of the words, Lacan also said that words create the world that we possess (*É* 65); Stevens values the theory of language for the same reason (see *CP* 345).

Stevens' fictions are not exactly thoughts but only sense-perceptions, probably because thoughts are more concrete in that they can be spoken with clarity in connected words; for these fictions to become words or connected words, as they finally do in his work, the external world where language exists is necessary. This is how they become symbols, words, or signifiers. If words constitute the life of the world, then the fictions are the life of an individual; that is to say, the subtle exchanges between past and present, which have yet to become words, are his noumenal being. The being is grounded, made into the subject's being-in-the-world, when it becomes a signifier or word, like "to be." Lacan's notion that there is being only due to the verb "to be" comes in handy here (see Fink 182n5). Stevens' view of the signifier is very close to that of Lacan as he speaks of the dependency of life on the words that evoke life (*CP* 287).

The poet-observer of reality, says Stevens in section XIII, is like an "ephebe" who walks alone. The word "walk" is often used by Stevens to represent the activity of perception and, thus, a way of looking at things (see, for example, "Of the Surface of Things" [*CP* 57], "Palace of the Babies" [*CP*

77], and "Idea of Order" [*CP* 129]). The ephebe's walk is solitary, unlike that of priests and proctors, who are serious masters of a serious subject for which they have tremendous respect but that is (or has become) useless now. Although serious like them, the ephebe is not concerned with the serious that is useless, since he does not dwell on the idea of Christ's return, which evokes the stale spiritual and its intolerable constancy. Instead, he intends to define a new spiritual that will lead humanity to experience divinity, which the stale spiritual has ceased to do. Thus the priests and proctors have dried up while the ephebe matures to "Professor Eucalyptus" (notice the use of capitalization) in section XIV. While the former still seek God in the sky, the latter seeks him in the ordinary, visible, near world since there is nothing else to choose from; what he can choose, though, is appropriate language to describe what he sees.

Acknowledging Bloom's brilliant exposition of section XII (320–21), it may further be argued that Stevens associates "cry" and "wind" with words emerging from "within" (*CP* 336), which explains the wind's cry as both an internal and external phenomenon (*CP* 336). In this sense, owing to Stevens' symbol of the night as the interior world, the windy night in section XII represents the words from the interior world as part of the poem, which is a reverberation or reverbalization of those words; this is an exteriorization of the interior, the point (as section XIV suggests) at which the outer reality is in some accord with the inner. The description of reality becomes a divinity at this point. Despite this, however, reality remains obscure owing to the *meconnaissance* principle. Yet, perhaps because of this human weakness, the description of reality elicits a definite elegance in language, imparting divinity to it. When Stevens says of Professor Eucalyptus that he seeks the divine in the ordinary reality, he is distinguishing between God and reality; this may be why he uses the verb "seek" twice in this section, thus perhaps avoiding "see." This becomes clear in the last three lines: the quotidian reality that we experience cannot substitute God since God is not perceived in reality; the reality we perceive is without its essence, its "real." This "real" of the real is what is probably a substitute for God—*because* it cannot be perceived well. In A. Alvarez's words, Stevens has great feeling for "the truth that lurks below the changing surface of appearances" (131). That radical essence, to use Stevens' words, is the "unreal" of the real, its "irrational," its "infinite." The conjunction of or flickering between the real and the "unreal" is the essence of poetry for him (*OP* 256), the reason why he often "skims the real for its unreal" (*CP* 272); their interrelation is made possible by the poet's sensibility, which makes both the real and the unreal fecund (*OP* 293).

The holiness has become abhorrent in section XV; it is necessary to establish a secular ground of belief. The poet finds this ground in the innermost self, which Doggett refers to as "the generic self" (132); Lacan would call it the Other. This change in belief is viewed as necessary for refreshing and renewing the desire; it helps to lift the rock of being from out of its hibernation. Both "was" and "as" are essential to Stevens' conception of the human "is." In section XVI he says that there is no image of time's "is" because, as he remarks in section XVIII, perception is always a matter of the past and does not allow us to see things in their present. Since knowing fact as fact is worthless (*OP* 237), the "as"-art of perception is valuable as it fills out the otherwise worthless facts of the body and its existence. Perception is made possible by the consciousness, whose existence depends on the blossoms in a possibleness, where it will be possible to view the shimmering of unrealizable or unrealized parts of the real, which the consciousness does or might perceive through its own truth. These are or would be the shimmering of the consciousness itself.

Speaking of the consciousness anticipates the central interior. Section XIX begins by noting how things pick up their character from some cogent source — for example, from the imagination. Each century had its own radial source in a man who became its center. However, the poet is concerned with the present, with the modern reality — which keeps narrowing all the time so that "colony" remains confined to the self in its present (*CP* 237). What could be the radial source in such a transient scenario? The poet answers that it is the Other, who speaks in the unconscious. The subject who hears the speech cannot understand it, though. Stevens' conception of the Ecclesiast chanting an obscure text recalls Lacan's gloss of the Other-as-language. If the conscious is, as the preceding section has suggested, aware of time, then the Other is the interior world without time and ever present, and Stevens is jubilant to be *there* with it; "Martial Cadenza" (*CP* 237–38) is an explicit example of this mood.

The poet's search for the ultimate real continues in section XX. Here, the town (as a combination of both the real and symbolic) exists in the unconscious. The imaginary conceptions of the town when it was first perceived do not go away; they exist in the unconscious as memory and mingle with its present images and the feelings evoked in the mind. It is here that the real is purged of the impure and can be experienced by the subject since, by way of his occupation with the unconscious, he also escapes the impure. However, this is possible only if he leaves behind the imaginary domain and the symbolic, since they are obstacles in perceiving the ultimate real; Lacan likewise places the real beyond them. As Ragland-Sullivan writes, our language and "self"-experience are very much responsible for our interpretations of the real; this composes "reality," not the "real," which is "both beyond and behind imaginary perception and symbolic description" (188). Stevens often uses the word "men" in the sense of the symbolic order that the subject assimilates from other people, through their language. The subject constitutes the reality of his habitation in this way. To see the "real" real or the ultimate real, however, the imaginary and the symbolic grids must be evaded; one must escape their attendant impurities, so that one is transformed into "a naked being with a naked will." This is very much a nostalgic desire for that *infans* stage ("naked being") before the infant's entry into the imaginary and symbolic orders, when the desire was naked as it wanted nothing except the body of the mother; it is a desire for the purity of the encystic stage of life when there was no separation from the mother. Perhaps the poet wants to go further back, even beyond that stage, so that there would be no question of the infant desiring the mother but of inhabiting "the hypnosis of that sphere" itself.

Is this return possible? Section XXI suggests that perhaps it is not. The necessity of being oneself, of becoming a human subject, is unalterable (*CP* 324); it is a will forced upon him by others, and there is no escape or other choice for the subject. However, like him, the others are also subjects: it may be that there is a universal will, which is further described as a constant romance that has become operative because of alienation from some vaguely understood, distant island. The "black shepherd" is the Other, the unconscious is his isle; he is present in the subject's hearing of him and his obscure expressions. It seems to the subject that he hears them coming from some is(olated)land, but they do not belong to any particular place since the unconscious is a continuity between inside and outside. Thus, although the severance between the subject and the unconscious is clear, there is no cause for sadness, since the senses can enjoy the other island — the phenomenal world — that is close to them and from which issue substitute romantic intonations. Stevens often uses the word "wind" to evoke (the movements of) the mind; in this section, the wind is of particular interest since it unites the two romantic intonations, upon hearing which the subject enters a celestial mood. Here the poet is, indirectly, again emphasizing the beneficence of the actual world around us (*CP* 155), for it enables a contact with the unreal, the irrational, the distant, or the unconscious. Doggett appropriately comments that "since a trust in the reality of things and selves fills out the void that would otherwise exist without a belief in a transcendental ground of being, the word *reality* holds an unconscious store of feeling in Stevens' use of it" (27). *An Ordinary Evening* has a particular value in the poet's bringing together the immediate (near) and the unapproachable (distant).

Section XXII celebrates what Doggett calls "the reality of things and selves," gorging on what he elsewhere calls the First Idea or the ever-early candor. Since the stance here is that of a preacher, Stevens himself is Professor Eucalyptus and also the poet who equates reality and God. In section VII, he has already condemned the hardcore realists who make reality lesser through objectification or exteriorization; now he must speak of how the poet's enterprise is different, how his creation is a re-creation of the unknown origin of things and of ourselves. The poet interiorizes things; they may be inanimate, but his brooding fills them with their ever-early candor. Once again we see that Stevens' search for reality is associated with a certain unity lost at the origin itself. If not for others, then for him, at least, it is an everyday feeling. However, he is not satisfied with — or rather, preoccupied by — that feeling alone, for it would leave him among the individuals or mad persons devoid of any relation with humanity. In his view, he must renew the world by renewing the creative art in such a way that it would think of the whole humanity by relating it to the unity at the origin. This would be true (re-)creation. All have lost that bright origin, the "real" real; using this fact in poetic art in order to recover the lost origin would satisfy the poet's creative desire. An illustration of such re-creation as a search is found in the final five lines of this section, where Stevens uses the image of the evening star for the Other and seeks to lend it credence so that others will accept its truth.

This is how the unconscious is viewed as the place of the ultimate real, where the poet finds what Doggett calls the "transcendental ground of being," and of the inanimate world outside as well. This is the metaphysical half of the phenomenal world; this metaphysical aspect or noumenality, Stevens continues in the next section, illumines and elevates the phenomenal world. He associates the noumenal with the maternal. The Other includes the mother in Stevens, who views union with her as his own unity and integrity. He feels that during the day this unity is dispersed in the multiplicity of self, but that in the night's sleep it can be experienced as the unifying principle of everything, of all multiplicity. The poet considers this sense of unity to be one's true identity, composed in the night-as-the-interior-world. At the same time, he is aware of the fatal outcome of such nakedest perception (*CP* 459); he sees fragmentations occurring within that unity with the (m)Other, as if that unity is death — as if death hides within this real. Thus, Stevens is seen backing away from that fatal desire ("adventure" from *venire*, or "come"), and the desire for the (m)Other remains unfulfilled.

Nevertheless, section XXIV suggests that the Other must take up Jove's place to avoid repetition. This augurs a new beginning, and preparations for welcoming the new era are under way: It is not yet evening, the time congenial for the Other to start expressing itself, or for the people to begin actually expressing their faith in it through their creative art (the "hand" as creative art). Though the people's thoughts are not yet fully ready, they are willing, since they know the novelty and significance of the new faith. This is something that takes place "within" and "without": the Other being a continuity between inside and outside, it touches both the space outside and the self alike. Stevens places the Other at a point where the sky and earth meet. This is an effort to bring the outer and inner realities together at a point, which was his major premise in writing this poem. This point is the essence of his poetry; it is from here that poetry springs for him. It is no wonder, then, to see his engagement with the Other in the next three sections.

The Other is the center of Stevens' theory of poetry and of life. Thus, there is the sense of the Other fixing him in section XXV, which speaks of the Other and its gaze. The Other is the one face of reality that remains constant in the otherwise impermanent nature of reality. It is called "hidalgo," literally meaning "son of something" (from Spanish *hijo dalgo*). "Son" is he who inherits, and "something" is a word used when what is known or understood cannot be specified or expressed; in modern usage, "something" is also used to indicate the importance of a person or thing. The Other is son in the sense that it inherits its nature from the outside world, itself inexpressible yet important. This is why the Other is portrayed as a mysterious figure. However, as is very often found in Stevens' poetry, the Other makes the real most unreal, most beautiful, leading the poet to think that isolations between him and the Other were untrue. Section XXVI begins with how, perhaps owing to the vicinity of the "hidalgo," everything on/of the earth (also meaning the self) undergoes an enervative change, but the Other has the last two stanzas. Stevens is enamored by it much as he is by the earth; although hard to perceive, he hears it whispering something auspiciously human.

In section XXVII, the poet again brings the external and internal realities together: the Other becomes the Ruler of Reality and the other, Not-Me world becomes the Queen of Fact. Although the reality of which the Other is the ruler is really the "unreality," as a spouse of the Queen of Fact he is the ruler of both the "unreal" and the real. In the face of these empirical propositions, Stevens is led to infer in section XXVIII that the mind is the habitat of reality, and, if this is true, that the real and "unreal," the physical and metaphysical, the concrete and abstract, the rational and irrational, are inseparable. Stevens begins to furnish examples of such couples, but he seems more bent on the unreal since, apart from the first example (which includes the New Haven of imagination before one arrives in it and the actual New Haven after one arrives), he speaks of places only conceived imaginarily. It was the poet's life-long cherished conviction that the essential poetry springs out of the interaction between the unreal and the real (*OP* 256); he believed—and the whole field of art bears this out—that by "engulfing" the real, the "unreal" "subtilizes" it and our experience of it (*OP* 240). In this sense, *An Ordinary Evening* lays bare Stevens' theory of poetry, which, its writer says, is its life. It is the imagination that brings people and poetry together; hence Stevens is sure that it should not be very difficult to show that the theory of poetry in general is the theory of life itself, because, like poetry, life is constituted within two opposites.

Stevens' interminable adventures into the unreal gave him confidence that he could use the unreal to re-create a different land altogether. This is what he probably meant in writing section XXIX, which was the ending section of the original eleven-sectioned version of the poem. There seem to be three lands here, not two as Vendler (*On Extended Wings* 293) and Bloom (333) have suggested: the exotic, "unreal" land of the lemon trees; the actual, real land of the elm trees; and the vaguely specified land of the big mariners. The mariners, however, have already left their land and come wandering to the land of the elm trees; this is a restatement of Stevens' belief that we live in a land not our own and, much more, not ourselves. The parable of this section has a close affinity with Stevens himself: his shifting from Pennsylvania to Connecticut, and his trips to the abundant tropical South, are reflected in the mariners' wanderings. Like the poet, the mariners have made the land of the elm trees their home, and both have been living their lives (their r's could be both their language and being) in the land of the lemon trees and have assimilated the exotic quality and richness of it into their language, enabling them to re-describe the exotic unreal.

In the land of the elm trees the mariners looked on "autumnal women, women more of earth and its ripeness than of the mind's desires" (Bloom 333). The women could not satisfy the mariners; they are much like the South in Stevens' poetry, which does not allow the imagination or desire scope to find, to discover, to search (recall Crispin's journey from South toward North, and also the Florida that was left in order to arrive at the North in "Farewell to Florida" [*CP* 117–18]). Therefore, the mariners kept desiring that which was not *here* in the land of the elm trees — they lived in and spoke *there*, in the land of the lemon trees of their desire (emphasis mine); thus, finally they came to the land of the lemon trees, where they felt being in the land of the elm trees itself— but with a refreshing change nevertheless. This is the engulfment of the real into the exotic unreal, which is a change that makes one feel both elated and at home all at once. It was a change brought about by the language, for it was due to the importance of the unreal that the language of the mariners picked up a definite panache, so that they were able to re-describe the particulars of the unreal.

Stevens' desire for reality thus continually urged him toward disinterring what he calls the unreal, but in this attempt he also effected an ecesis of the ordinary reality, and both created psychical *belvederes* that afforded him unusual *jouissance*. This exercise was aimed at entering a different life, a life beyond the ordinary life and "brighter, perfected" (*OP* 101). This forced him to go further beyond, as the poems that I call his "apogees" testify.

CHAPTER 6

Apogee

> The wonder and mystery of art, as indeed of religion in the last resort, is the revelation of something "wholly other" by which the inexpressible loneliness of thinking is broken and enriched. (*OP* 237)
>
> The sense of being changes as we talk. (*OP* 109)

The repression or loss of the phallic signifier in Stevens made him understand its significance, for it is what is lost that attains an unusual importance in man's desire; he kept speaking of this "Ur-syllable" in various disguises (Reddy 11), often using the terms "syllable" and "alphabet" to speak of it. The loss (repression) of the signifier is the loss of its meaning for the subject. When Stevens gives expression to this loss, he does so obliquely—for example, in "To the Roaring Wind," he indicates the loss of a syllable, but does not specify what syllable he is speaking of; moreover, he imputes the loss to a "you," who is qualified as "Vocalissimus" (*CP* 113). As I suggested in the preceding chapter, if "wind" is treated as "mind," then the poet can be seen as addressing his own mind, so that the "cry of the vocalissimus-as-wind" (*CP* 336) is the cry of the "shifting" (*CP* 83–84), shuffling, restless human mind. However, there are two instances where Stevens is more direct: In "No Possom, No Sop, No Taters" (*CP* 294), he writes that it is in the solitude of (the mind's) winter that he hears a syllable intone its lack. The syllable emptied of any meaning, however, finds the most direct expression in the last volume, in "Prologues to What is Possible" (*CP* 516–17), where the verse seems to sum up Stevens' life-long loneliness and the struggle to end it. In the last few lines of the poem's first section, he imagines himself to be a lone voyager lured on by, and eager to enter, the syllable (*CP* 516). Although it is not easy to see if he was able to dialectize this master signifier, it may be suggested here that he could have succeeded in his attempt to some extent since the later poetry shows his struggle to subjectify the cause of being and (the object of) desire—object(a)—which is not possible without the dialectization of the phallic signifier. However, this does not necessarily mean that he finally recovered from his illness, since poems like *Chocorua to Its Neighbor* (*CP* 296–302) and *The Rock* (*CP* 525–28) seem to shatter that assumption. *Chocorua* (first published in 1933) and *The Rock* (in 1950) both belong to very different periods, and though the poet's stance is different in both, it nevertheless negates the assumption that he might have recovered.

Among the poems discussed here, "The Motive for Metaphor" (*CP* 288), *Credences of Summer* (*CP* 372–78), and *The Bouquet* (*CP* 448–53) seem to form a logical progression toward the subjectification of that radically lost cause; therefore, it would have been logical to discuss them in order. However, the assuming of that foreign cause cannot happen without dialectizing the phallus. Discussing these poems together would not only be assuming that Stevens did dialectize the phallus but also asserting the poet's cure from the crisis. *Chocorua* and *The Rock*, also discussed here, undermine that possibility, for each appears in the *Collected Poems*, chronologically speaking, only after what might seem to be a stage of recovery on Stevens' part. Both poems reflect the desire for the (m)Other, precluding the possibility of an end to the poet's crisis. This study, thus, must leave the question of his "cure" open-ended.

The phallus is the signifier responsible for the subject's sense of being an individual, separate from the (m)Other. Thus, in "Motive for Metaphor" (*CP* 288), it is described as the fundamental signifier. It is also supportive of the symbolic order in which humans alone cherish the fantasy of their existence—as if, as Stevens puts it, life depends completely on this signifier (*CP* 287). As a substitute for the lost object(a), this signifier is the arch-signifier thereof. This ultimate *point de capiton*, as Lacan refers to it, gives all other signifiers their function as they seek to combine with it and serve as its metonyms. Thus, it is the chief motive for any metaphor. Reading this poem on the phallus requires special attention to the clever use of the pronoun "you." Since the pronoun "one" does not exclude the "I," as discussed in chapter 2, the pronoun "you" is preferred in order to preserve the ambiguity regarding the inclusion of the "I." Its use helps the poet to detach himself from the whole scene. This impersonal attitude allows him to state a universal truth, yet it would not be wrong to believe that the pronoun and the universal truth must implicate the poet-speaker as well, since "you" is colloquially used to designate "everyone" or "all." However, the fact is that he only includes himself in the scheme of things later, in the third stanza, where the first use of the reflexive "yourself" clearly suggests that the "you" of the line is singular. The question is, what to make of it?

Initially (in the "spring" of life), one's journey into this world begins with oneself as the object of parental desire. This desire, insofar as it is expressed in language, is symbolic; in other words, it is the discourse of the parental Other. This parental desire ensures one's entry into the symbolic order even before one's birth, even before the conception. It is this desire that one must make one's own if one is to come to be as a human subject. However, for this the infant has to go through the *Name-/No-of-the-Father* (i.e., through castration). Castration is also a revelation, for it reveals to the subject what he does not have or what the (m)Other desires. It is the phallus that, thus, becomes the imaginary object of his desire. In his youth, the subject is likely to attain the all-important sense of having or being the phallus, though in reality it is only a sense and not a fact. What really happens here is that he only dialectizes the phallus-as-signifier. It is here that he can give up castration and experience *jouissance* as a result of the "further separation" from the (m)Other that is responsible for that sense of being (this marks the "summer").

"Autumn" is that period of life when one has already experienced the fullness of "summer," the *jouissance* of the phallus. This human season may be viewed in terms of the loss from which one seeks to recover through forming an imaginary relationship with the bygone "summer." Stevens describes such seasonal relationships in the last two stanzas of section IV in "An Ordinary Evening" (*CP* 468). And yet, at the same time, having had the experience of "summer," one's desire seeks to go further beyond the "autumn"—to bring into view or vicinity what Lacan refers to in Seminar VII as the aim or site of desire. It is here that one dates one's death or, as Freud said, the "beyond" of the pleasure principle. "Summer" is beautiful indeed: it is in the "summer" that one's body is most beautiful and energetic—this is true even of the external nature. In a way, this is the limit. Nevertheless, the desire is merciless, for in "autumn" it seeks to transcend the limit of phallic *jouissance*. To use Lacan's words, whereas "summer" or its beauty had a "blinding effect" on desire when one was full of youth (S VII 281), now in "autumn" the desire overcomes the effect and seeks to make visible the aim of desire itself; this is the *ektos atas*. Lacan uses the two terms, *Atè* and *ektos atas*, in Seminar VII in relation to *jouissance*; by the former he designates the human limit of symbolic *jouissance*, and by the latter he means a crossing over of that limit and virtually meeting with death as desire (262–63, 277, 280–83). The desire purging itself of the "blinding effect" of the beauty of "summer," of the symbolic *jouissance*, is nothing but dissatisfaction with the phallus-as-signifier and a search further beyond for the phallus-as-thing. It is nothing short of fixing an appointment with death. Lacan illustrates this in his discussion on *Hamlet* ("Desire" 11–52). To return to the Stevens poem, this is how the subject is divided in his "autumn"—between his "summer" and "winter," between phallic *jouissance* and death, or, in other words, between the phallus-as-signifier and the phallus-as-thing (since the latter is the aim of desire, desiring it is the death instinct). One cannot be or have the phallus; any attempt at striking it is an *ektos atas*, a crossing of the human limit that one can only briefly cross and then meet death.[1]

One is "oneself" in "summer"; therefore the desire to be oneself properly belongs in one's "spring" and "autumn," when the lack of the phallus or of the sense of "self" is observed. Thus, one does not desire to be oneself in "summer." It is necessary to see that Stevens is speaking of "summer" in the third stanza. The dash at the end of the second stanza makes the poem glide almost imperceptibly from "spring" to "summer." This growth from childhood to mature youth, from the lack of the phallus to the sense of having it, is made possible by the imaginary relationship with the phallus, whereby it is symbolized and dialectized. This relationship brings into view the world of fantasy and *jouissance*. The poet-speaker has experienced that world and addresses himself as an other, as "you," with respect to his own "summer-time" persona in line 11. It is only here that he includes himself in the "you" and speaks to himself as an other. Stevens could have easily written the line without the first "yourself," but he does not do so only in order to indicate that the "you" in this line is different from that used in the first two stanzas. It is only now that the reader is allowed to retroactively determine the presence of the poet-speaker in the "you" of the previous stanzas. Without that "yourself," the poem would have looked like a general statement of the human condition without reference to any particular individual, since then the "you" that immediately precedes it would have been rendered indistinguishable from its previous occurrences. However, it was necessary *for* the poet-speaker to include himself as well; in fact, specifically so. The reasons for this will be discussed a little later.

In "summer" (i.e., during the period when one cherishes the sense of having the phallus or being it), one enjoys what Lacan refers to as the phallic or symbolic *jouissance*. In an instance of this experience, the phallus as the master signifier (S1) is brought in relation with another signifier (S2), and the subject experiences a contact with the real.[2] The S2 here may be an *objet petit a*,[3] an object from the actual world of direct experience, which the subject desires but which can only satisfy his need and not desire, for his desire is always for *something else* that can never be seen or said. The mirage of this "something else" as object(a) behind the need-satisfying object lends it the status of a signifier (S2). It is in this bridge-building between S1 and S2 that the subject senses he has (re)discovered the original object of desire, object(a).[4] This is a moment of *jouissance*, no doubt; however, it is the dialectization of S1, the phallic signifier, that makes it possible. Moreover, since object(a) is not an object as such but a signifier, the subject — rather, "man," as opposed to or distinct from "woman" — experiences only the *jouissance* of the signifiers, a "symbolic *jouissance*."[5] The role of language is nothing but to symbolize, to make present something (that is absent or) in its absence. The basic processes through which it happens are metonymy (word-to-word connection) and metaphor (substitution of one word for another); the absent word has a metonymic connection with the present word (or signifying chain) that takes the place of the absent word, as in a metaphor (parentheses mine; *É* 156–57). In other words, it is the absent word or signifier that is responsible for the presence of the present word or signifier. The phallus as signifier in Lacan is that absent signifier, which is responsible for the subject's discourse that is thus always metaphoric. This is why, as Stevens says in the poem, the phallus motivates all metaphors.

As the subject can never establish a direct contact with the cause or aim of his desire, that primally lost object(a), except in his sense, to approach it directly is to go beyond the phallic signifier or beyond the limit of the symbolic, which is the human limit. It is to approach the phallus as an actual object or thing. Crossing this limit and approaching the real object of one's desire must be a moment of *jouissance*, but its intensity is such that it is unbearable for the subject[6]; thus, it is also a death instinct. Therefore, it is necessary for the subject to "shrink" from it and be at the level of the phallus-as-signifier or at least within this limit; this is precisely what Stevens says in the last three lines of the fourth stanza of "Motive for Metaphor." Here, it is not clear whether the poet is referring to the phallic signifier or object(a); however, this ambiguity is constructive: the subject owes his sense of self or being to the phallic signifier (S1), and the being as object(a) is always absent for him who shrinks from it, which has a metonymic relationship with the chain constituted by S1 and S2, where the latter could be the subject himself as a signifier.[7] This ambiguity is also complementary to the subject's "autumnal" division between his "summer" (*jouissance* of the phallic signifier) and "winter" (*jouissance* of the phallus-as-thing or of object[a] qua object). The final stanza, in continuation with this ambiguity and division, is therefore in the difficult position of describing the phallus as both signifier and as object. Having said this, it could also be argued that the poet is referring to the phallus, and not to object(a). Stevens' reading of Shakespeare could have been responsible for this: In *Romeo and Juliet*, Mercutio, in describing the time of the day to the Nurse, uses two Elizabethan slang terms, "dial" and "prick of noon" (literally, "point of noon"), respectively meaning "female genitals" and the "penis" (Act II, Scene iv, ll. 111–12; Easthope 17, 37). Stevens has just replaced the word "prick" with "primary," and, as usual, made the reference to the phallus a matter of secrecy. The final stanza, nevertheless, evokes the image of the erect phallus, in flesh (i.e., the phallus-as-thing). Lacan has said that the phallus is perceived "only in sudden manifestations ... in a flash, by means of its reflection on the level of the object" ("Desire" 48); in this sense, the mention of the momentary auditory and visual experience of it in lines 2 and 4 of the final stanza, as if of some audible or visible thing or object, is noteworthy. Yet the poet does suggest the difficulty of apprehending it in saying that intimacy with it is impossible. Thus, it is at once a real and unreal (fantasmatic or imaginary) object. The poem's last line appropriately sums up the importance and fatality of the phallus; more importantly, its status as a master signifier without meaning is noted — like an algebraic variable having no meaning in itself, it is symbolized by an X.

Here, Stevens' X has a close affinity with what Lacan said of the "x" in his formula for metaphor, which is found in "On the Possible Treatment of Psychosis" (see *É* 200). In that formula, the "x" is a variable and can be replaced with any signifier having the potential to evoke the phallus. Stevens' dissatisfaction with the many substitutions for it finally leaves it simply as X, keeping alive the possibility of inventing more metaphors for the phallus.

Going back to the question of the use of "you," the poet's inclusion of himself as late as line 11 suggests that the poet-speaker is hiding himself. Is it due to the poet's penchant for impersonality in his poetry? However, if it were simply for that, then he could have eliminated the first "yourself" in the third line of stanza 3; that is, he could have chosen not to include himself at all. One would do well to recall what Vendler says: "[T]he emotional heart of a lyric by Stevens is likely to be found in the middle of the poem," since it is there that one finds the poem's "point of origin in feeling, which, though it comes late in the poem, serves as the center from which the other lines radiate" (*Words Chosen* 44, 12). The point is, despite the poet's impersonal attitude in his poetry, his personal experience or feeling is very much at the heart of any poem. Vendler is therefore correct in her recommendation "to substitute 'I' whenever Stevens says 'he' or 'she'" (*Words Chosen* 44). Here, she misses out on "you" and seems too radical in her recommendation, since she might not have thought of Stevens' treatment of the other and of the Other, both of which retain their otherness and hence are often referred to in the poetry in the third-person singular; this is especially noticed where it is a question of the Other. The question is why Stevens should hide himself thus. Lacan's comment on the neurotic's behavior, which has already been discussed in "Prolegomena," is useful here: this neurotic's strong ego functions as a protective cover whereby he hides his castration — successfully, one might add, for many people have spoken of Stevens' egotistic attitude and generally imposing nature but they never suspected any problem in it. Stevens' incisive, insulting sense of humor and his general downplaying of the persons in the field of literature not only suggest his ego's strength but they also point out his desire to annihilate any semblance of a chance that might become the source of *jouissance* for *those persons*, who were (collectively) an Other to him. His aloofness from people, his uneasiness with or even hatred of the contemporary literary artists (or his equals and superiors in general), his reluctance to give public speeches, his avoiding talking to and answering the questions of the audience after talks — all these traits in his character point to the fact that he was strenuously avoiding the "sacrifice" of his "difference," of his "castration"; he did not want the Other(s) to enjoy his castration (*É* 323).[8] One of the best examples of this is his insultingly abrupt response to Richard Bissell, who wanted to know about a legal case that Stevens had lost (B 21). Since Stevens was heading the case, he must have imagined others thinking of the loss in terms of his failure. Here, Stevens denied his boss any enjoyment of his own shortcoming or failure.

It is no wonder, then, that Stevens postpones his inclusion in the "you" of "Motive for Metaphor"; in this way he could hide himself and talk about others. At the same time, though, he must include himself. However, when he does it is very important. His emphasis is literally on what he says in line 11, where he willingly brings himself in. Without being fooled by his negation of his own self, the reader must see that in this antiphrasis the poet is, in fact, emphasizing and celebrating that sense of his "self" when he was in his "summer." It is the uniqueness or the ecstatic feeling of the sense of self that necessitates the negation; it is a figurative way of asserting the self, a rhetorodetermination of the self. The lack of that sense is common in "spring" and "autumn," which he is wont to take as his lot. Stevens was very much a "normal" person in his youth when he was still courting Elsie, before his quarrel with his father; this, roughly, is the period that line 11 recalls. In that line, he reminds himself of the fact that he, too, once had the phallus. This fact cannot be told at the beginning of the poem, for that would make it too conspicuous; more importantly, it could give rise to a spate of questions such as "Has he lost it?" "Does not he have it *now*?" "Is he castrated?" — questions that might give the Other(s) an opportunity to enjoy the poet's "difference." Lest this should happen, he must make inconspicuous even the fact that he did have "it" once. This is the "emotional heart" of the poem; Vendler might further argue that it is from the nostalgia of the lost phallus that the other lines of the poem "radiate." This nostalgic feeling for the lost world of his "summer" is what must be perceived in the poem's third stanza.

However, this does not mean that Stevens showed no improvement insofar as his recovery was concerned. There are indications in his poetry that he may have rediscovered the phallic signifier. The change in his relationship with the reality could support this suspicion. The poetry of *Harmonium* days is full of the loss of reality, even of a reality-phobia of sorts at times. Poems like "Snow Man" (*CP* 9–10), "Domination of Black" (*CP* 8–9), and "Valley

Candle" (*CP* 51) are powerful expressions of a potential threat of the reality principle, while poems like "From the Misery of Don Joost" (*CP* 46–47) offer a clear statement of his inability to cope with that loss (*CP* 46). However, the poetry from "The Blue Guitar" onward shows a comparatively positive change; many poems of *Ideas of Order* and *Parts of a World* especially reflect the poet's attempts to recover as they aim at creating order out of his chaos. There he seems to have accepted the fact that our world is "imperfect" (*CP* 194), which suggests distance from the obsessive character of his interest in reality. The seeds of this distance were found in *Sunday Morning* itself, in its moving away from the fear of or obsession with death. The relationship with reality is essentially imaginary, and it is the imaginary domain that needs to be reordered if a patient is to recover; in this sense, "The Blue Guitar" is a very important poem. Without such reordering of the imaginary, a poem like "Study of Two Pears" (*CP* 196–97)—where Stevens studies both imagination and reality objectively, and suggests the impossibility of resisting the imagination's intervention in reality perception and, at the same time, of perceiving things as they are—would not have been written. In fact, Stevens could reflect an/on enjoyment of reality, as is obvious in many of his poems, among which "The Latest Freed Man" (*CP* 204–5) and "Of Bright & Blue Birds & the Gala Sun" (*CP* 248) easily stand out. Nevertheless, it is also true that there are other poems or verses even in *Parts of a World* that might be suspected of showing the same old obsession with reality. Could it be that those poems or verses are merely recollections from the past experiences? Could his past experiences have provided food for later meditation for a poet like Stevens, who was a keen observer of psychic phenomena? While believing that he never recovered would be an injustice to him, asserting his recovery would be a hasty judgment.

Stevens' later poetry has something different in store, which it is difficult to view as a sign of normative desire since it reflects too much of what he craved in the early poetry. Certain poems of *Transport to Summer* root this suspicion. *Credences of Summer* is important for two reasons: on the one hand, it shows that stage of Stevens' development when his quest for a desired relationship with reality seems to have attained its peak—a perfect relation, one might say; on the other, it celebrates the enjoyment of reality with such an emphasis that one wonders whether he transcends the human limit of the enjoyment. It almost leads to the thought of his going beyond the limit of the phallus-as-signifier and reaching out for the "other" kind of enjoyment that goes by the name of Other *jouissance* in Lacan; there, he seems to hook himself onto the real, to virtually map himself onto the real order—this could well be the cause of the obscure projection of the "rock" in *Credences*. The other two poems discussed in this chapter, *Chocorua* and *The Rock*, seem to confirm this suspicion. *Credences* thus could be seen as a point in Stevens' life where things turned in a different direction.

The "Motive" might lead to speculations regarding Stevens' regaining of the phallus, but in the end it remains an X — meaningless. This, unfortunately, throws him in the dyadic closure with the Other — perhaps ever more radically. *Chocorua*, placed seven pages after "Motive" in the *Collected Poems*, is a forceful expression of that potentially dangerous closure. It is one of Stevens' most polemical poems, and the most neglected of his longer poems. While Bloom rates it along with *Esthétique du Mal*, *Description without Place*, and *Credences of Summer*, he says of the poem's neglect that "it has *Notes* on the one side of it and the other three long poems of *Transport to Summer* coming after it" (222). This reasoning seems inadequate since the ever-intensifying quest for new findings in Stevens would not have left such a forceful poem wanting commentary. Rather, the neglect perhaps stems from the poem's language and subject matter: The language, Bloom observes, is "less aphoristic" than that of *Notes* (222), and leaves little space for the critic to intrude; however, it is more difficult to figure out the poem's subject matter. It is extremely necessary for any commentator of the poem to first have a clear idea of the poem's central concern precisely because it presents a very sustained, integrated, and forceful argument through its twenty-six sections. Such argument, however less aphoristic, should in fact enhance the cause of commentary once the subject of the poem is identified. Without having a clear idea of what the poem is about, the total effect of the poem's language is that it produces a "hovering effect" (Bloom 222), because one cannot shake off the feeling that the subject of the poem involves a certain degree of sublimity.

"Chocorua" is the name of a mountain, but who or what is the "neighbor"? The role of the mountain in Stevens owes much to Cézanne's paintings, which reflect in the painter's late period a singular important image of a particular mountain. Fred Robinson and Betty Buchsbaum have discussed the infiltrations of Cézanne's mountain-art into Stevens' poetry. Both painter and poet were interested in the mountain because of its standing as "an elemental force and power ... identified through the ages as a place of spiritual aspiration and metaphysical revelation" (Buchsbaum 311); for both men it was the symbol of their quest for the ultimate reality. The ages might have looked upon the mountain as a place of spiritual aspiration and metaphysical revelation, but — if Cézanne does — Stevens hardly shows interest in a reality revealed through spiritual or metaphysical speculations. The reality Stevens sought has much more to do with the actual world around us, the world of concrete facts and our experiences of it. Such a reality may be wholly, radically other, yet it can be felt or experienced concretely and not vaguely like, say, a glimpse of God in a religious fantasy (but still comparable to it). If Cézanne, "an observant

[C]atholic," often spoke "of his artistic vocation in religious terms" in the last decades of his life (Buchsbaum 307), Stevens preferred not to do so. Rather, he thought that the world's glory is God's own glory and sought the spiritual in the reality that makes this world (*OP* 178). To say that *Chocorua* leads to "the Emersonian realization ... of a transcendental realm" (Bloom 224) seems an imposition; it is to be heedless to Stevens' rejection of Plato's "asceticism," which takes us away from the reality surrounding us and seeks objects "apprehended *by thought* and *not sense*" (emphasis added; *OP* 236). The poet preferred the world of sense to that of thought. Sense establishes a communion with that which can be empirically known and realized; thought often does so with that which is purely conceptual and remains unrealized. This is the difference between Plato's (or for that matter Emerson's) conceptual, transcendental, and hence "decadent or barbarous" reality (*OP* 236) and Stevens' empirical, sense-able reality. The mountain in Stevens, far from being a concept or an image of spiritual aspiration, is real. And yet it becomes equally "unreal" in a poem like *Chocorua* through Stevens' poetic act or treatment of it because he makes the mountain belong to some "another dimension" (*OP* 239). It is this dimension that must be seen if one is to comment on this poem.

Stevens certainly looked upon the mountain as the most imposing part of the world of actual objects. It is this very quality that, through the subliminal processes in the mind of the perceiver, makes the mountain enter into the dimension of the "unreal." There is obviously an aspect of the perceiver's individuality involved in this kind of transfiguration and sublimation of an object, in the sense that the way a particular object affects him is unique to himself; he sees it through his own experience of it and, therefore, like the genuine artist, he is never true to what he sees (*OP* 237). This is how Stevens came to designate the non-real-seeming aspect of the real as its "unreal" (e.g., see *CP* 272) or as its "infinite" (*CP* 451). The more imposing or interesting the object, the greater its engulfment into the "unreal." What Stevens means by "unreal" is the polyvalence and transfigurations of the object as it plays with the mind. He was aware of this when he wrote, "Things seen are things as seen" (*OP* 162), with "as seen" pointing precisely to the mind's play and poetic act or treatment with respect to the object.[9] Stevens' sense of reality is largely composed of his meditations on the unseen part of actual things, which thus become both his "difficulty and inamorata" (*OP* 241), from which originates the dimension of the "unreal." Such "unreal" of an object is, however, merely an individual's perception, and therefore is never a complete description of the object. It is only a glimpse into what Lacan would call the real of the object under one's gaze. This is why, like the "unreal," even the actual attracts the poet's attention, for it retains its objectivity without ever fully giving itself up to the perceiver. However, it must be mentioned that both poet and psychoanalyst, while they affirm the objectivity of the real, maintain that saying or seeing the real objectively is not possible; Stevens compares the activity of the "unreal" in reality with the activity of a hallucination in the mind (*OP* 240), where the "hallucination"—the "unreal," going by the comparison—is the doing of the mind itself, which, in the comparison, stands for the real.

The mind is indeed real, like the outside world—veritable and existing. If the mountain is the most imposing object of the outside reality, who or what can be its "neighbor"? Neighbors, from cultural standpoint, are those who are of similar social standing, are similar in some respect, identify with each other, and share things among themselves. Considering the force of the mountain image in Stevens and his deep interest in the unconscious, there is no better neighbor to the mountain than the Other of Lacan, for the Other is the most imposing part of the inner reality. The unconscious owes its existence to the outside world, including other human subjects and their language and culture. What the outside world is to the unconscious, or the "mountain" is to the Other—that is, the other is to the Other—is precisely what is implied by the title of this poem. It does not indicate a discourse *as such* of one mountain with another, but implies a relationship of the other to the Other. The whole poem is an apostrophe to the unconscious as the Other. This is obvious in section XX, where Stevens concedes the Other's prominence, which is of no-thing, not a thing, in the sense that it is not available to the senses, and yet is very much present. The unconscious manifestations are experienced more clearly in the dream (night), which in day-ly life is often not remembered very well and is forgotten as having no great significance; yet the unconscious does *in*-sist, even though in disappearing it "ex-sists."

Despite this realization of the poem's subject matter, the problem of the speaker persists, complex as it is. One might point to the line "Now, I, Chocorua, speak of this shadow..." from section XX to suggest that the "I" is Chocorua the mountain, who speaks of that "shadow" (the Other). This is, in turn, suggesting that the "he" who begins speaking in section X and continues until section XII is that "shadow." However, if this "shadow" is so congenial as to speak to Chocorua in so clear a tongue, would it have remained the object of desire—as it indeed does remain throughout the poem—anymore? This is an essential question with regard to Stevens' poetics. In fact, if Chocorua as a mountain is the other, so is the "I": *Je est un autre*; the "I" who speaks is an other to himself who listens. Stevens has demonstrated this Lacanian observation in some poems discussed in chapter 2; "A Dish of Peaches," in fact, dramatizes this experience. Thus, the "he" who speaks in sections X, XI and XII is the "I" speaking *as* an other. Both "I" and Chocorua the mountain are thus the other. It is in this way that they are comparable, not identical. This is very much the essence of identification between man and the outside world. Without this desire for the other, there would be no subjectivity, no unconscious, no Other. At best, the line quoted above from section XX could be read as "Now, I, an other, speak of this shadow..." To conclude the argument, it is imperative to leave the question of the speaker open-ended, as Stevens does in "A Dish of Peaches." It would be in keeping with the poet's poetics. In *Chocorua* Stevens does show the awareness of hearing-oneself-speak or of the otherness of one's own speech, which becomes his own after he identifies his voice with another voice (*CP* 298). This is in perfect accordance with Lacan's thought on the matter. Therefore, the "I," the speaker of the poem, is not to be confused with the mountain, but should be considered as speaking with a sense of an otherness to himself; the speaker and Chocorua are identifiable insofar as both are in an otherness with respect to the speaking voice(s) in the poem. The poem reads better if considered as a discourse on otherness and the Other through which the poet seeks to approach the real "upon [his] mountain" (*CP* 249).

Indeed, the poem begins on the note of otherness that is mitigated through the identification involved in speaking and its hearing. The human subject's quest for wholeness is the cause of the identification process, which grounds the sense of unity with the outside world. To see human beings through such a psychoanalytic frame is to see them without their physical existence. Nevertheless, it is by no means a movement or progress toward that wholeness or enlargement, since the enlargement Stevens sought was that of an individual and his inner world.[10] That enlargement, in Stevens' thought, would come only through the "desire of the Other" (*É* 312). While the subjective genitive ("of") in Lacan's phrase is suggestive of both "desire for the Other" and "desire for the Other's desire," Stevens exhibits only the former aspect of it in *Chocorua*. It may be noted that even the identification with the outside world is marked by a sense of an otherness (note the use of "you") in section I. The very first sentence in this section hints not only at that otherness but also at the desire to be like the "you." It reflects a desire to be the "neighbor" to the "you," a desire for identification with "him." It is a desire for the Other. The moment of confrontation with the Other is over and the present tense of section I is replaced with the past tense from section III onward, even as the "you," which is used colloquially to also include the "I," of section I changes to "he" in section IV. The poem will now ruminate on and report the experience of the unconscious manifestations that were observed during the twilight at the end of the previous night.

Twilight and night are special times in Stevens since they obscure and obliterate the clear contours of things, such that intellect gives way to emotions

(*L* 170–71), allowing perception of the invisible things (from the unconscious) that may be primitive but are attractive and desirable nonetheless. The unconscious manifestations can be observed with more clarity during night since it is a time when the imagination sleeps (*CP* 47), which eliminates the possibility of *méconnaissance* or mis(re)cognition. However, the Other never sleeps (*CP* 171); he is like the thought that does not fade (*CP* 55). It is during night that the inner voice responds more truly (*CP* 137–38). However, *Chocorua* suggests the end of night as preferable. Stevens associates day with desire and night with sleep in "The Blue Guitar" (*CP* 167). It is not that there is no desire when one is sleeping at night, but—it is a common experience that dreams that come at the end of night are remembered with more clarity—a more vivid experience of the Other, *as if* in a state of consciousness or desirousness, was a prerequisite for the poem. Though the Other responds in nighttime (or in the unconscious-like state of the mind), Stevens prefers the transitional period between night and day. It is in this favorable light that the Other manifestations are more tangibly and sharply felt and vividly remembered. Having experienced this sensation late in the night or very early in the morning, the feeling was remembered throughout the day.

From the middle of section III until the end of section VI, we have the first information report on the Other. The reference to Liadoff recalls the "Two Tales of Liadoff" (*CP* 346–47). Besides being the name of a Russian composer, as Bloom points out (224), "Liadoff" is an anagram for "laid off," alluding to the Other's otherness or aloofness, even as the Russian connection brings to mind the Other's description in "A Dish of Peaches" (*CP* 224). "Lay off" also means "dismiss"; recall the Other's remaining "dismissed" if there is no dream (*CP* 464). The death of Liadoff, referred to in the first of the "Two Tales of Liadoff," is thus the vanishing of the Other from the reach of perception. Stevens refers to such vanishing in section VIII of *Chocorua*, and then declares the Other to be tragic. A very similar way of imputing the perceiver's own feelings onto the perceived is found in the Liadoff poem as the speaker hears Liadoff's tragic intoning (*CP* 346).[11] In fact, in both poems it is the speaker who is sad as the Other disappears beyond the reach of perception, it being the object of the perceiver's desire. This kind of pampering of himself only betrays the perceiver's intense desire for the Other.

Section V of *Chocorua* portrays the Other through its ever-fading contours, finally becoming altogether imperceptible; in fact, both sections V and VI attempt, through their metonymic rhetorocity, a realization of the Other as they seek to catch the moment of the Other between transparency and opacity, in that difficult light which marks one of the limits of the perceptive reach or of the scopic drive. In this difficulty, the Other becomes tangible, but only for a moment. It is admittedly a sort of union of the intangible and the mind. The Other existence is felt, and accepted; yet, as far as the knowledge of it is concerned, there is none. Thus, what Stevens does in the rest of the poem is to see it in the tangent of his experience and feelings of the moment.

In alliance with the preceding two sections, section VII depicts the Other's substantial nonsubstantivity, and shows the awareness that it belongs to the unconscious. As belonging to the unconscious (i.e., to the human), Stevens has attempted its personification in section V, attributing human limbs to it — even breathability in section VI (also in section VIII). However, by virtue of intangibility, the Other always exceeds what is perceived of it, or of it *as*. The dilemma of whether to call it human or more than human is vented in section VIII; this is a restatement of the problem preserved in section XII of "The Blue Guitar" as it concludes that, despite its otherness, the Other is also "I" (*CP* 171). In fact, Stevens goes so far as to speak of its inhumanness and savagery (*CP* 328); God is a tyrant in Stevens' conception, for gods rule us through our fear of them (*CP* 262). Section XVI of *Chocorua* equates the Other with fate, as an irresistible power controlling us; the Other controls all our behavior, leaving nothing outside its domain (*É* 163; ERS 3). The section further describes it as a triad of darkness, desire, and humanity. Like the metonymic revelation of God, it is perceived in parts while much of it remains dark. It is the object of human desire, like the God of religious desire. And it is human just as God is modeled on human attributes (*OP* 213). All the three glosses on it seem to form a parallel with the trinity of the Holy Ghost, the Father, and the Son, respectively. The Holy Ghost represents that part of God which remains unknown, and the Son signifies His humanity. The Father, in the parallelism suggested, represents man's desire. Lacan's concept of the phallus has its origin in the *Name-of-the-Father*, and both are what he refers to as the "third term" responsible for the "emergence of desire itself" (*FS* 36), thus enabling the above comparison.

Section XVI further speaks of the Other's collective nature; the relevant lines indicate that by "collective" the poet means "universal"; at the same time, he destroys the Other's collectivity or universality in the second line by suggesting that each man has an Other. Stevens is almost identifying the notions of "universality" or "collectivity" and "particularity" or "individuality." Lacan eulogizes Hegel for identifying the particular and the universal as the same thing, and further adds that psychoanalysis must reveal that both are merely mirages (*É* 80). While Stevens refers to the Other's universality, totality, and wholeness, he also splits it into particulars in speaking of its existence within each individual. The Other as language (*l'Autre langage*) is universal, total, and independent, but it cannot be separated from a particular subject whose desire, invested with the particular environment around him, makes that language particular to himself. Or, as Lee writes, when language as universal is conflated with the subject's desire, it "always aims ultimately at recognition by particular others" (75), thus disrupting its universality. Simply stated, man learns to desire from the others around him insofar as they express their desires through language, and these others and their desires change with respect to place even though the language used for expression does not change so radically, with respect to place, as the desire's particularity or peculiarity can change it. In short, each human being has at his disposal a particular language, which becomes peculiar to himself through its combination with his desire, forming his Other. Hence, the images representing the Other in section XVII come from different environments, suggesting that the people living in different environments would call the Other by a name peculiar to their respective environment.

The Other's complex modes of functioning and aspects are conducive to the process of "enlargement" of the one who has diminutive feeling (XVII; it perhaps refers to the excessive castration that Stevens underwent during 1908–1911, and probably kept undergoing, as he continued to feel guilty of his father's death for a long time after it occurred). These modes and aspects help to bring about a change in the lives of those who feel lost, helpless, and frustrated, as in the Arabian nights. In other words, the alienated neurotic desire finds satisfaction in seeking the Other. While the umbragenous imagery dominating section XVIII creates a mysterious aureole about the Other, it also conveys the consolatory feeling of "comfort" that the neurotic desire seeks in the Other, a feeling of strength (com + *fortis*, "strength") resulting from the neurotic's imaginary relationship of being a confidante (the Other becomes a confider who speaks to the neurotic), since its secret speech — that the neurotic seeks (*CP* 328) — belongs only to the one (the neurotic) who listens to the Other's speech (conspirator = com + *spirare*, "breath," hence "speech"). And yet its voice and what it speaks are not superhuman since, as in Lacan, it is a formulation derived from other human beings and their language. However, the poem evades answering clearly regarding where it speaks from, about whom, and in which voice; it is this unconscious, unknown dimension of its place and voice that makes its speech more acute (XIX). The Other is the foundational structure of human psyche (XXI). The modern French word *fond* was written as *fonz* or *fons* in old French, meaning "foundation"; in using both the archaic and modern spellings, the poet might be suggesting that the Other has been there since time immemorial as the basis of human mind. Although Stevens earlier evaded commenting upon the nature of the Other's speech, he now refers to it as "glubbal glub"; the second word of the expression is an inarticulate sound as such, and the first means "a band, company, troop" (*OED*). In Lacan's thought, the Other or the unconscious is an "ensemble" of "imagistic material—including many images that are phonetic" (ERS 13); he has often said that the unconscious is "structured like a language" (*É* 234; S III 11, 119, 166–67). These glosses may be recalled because Stevens is speaking of the Other as language at this point in the poem; he is perhaps suggesting that it is (also) an ensemble of inarticulate sounds—hence it is difficult to interpret its speech. All the same, he finally declares that it is human (XX).

The fact of the Other's existence can be ascertained if the mind's eye is sharp, for it soon vanishes into the mind's limits. Its perception by the mind's eye is a transfiguring, enlarging experience since "where/He is the air changes and grows fresh to breathe" (XXII). Just before this Stevens has written "where he was," suggesting "his" disappearance. In these two lines, the poet seems to exhibit the fetishistic desire of the human subject to inhabit the place of the Other. In fact, probably borrowing consciously from Freud, or more probably realizing from his own experience, Stevens writes an absolutely Freudian bit in the fourth line of section XXII: "where he was, there is an enkindling." Paralleling Freud's "*Wo Es war, soll Ich werden*" ("Lecture XXXI" 80), much celebrated by Lacan, Stevens without a doubt depicts the Other as the place where the human subject is realized, as the place of the real (of the) human subject. The Cartesian philosophy confuses the real place of the subject with the *moi* (ego); Lacan destroys the Cartesian notion systematically in "The Agency of the Letter in the Unconscious." For Lacan, the subject really thinks in the unconscious; as Bowie remarks, "all thinking is 'thinking other'" (133). The thinking associated with the ego is a mirage, hypocrisy, a rejection of the ego's "ex-centricity to itself" (*É* 171). In the same essay, Lacan translates Freud's dictum, "*Wo Es war, soll Ich warden,*" as "I must come to the place where that was," and glosses this "coming" as a kind of reunion with the real "I" (*É* 171).[12] The happening anticipated in Freud's dictum is momentary, but it marks the sole objective of man's endeavor; the moment of *Es* is one of human reconciliation, unification of the alienated *moi* identity of man with his real "I," as Stevens agrees in section XXIV. It is a moment of the subject's overcoming his ex-centricity or ex-sistence with respect to his own reality, thereby allowing him to take hold of his being, his true existence, which stands apart from his everyday false sense of existence.[13] What the Other *jouissance* implies is precisely this "coming to be there where *it* was"; it is at this point of *jouissance* that Lacan distinguishes the not-so-absolute categories of masculinity and femininity. The *jouissance* that the neurotic seeks is different from the phallic *jouissance*, which is made possible by a giving up of castration and is both the determining factor of masculinity and the limit of man's *jouissance*. While women are capable of the phallic *jouissance*, they also have the potential to go beyond it and experience another kind of *jouissance* called the Other *jouissance*, which may also be described as the hysteric's *jouissance*. In a woman's case, therefore, the phallus enjoys an inferior position as compared to the Other that is beyond and above it. Designating the phallic signifier as S1, Fink comments that although S1 is an end for men, it is an opening for women (107). In other words, the neurotic desire for the Other is mediated through the phallus that is repressed (not foreclosed as in psychosis). Insofar as Stevens' poetry reflects the desire for the Other, it is neurotic, revealing feminine structural potential at the same time. *Chocorua* speaks of both kinds of *jouissance*, as is discussed below.

The desire for the Other is very obvious in the poem. The poet demonstrates it in yet another way by declaring the Other to be Big Brother in section XXI. In the *Esthétique*, he qualifies the Other as brother to the father (Stevens' malady would not allow the father the status of the mother's desire, which is why it becomes a Big Brother here) and as half-expressed by the mother (*CP* 317). In any case, the father-like figure is equated with the Other; besides, as half-expressed in the mother's speech, it is the mother's desire. Since the mother speaks of this Big Brother, he could be (in) what the mother says. This is also indicative of Stevens' relation with the Other as the mother's demand. Lacan's concept of the phallus originates from the *Name-of-the-Father*, and both are treated as supportive of the symbolic order. Stevens here distinguishes the Other from the phallus in denying it the status of the father; more importantly, in referring to it as brother, he asserts a fraternal love for it. This is similar to Sophocles' Antigone's rejection of the pittance of Creon's law and her radical expression of love for her brother Polyneices.[14] Antigone ignores or finds no satisfaction in Law (this is a repression of the phallus-as-Law through transgression), and thus crosses the limit of phallic (symbolic) *jouissance*, because she seeks the real that is her brother, whom no law could replace and who has already crossed the law of the state and, having died, gone beyond the point of return. The law by which Antigone regards her brother is beyond the symbolic (see Lee 127). She stresses the uniqueness of her brother and laments. Stevens' rejection of the status of the father and his granting of the status of "brother" to the Other of his desire cannot be accounted for except by comparing it with what Antigone does.

However, Stevens does not go as far as Antigone does. He does not forget his ex-centricity as a subject even though he undoubtedly seeks the Other *jouissance*, the cause of his enlargement, as is obvious in section X. In the relevant lines from this section, Stevens seems divided between that enlargement, where there is no question of identity, and the human subject's need of identity. Here, the question of "What am I?" is, of course, indicative of the cut that language introduces into the individual, making him its subject; Stevens was aware of this subjection when he wrote of language as man's Lord (*CP* 322). In section X, he speaks of falling back from the moment of enlargement:

the *Atè*, Lacan's term that designates the limit of human existence as subject and even as an individual life. Antigone's going ahead with her brother's burial against Creon's prohibition of it marks the *ektos atas*, her going beyond the limit where human life cannot survive for long (S VII 262–63).[15] Though the speaker of *Chocorua* approaches this limit in placing his *moi* "where *he* was" (emphasis mine; XXII), at the same time he is able—to use Lacan's playful allusion to Heidegger—to "eat his Dasein" (*É* 104)—that is, to digest his being in the world as a subject, to accept his ex-centricity. Thus falling back or returning from the *Atè* also means accepting castration, which binds the subject to the phallic signifier. This is how the Stevens poem oscillates between the symbolic and the real, between Lacanian conceptions of masculinity (desire for the phallus) and femininity (desire for the Other). This polarity is also found in Stevens' *Collected Poems* in "Re-statement of Romance" and "Motive for Metaphor," with the former poem evoking the feminine structural potential and the latter the masculine. *Chocorua* seems to have resolved this bipolarity by holding on to both; however, it must be conceded that the poem fails to shake off its bent toward the desire for the Other. In fact, most of Stevens' poetry reflects this abnormal desire.

The moment of "enkindling" sparked by the subject's momentary sojourn in the place "where he was" is associated with desire and its fulfillment in section XXIII; it is the moment of the desire's fulfillment, of the subject's enlargement, the moment of his reunion (XXIV). This is a satisfaction of desire that nevertheless marks the "fall" from the *Atè*; it is merely a mirage of the satisfaction of desire, without which, ironically, it would be impossible to return from that limit. The return is necessary, for otherwise the subject will not remain a subject but will be transported into the field of the Other, achieving a unity with the Other, where his life cannot last long; this is more dangerous than the subject's position in the dyadic relationship with the Other. Lacan warns of this danger in Seminar XVII through the story in which the Other is represented as a big crocodile threatening to devour the subject (112). This is what is anticipated in *ektos atas*, where both Hamlet and Antigone go; there, they do not remain human subjects in the sense that they take their desire upon themselves, thus subverting their intrasubjective intersubjectivity, which is the basis of desire's eternalization. They allow, willingly, the "crocodile" to devour them or, in other words, they do not give up the Other *jouissance*.[16] What makes the human subjects human is their alienation from the Other (see also *FS* 26). Ironically and tragically, they cannot fully *assume* their desire, yet what makes them human is their alienation itself (*CP* 328; also see ERS 93). What sustains our status as subjects is our inability to achieve "the ultimate in satisfaction" (Lee 141–42). Complete satisfaction of desire is an illusion, but this is what saves us and supports our subjectivity, and even guarantees life. On commenting about Lacan's characterization of desire as a defense or prohibition mechanism guarding the subject from crossing a certain limit in *jouissance* (*É* 322), Lee observes that *jouissance* proper "envelops the functioning of the human subject"; further — characterizing the double meaning implicit in the ambiguous "desire of the Other" in relation to *jouissance*, where the duplicity of interpretation is suggestive of the oscillation between masculine and feminine structures — Lee also adds that Lacan in his later work associates *jouissance* only with women's sexuality, leaving its meaning as *plaisir* to characterize men's sexuality, thus aligning it with the restricted notion of phallic *jouissance* (142). *Chocorua* already suggests in clear terms that its speaker reconstitutes himself as a subject when he speaks of the cry of subjectivity against the moment of *jouissance* (X); this also implies alienation from the Other. Section XXIV, which follows the description of the moment of enlargement in the preceding section, also indicates the alienation as the speaker hears the Other's "loud speech" ("fortellez" may be split as *forte*, "loud" + "tell").[17] Sections X and XI follow the same path of the moment of enlargement followed by the speaker's awareness of the Other's speech. Though it is difficult to perceive or touch the Other, the very fact that it speaks to the one who listens constitutes intersubjectivity that is essentially intrasubjective. The constitution of intersubjectivity within an individual makes him a subject, a *human* subject. All this clearly implies the speaker's giving up of the ultimate *jouissance*, which is "tamed by the subject's structure and replaced by the moderate satisfactions" (Lee 142).[18] This is how, despite his desire for the Other, he relinquishes the Other *jouissance* and returns to the human limit.

Section XXV gives indications of the end of the poem as it circles back to the twilight imagery of section III, which is the proper beginning of the experience contained within the poem. Both the sections depict the realization of the Other as an-Other as opposed to the speaker's near closure with it (epitomized in section XXII), toward which the other sections strive. The difference between section III and XXV, however, is that the former reflects the speaker's anxiety through the atmosphere of awe created in it around the Other, while the latter seems to relieve him as the desinence of the section speaks of the speaker's "pleasure of his spirit" (paralleling Lacan's "*jouissance* of the Other"). Thus, the pleasure of man is the pleasure of the Other, or, using Lacan's gloss on desire, "the *jouissance* of man is the *jouissance* of the Other." However, again, one must not forget the ambiguity inherent in "*jouissance* of the Other" introduced by the status of the "of" as subjective genitive: "Other as *jouissance*" and "Other's *jouissance*" are the possible variations. The former is what Lacan refers to as "Other *jouissance*." However, since the poem's speaker has already given up the Other *jouissance* and returned to the limit of the phallic domain, the "pleasure of his spirit" is properly equated with the

"Other's *jouissance*" (thus, it is read as the "pleasure of [the Other's] spirit," which points to the object of the Other's desire). This reading already introduces a gap (*béance*) between the Other and its *jouissance*; in other words, the speaker of the poem seems to have realized the Other itself as lacking or desiring. This divides the Other, as Fink shows (118), into two parts: the Other as signifier (i.e., barred like the human subject) and the object that it signifies (object[a]).[19] The object(a) is the cause of the Other's desire, and since man's desire is the Other's desire, the subject is brought into relation with that object. This "further separation" from the Other is crucial for the subject to have "a greater degree of subjectivity" (Fink 187n21) or to become a desiring being himself.

In this way, the human subject is realized in its separation from the Other; this may seem paradoxical, but there is no human subject without this otherness in his or her relation to *an-Other*; said differently, the human subject will have no existence without standing apart from or outside of the Other. The final section of *Chocorua* is therefore a tribute to the Other. It is the Other that, in the first place, introduces the subject to desire through its "demands" (the Other as language). Its description in this section suggests that there is no Other of an Other since, with respect to the subject, both the Other and its Other are equally greater presences and therefore are equal to each other. In the Other's division as signifier and object, one sees the presence of an object that is absent (object[a]); the absence of this object, in fact, brings in an array of substitute objects that help one accomplish *jouissance*, of one's own, to a certain degree, and therefore they are extremely important absences/presences. Even if the subject subjectifies them, he does so in his imagination or fantasy, for they remain in the field of the Other owing to their presence *as real*. The Other is, thus, their companion insofar as they maintain their Otherness with respect to the subject. However, this is very much how one realizes oneself as a desiring subject, of which the Other is the pivot (*CP* 302).

The dyadic closure with the Other means a loss of the external reality. While much of *Parts of a World* relishes the happy liaison with the external reality, *Transport to Summer* seems to enjoy both the inner and outer realities. In other words, Stevens keeps shifting and tossing between the two. Just released from a near closure with the Other experienced in *Chocorua*, the memories of the experiences of the unconscious are still fresh, and there is a desire to establish a contact with the external reality. *Credences of Summer* brings both the interior and exterior worlds together. It may be looked upon as Stevens' desire to reestablish his contact with both the worlds; however, here—as is usual in Stevens—the external reality is devoid of human beings.

The first section of *Credences* is obviously a description of the peak of one's "summer." It depicts the mature youth when thoughts take deep roots, and the mind becomes capable of serious meditation as the childhood desires and imaginary indulgences do not exist any longer except as mnemic traces, since the mind is very much assimilated into the symbolic order of language and culture. The "summer" is that period of life after the castration complex when one touches the limit of the symbolic order and is closest to the real; this is what, in Lacanian terms, may be called the dialectization of the phallus. Here one lacks nothing, so to speak, since there is no distance between oneself and one's desire; distance is related with time, is directly proportional to time. Having touched the limit of time, one inhabits the real that is timeless. This is a fulfillment of desire, which vindicates and asserts not only both time and timelessness but also the imagination, for the imaginary has a correlation with lack through desire.

Since the phallic signifier marks the limit of the mind's or desire's reach, even thoughts and feelings will progress no further since, like the imaginary, they are the means of the fulfillment of desire, which is comforting. The inscription or dialectization of this signifier helps one get rid of what Stevens calls disastrous relationships. The last three lines of the section depict the stages one invariably goes through during one's growth from childhood to youth: the "father" signifies the principle of castration, the "mother" suggests the desire of the mother, and the "lover" is representative of the principle of imaginary identification with the other. Failure to overcome or achieve them is disastrous, but it is false since none of these is the ultimate object of one's desire, and also because they make one their dependent and resist one's advancement toward that object, the true desire. The true desire—which is also a disaster since, as the poet says in the next section, nothing more remains to attain and the life of desire ends—must come when one has become self-sufficient (i.e., has acquired one's own desire or has become a desiring being oneself), which is possible only after dialectizing the phallus. Nassar almost says this as he reasons, "These are 'false disasters' because one can surmount the sorrow of their loss [the loss of fathers, mothers, and lovers] through the imagination" (175); Lacanians would want to replace Nassar's "imagination" with "acquisition of their desire." This happens in the "summer." However, what this analysis of "summer" required was the mention of everything *else* except "summer." Why should one take so many pains to describe or see it, and moreover, objectively and with undesirable regard to everything *else*? Hence the resolution to see the "summer" itself that comes in the next section.

Stevens has been thinking about "the thing itself" for a long time; seeing it required an intense subjective involvement to avoid a completely "objective impression" (*L* 134). Seeing with intense subjective involvement would accomplish the desired vision, and whatever is unimportant from the viewpoint of desire will automatically be gotten rid of; it is the unimportant that hinders the sight. The second stanza of section II speaks of the process of symbolization without language at all. However, language, a construct of signifiers, is there as that which has metaphorically replaced the phallus. In fact, even the phallus is a signifier (hence a metaphor), since any signifier comes into existence due to the lack or absence of something, as a replacement for what is lost.[20] Thus, neither language nor the phallic signifier will suffice, since the phallic signifier comes into existence because of the lack of the ultimate object of one's desire—object(a). The sun in this section may therefore be equated with this object. It is the loss or lack of this object that gives desire its function; in this sense, one always desires what is lost. Once this object is achieved, the desire will not exist, nor will that which has replaced it, and the object(a) will give rise to nothing else since everything else is a function or result of its lack; thus, this object, our desire, will exist in its complete nakedness. Both object(a) and the subject are productive things: the former creates by virtue of its very absence and the latter, due to his lack, creates during his seeking of the object, and there is nothing beyond it to seek or attain.

Attaining object(a) is the moment of *jouissance*, the center of human desire. It must be preserved since it is only momentarily that one attains to it. In order to preserve it, though, its fixation through symbolization is necessary. The leaves of language, with or in which one symbolizes it, must give such peace and joy that a possibility of change in the language or in the view of that object may be ignored, since what is important is to arrest peace and joy. Once this is done, any change, even in the object, will not matter, since happiness is the highest pursuit for Stevens (*OP* 157). This is what the poet proceeds to do in section III.

As Hines says, the metaphors used to describe the object of desire "expand and change with each stanza" of the third section (222). First it is described as a tower, then as the tower on a mountain, and then as an old man on the tower on the mountain. Each metaphor increasingly distances the object from the perceiver. This suggests that the original object of desire keeps receding, thus evading desire through substitution of surrogate objects between itself and the perceiver. However, where Frost would use stylistic devices to stop such unending loops, as in "Stopping by Woods on a Snowy Evening" (275) or "The Pasture" (epigraph to his *Collected Poems* and the leading poem of his *Complete Poems*), Stevens does it with humanization of things. For example, in "Landscape with Boat" (*CP* 241–43), the search for truth ends with the belief that oneself is the truth or that everything belonging to the humanized reality is the truth (*CP* 242); the same could be said of "On the Road Home" (*CP* 203–4); similarly, the concept of "freedom" in "The Latest Freed Man"

(*CP* 204–5) originates from the humanization of the actual world. Such humanization is symbolization through intense subjective involvement, fixing the thing itself in the foliage of sense. The introduction of the human element in the form of the old man seems to serve the same function. Yet the repletion of images and metaphors in this section shows that "the immanence of metaphor is accepted as intrinsic to even the purest perception of the nakedness object" (Patke 161). There is no object that is "naked" for us. And when it is a question of object(a), one must satisfy oneself merely with the *sense* of having attained or humanized it. This is only how one can map oneself on to the real. The "real" real thus resides beyond human reach; it is *there* that the "sun" resides happily and peacefully. Stevens might well be playing with "sun": read it as "son" and his "sleeplessness" becomes his restlessness/desire; it is only in his desire that the son, the human child, can be happy and at peace or can graft himself on to the real and gratify his desire and be at peace.

Object(a) being the ultimate cause of human desire and existence, each demand, every need, and the desire of man is the function of its lack. It is the ultimate real, the final destination. Its description as "refuge" created at/by the "end" should easily recall the often-quoted line from *Sunday Morning*: "Death is the mother of beauty" (*CP* 68). It is death that gives rise to this object that one desires. Lacan has it too, but in a different way; for him, desire is always the desire for death, and beauty has a "blinding effect" on the desire. The effect of beauty on desire keeps death away. In this sense, Stevens' use of the word "refuge" is remarkable, for it takes on the protective function of the beauty's "blinding effect." Perhaps Stevens has not attained this peak since its beauty has mesmerized him.

The final stanza is very peculiar and difficult in the sense that there is no differentiation of man and object(a). While the old man on the tower is a metaphor for object(a), it also suggests man's achievement of it. Insofar as this achievement exists only *as* sense, it is beauty, but it is death if it becomes a reality. Therefore, not surprisingly, there is an indication of the man's age, when the "blinding effect" of "beauty" fades and paves the way to go beyond the human limit, as has already been discussed. This fading of the effect of beauty or of symbolic *jouissance* that belongs in one's "summer" is what is probably suggested by the "absorbing" of "summer" by the man's old age. Further, the reference to appeasement and fulfilling of age, and the closure of feeling, evoke death even as the desinence of the stanza and the section creates "the sense of an ending."

Though only in sense, attaining object(a) is a momentary experience; the subject cherishes the moment's memory for a long time nonetheless. Section IV tries to catch the effect of that moment on the subject. The desire is satiated during the moment, but it soon returns to its poverty and begins looking out for the same *jouissance* again; it is then that one's interest in the actual world increases, for the desire seeks that object in this world. In short, it is the mirage of object(a) in the things belonging in the actual world that lends them the status of *objet petit a* (see note 3 to this chapter). This status is the limit of this world. Stevens tries to describe this limit with reference to the summertime Oley valley in Pennsylvania. Lacan's real order includes the corporeal world as well. In this section of the poem, as in many instances in his poetry, Stevens brings corporeality ever closer to what may be called purely psychical reality—that is, he finds the spiritual in the corporeal (*OP* 178); this must result in a great satisfaction, as corporeality gives of object(a). This object then exists very much around oneself and the eye of the imaginary does not need to be visionary, since the scopic drive is gratified.

In Seminar XI, Lacan proposes that this drive helps the subject construct himself because, as Lee writes, the relation established by the drive between the subject and other subjects or objects involves an activity that ultimately governs the subject's imaginary—hence his identity or its construction (153). Insofar as the other satisfies the drive, it is the process of identification that is involved between the subject and the other; during this process "the ... subject fades into an identity with those mysterious, but real, *objets petit a*," which function as signifiers (Lee 153). Even though such identification is purely imaginary, is not real, it is nevertheless constructive of the subject himself. Thus, when Stevens speaks of the satisfaction of the drive related with the eye in the first stanza, or of that related with the ear in the second stanza,[21] he is speaking of an identification with the summertime Oley environment, which is the other, a substitute for object(a). Lacan's concept of the drive involves the fading (*aphanisis*) of the subject, whereby he "drifts" in the direction of the other. Identification with the other is the most that can happen in the subject's relation with the other. However, it also helps the subject in constructing or *making himself* (S XI 195), imaginarily. What is involved in this "making oneself," however, is also the signifierization of the subject by the "symbolically approved" objects or signifiers from the symbolic world. This is how he progressively keeps getting steeped into the symbolic order that he enjoys; this is the joy language offers (*CP* 322). Stevens celebrates these happenings in the last few lines of the section.

The first six lines of section V require an understanding of the next few lines for interpretation. The singular day, woman, and man represent and enrich all other days, women, and men in the sense that they give meaning to the rest of their kin. They are sort of epitomes or paradigms that take all other days, women, and men to replace them. However, the question in line 4 speaks of the importance of the other days, women, and men for the enrichment of the singular day, woman, and man. This kind of possibility of substitution of one thing for another is very characteristic of signifiers; it is precisely the function of metaphor (see *É* 156–57). Thus, all of them are signifiers, for, like signifiers of a language, the single day, woman, and man stand in a relation of difference or opposition with the other days, women, and men. Yet the poet does uphold the singular day, woman, and man for their strength, majesty, or loftiness. In this sense, the poet's attempt at approaching or apprehending the most potent signifier becomes manifest even as he ends the section with words of power. Thus, the soldier of this section seems to be the most powerful signifier: just as the other days, women, and men are represented by the singular day, woman, and man, so the singularly important day, woman, and man must be represented by something else — this soldier. The soldier, therefore, is comparable to the phallus, the primordial signifier that mediates between the ultimate real and lack. A passage from "Repetitions of a Young Captain" speaks of the soldier in terms of "real" and "lack" (*manqué*) (*CP* 309). Stevens has already celebrated the entry into the symbolic order in section IV of the *Credences*. Section V seems to seek what is lost as a result of this entry. The little satisfaction that is obtained is from the male sexual organ, for here Stevens speaks of the phallus more as a physical organ than as an imaginary thing or signifier. The passage from "Repetitions" referred to above also celebrates the male sexual organ as compensation for the lost real and as a substitute for the native incompleteness. The difference between these two occurrences of the phallus is probably that the passage from "Repetitions" tends to treat the phallus more as a signifier than as a thing, though in both poems one sees (Stevens') confusion of it as a thing and as a signifier.

The unconscious assimilates the symbolic order. The phallus, being the one signifier that gives other signifiers any function, enriches the symbolic order. Stevens says as much in the first few lines of this section. However, it is through the other signifiers that one ultimately comes to "dialectize" this master signifier in one's "summer" — hence the question in line 4. At the same time, the poet shrewdly isolates the phallus from the other signifiers, disguises it as a queen, and suggests that it is merciful to the other (signifiers). (It is certainly not merciful to the neurotic, whose discourse becomes problematic due to the repression of the signifier.) Hence Stevens' return to his initial stand, lending primacy to the singular day, woman, and man that together represent what Lacan calls the *points de capiton*: the phallic signifier enriches the symbolic — not directly as such but through its "veiled" or repressed state. Thus, Stevens shows awareness of the status of the phallic signifier as the ultimate *point de capiton*.

For all the attempts of Stevens' critics to describe the rock of section VI, it has evaded their linguistic apparatus to a large extent. It is neither the "bare reality" of Sukenick (195) nor the "objective certainty" of Mills (98; also see

Riddel 220). Riddel comes closer to it, though, when he writes that it is "the physical transmuted in imagination and raised to a vital form" (220). Yet he wrongly adds after "vital form" the words "(metaphysical) of poetry," which are not necessary. However, even that "vital form" keeps receding in the poem, so that any certainty of it is already questioned. One could say — and *The Rock* makes this clear — that it is really the subjective uncertainty of an objective certainty which is *therefore* raised to a vital form of grandeur, thereby lending it a certainty in the hope of asserting the subject's certainty of it. Desperate as Stevens is for a will to credence and as difficult as it is to articulate the "rock," neither the critics nor their language is at fault. However, Riddel is at fault if he meant to align Stevens with the traditional Romantic poets, whom Stevens adversely criticizes in the very next section, perhaps deliberately. It is true that the imaginary works upon the actual objects around and the subject perceives their "real," though metonymically. However, Stevens is not concerned with the actual world at this point. It is true that the "rock" emerges out of the actual reality, yet the aspect by which it engulfs the actual is important to the poet; here the reality functions merely as a signifier. Just as (in Lacan) the signifier is responsible for creating the possibility of there being a signified, so it is from the concrete, physical reality that the "rock" emerges. Lacan emphasized the role of the signifier in symbolizing the real, in bringing it into existence; yet he was aware that language can never bring the whole of the real into the symbolic order, for "a residuum is always left" (Fink 26). This is the reason why Stevens can only partly measure the "rock." The rest of it "ex-sists," stands outside or apart from, or is extimate to, the hominized world. Nevertheless, it begins to be in one's sense — one becomes certain of its existence even though it remains largely intangible.

Therefore, as Stevens' denial to lend the rock-as-object(a) the status of residing in a hermitage suggests, it is not something that is completely isolated and unknown or unknowable, nor does it forever remain a meaningless signifier; it is not something belonging in the purely conceptual or "ideal" reality of Plato. Stevens goes so far as to assert that it exists since it becomes tangible. The utterly other becoming tangible easily recalls Lacan's concept of "the traversing of fantasy." The fantasized object is nothing but object(a), which is responsible for one's birth; it is this utterly foreign cause that traverses into one's sense and is thus subjectified (Fink 62). This further separates the subject from the (m)Other and makes him a desiring being, enabling him to procure his being. Therefore the moment of the subjectification of object(a) affords the peace and joy that guarantee our being.

The object(a) is the last thing that one may have, or rather, desire to have. This can happen in one's "summer." Yet it would be a mistake to think that the subject symbolizes it once and for all, since "a residuum ... always" remains unsymbolized (Fink 26). This part or aspect of the "rock" is described in the section's final stanza, using the metaphor of an extraordinary light. Owing to the difficulty — even impossibility — of symbolizing object(a) completely, or to this human poverty, object(a) becomes a signifier in Lacan's work. This is what lacks in Hines' otherwise adequate comparison between Stevens' "rock" and Heidegger's "Being" (227), for Stevens' "rock" is more like Lacan's object(a), as the poet refers to its status as a signifier, a signifier having a definite (though spiritual and almost incommunicable) meaning that might be revealed to the subject if he has adequate strength of desire.

Perhaps the "hermit" and "hermitage" of section VI reminded Stevens of the Romantic poet among nature. The first eight lines of section VII muse on possibilities of "difference" with reference to the demerits of the Romantic tradition.[22] Simply stated, the problem with the Romantic poets, in Stevens' view, was that their poetry was dominated either by themselves or by nature (recall Wordsworth's extensive use of "I," on the one hand, and the domination of nature in general, as in the various odes, on the other). Thus, Stevens accuses these poets of never being face to face with the object of which they sang — that they either averted themselves, as in the odes (recall Keats' "Ode to Autumn"), or else averted the object by being egotistic like Wordsworth. Even their object of desire was very commonplace, which cannot really be the object of desire since desire must be made to move frantically by that object. For the poetic energy to be fully released, it is extremely necessary to place the object (or desire the object that is) beyond the reach of desire. Such an object would be the phallus or object(a) that one can never really have, but may come face to face with,[23] as Stevens did in the previous two sections. What happens in such an instance is described in the remaining lines of this section, though the description has baffled many readers of the poem; thus, Thomas L. Martin feels, "[N]o commentator ... has ever done justice to the 'thrice concentred self' of *Credences of Summer*" (47).

These lines should easily be one of the most enigmatic, most compressed, yet the fullest statement of the central concern of Stevens' poetic practice. To interpret these lines, Hines would suggest the use of Husserlian tripartite method of perception (rejection, reduction, and decreation) (36); however, as Leonard and Wharton rightly suggest, this "equation is no more than superficial" (89), for it does not account for the self's "thrice concentred" nature. The expression "concentred self" is the key to a better understanding of the section. The most important question is why the poet would need to use the word "concentred" before "self." The noun qualified by "concentric" or "concentred" must be in the plural form, for it is only then that the question of having the same center would arise. As discussed in chapter 2, the picture of the self emerging out of Stevens' poems is essentially tripartite. Dictionaries do not list the word "concentred"—they have only "concentric"; despite the poet's knowledge of the word "concentric" (*CP* 319), his preference for this coinage obviously reflects his concern with the process or action of the selves coming together.

Many of Lacan's readers identify the *je* with the symbolic, the *moi* with the imaginary, and the Other with the real; the other and the Other both are constructions of the three orders, though. Although it is undesirable to make such distinctions, analysis shows differences in the logic of the imaginary and the symbolic in perceiving the real: the logic of the imaginary is "identificatory, fusional," and that of the symbolic involves "naming, coding, and legalizing" (ERS 131). Since all human effort is directed toward the real (*OP* 165), the real is no less a part of the mind or self. This is how the three orders constitute the self, which is thus essentially plural, which explains both the self's "thrice concentred" nature and its taking hold of the object thrice. The self is also singular in the sense that one experiences the unity of self in a moment of *jouissance*, when all three orders or divisions of the self become indistinguishable. It could also be true that the center Stevens obliquely refers to is the object(a)—that Other desire the subject seeks with his trivision, which includes his body (the real) as well (this is how the peaches are tasted [*CP* 224]). All this shows Stevens' mature analytic ability.[24] Thus, the self (be)holds the object thrice: First, it scrutinizes the object to capture it. Here the role of the *je* in scrutinizing the possessed object is understood; of course, the role of the *moi* cannot be dismissed. This is pure and simple perception, or it could be equated with the process of introjection, an imaginary activity. Second, the self attempts to symbolize the object, or gets himself symbolized (*aphanisis* of the subject). The symbolization could be imaginary, as in the child's imaginary symbolization of its own body parts as it looks at its image in the mirror. The self symbolizes it, or "fades"/"drifts" toward it, recalling the concept of "drive." Third, the self is disengaged from the object, but the "capture" yields a "meaning" to the self. A momentary phenomenon, it could be the object's capture by the self or the self's capture by the object; yet both suggest the subject's "precipitation" as "being" and "meaning," as in the process of "dialectization" of a master signifier. This is how the object becomes part of the humanized reality. Looking at the pleasure it affords in the stanza, that object could be the object(a); it, therefore, will not be fully realized but will yield some incommunicable and untranslatable "meaning" to him. Yet this is a (re)constitution of that original object, and its loss as well; even though the loss is inevitable, the subject cherishes its memory for a long time in his unconscious. There is obviously the sense of achieving the prize of "being" that is involved here, giving "meaning" to one's existence. The "object" that the poet speaks of here is not easily available; it is an object that the desire is hard put to find; it is object(a) that can never be found except in one's sense of it. Standing face to face with it is a rarity, even impossibility.

The next section is a sequel to section VII; it describes the momentary experience with object(a) as, after its loss, it survives in the unconscious as memory. Section VII could be paraphrased in terms of the self finally attaining that object, yet section VIII does not speak of just resuming but of a new beginning. It has already been discussed that the mirage of object(a), which is always already lost, nevertheless gives an object or objects from the actual world the status of *objet petit a*, which the subject *therefore* desires; this makes the actual world around beautiful for him. Thus, the section depicts something more than the morning scene/seen. This morning as *objet petit a* is a surrogate for object(a). Stevens is aware of this deception, perhaps, but faces it boldly, singing in its face. It is the truth of human life and must be faced, since one can never fully (re)discover the ultimate object of desire. The drive, inaugurated by the original lost object, seeks fulfillment through substitute objects; this, however, requires the subject's symbolic castration. This is precisely what Stevens underlines in the first two stanzas of this section.

The final stanza of section VIII, however, falls back on the division of the mind or self suggested in the previous section. Stevens is aware that despite its divided (or trivided) nature, the mind's speech is that of only one man, that it is a solo battle for the real. This realization is not a belittling of the mind or the subject, but in fact makes the mind respectful since its loneliness makes it strong in order to avail itself of the opportunity to perceive the ultimate real. The trumpet here might suggest all types of human discourse, including the poetic and the philosophical; the time of morning would recall the morning-time discourse of the doctor of "The Latest Freed Man" (*CP* 204–5), whose mind grows venerable in the actual world. One may hear a question in the second stanza of this section: Must this actual world take the place of the primordially lost real in our sight and memory; must what is possible replace what is lost? The question is not answered, so it becomes a cry. The mind's cry, of "what I am" (*CP* 298), is the anguish at its internal fragmentation. But languishing under it is useless; one must yet "sing" in the face of this fact. Instead of getting hopeless and frustrated, it is better to accept the human inadequacy and have faith in the mind's (re)generative capacity, or "cure" (*CP* 526–27), which alone proffers any chance of elevating one's self.

Though sections VI, VII, and VIII allude to John's apocalyptic vision in Revelations, as Bertholf suggests and Hines seems to accept, or follow the meditative technique of seventeenth-century writers, as Martz suggests (see Hines 228–32), one cannot overlook the possibility that in using the allusions and technique, Stevens is only masking his own theory of cognition by matching it with the supreme religious discourse in order to assert his own theory surreptitiously, as Lacan often did. Perhaps it is better to say that the supreme and incommunicable experience does not belong to the religious domain alone but also to the common, ordinary, secular world; that man's mind can grow respectable even in the quotidian world of secular beliefs (which the "believers" spurn). In this sense, Hines' comment that "the 'Credences' are [not] religious. In fact, the reverse is the case, for Stevens' concept of being is fully secular" is very much acceptable (232).

Section VII has celebrated the sense of "being"; it is the moment when one maps oneself onto the real or, in other words, the subject experiences having or being the phallus, though only in his sense. Except for that moment, however, the phallus can only be seen as a "flash" on the level of an object. The penultimate section of *Credences* dwells on the necessity of remaining within the limits of the phallic or symbolic *jouissance.*

In section IX, Stevens is probably referring to the self as brightened by "cock," a slang term for the human phallus. There is an indication of the heightened sense of self owing to the phallic experience. Stevens exhorts this elevated self to control itself through the imperative expressions involving "fly," "stop," "let," "watch" (reminiscent of those in "The Emperor of Ice-Cream" [*CP* 64]). The obvious question is why the self should need to thus control itself. It may be pointed out that the exhortation is immediately followed by an image of death, and then by a reference to sexuality. Sexuality juxtaposed with death again reminds one of "The Emperor of Ice-Cream" (*CP* 64) and "Two at Norfolk" (*CP* 111–12). The garden is a place of joy, of "repose," as Andrew Marvell would say (Gardner 255–58). The reference to sexuality recalls the symbolic or phallic *jouissance* contained in sections V, VI, VII (despite the seemings of object[a], especially in VII, "man" cannot exceed the limits of the symbolic *jouissance*; thus object[a] is also a symbol or signifier). The reference to sexuality is intended to suggest dissatisfaction with, or something undesirable in, the phallic or symbolic *jouissance.* As discussed earlier in this study, man must remain within the bounds of the symbolic *jouissance*, but the poet's language points to the self's desire to transcend it, which means *ektos atas* (embracing death). This seems to be the function of the death image in the first stanza of this section. Stevens, therefore, rightly exhorts the self to control itself and be content. The phallus, being the "scourge of unity" (ERS 292), keeps the self divided between the phallic *jouissance* and the *jouissance* beyond it — the Other *jouissance.* Due to this division, or to the realization of the death associated with the Other *jouissance*, the self returns to and remains within the limits of civility or of the symbolic order, thus respecting the cycle of life and death, of joy and grief. The sense of death is responsible for the poet's advice to the self to stay within the limits of the symbolic.

Yet this does not portend hopelessness, for the self may enjoy more and different emotional moments and experience the phallic *jouissance* again, which will satisfy the self with its raw, unpolished nature, or with its "salacity" that will not seem "weedy." And then the self will rejoice again; it will, then, not be part of the false *moi* ("listener") sense of self, but real. In this way, Stevens accepts man's limitations and yet is hopeful of experiencing more moments of *jouissance* in life. But the key signifier in these experiences will be the phallus, which is described in the final section as an author who writes the script of man's "summer," where the several joyous experiences associated with the ego play the characters.

The phallic signifier is not directly involved in the play, however; yet its existence as an author of a play cannot be overruled. The final section emphasizes the author-ity of the phallus. This phallus-as-author meditates in isolation. (Here Lacan's description of the phallic signifier as the ultimate *point de capiton* governing all human discourse while remaining outside it might be recalled.) The "characters" of human experiences disguised in various garbs are the metaphorical substitutes for this "author." The author, like the unconscious, is the real place where the real play is played out; his characters, like the subject's splitting into many egos, are the function of the imaginary and are, therefore, presented as belonging in the symbolic universe of the play. Thus, they may not be as real as the "author," yet they are inevitably related to the real. Their nature is mixed, as they are at once imaginary and real, whose colors they wear. At the same time, they are very much part of the symbolic order of language and culture evoked in their "knotting." Despite their mixed nature, these "characters" have their own identity and create a discourse of their own, and play their roles happily, since they have the freedom from the subject's cry (of "what am I") and the sadness thereof. This is a complete picture of human existence, which relies on the idea of a perfect relation with reality where happiness is the last credence.

The moment of the phallic *jouissance*, however, does not last long, and Stevens would not tire of searching for it. In fact, his desire would not be satisfied in the humanized world of reality but would seek to achieve the beyond. Thus, toward the end of his poetic career he focused his attention more on the unsymbolized, ultimate reality. To speak of such reality obviously required the invention of terms and images that would be central to a poem; Stevens had been doing it throughout his poetry, but the terms or images, or symbols, were not always as central to the poems in which they appeared — except the symbol of "the blue guitar" — as they are in the later poetry, or were not always as cogent as they are in the later poetry. These symbols attain centrality after their use in the earlier poetry, or after the use of the analogous symbols in the earlier poetry: the "primitive," the "bouquet," and the "rock" are the major symbols in this respect.

As is true of any poet having a definite line of thought and a subject, one aspect of Stevens' poetry is that certain images are employed recurrently and have certain fixed connotations, although, of course, the possibility of various nuances of a particular connotation can never be ruled out. The image — rather, metaphor — of flowers, as in "Last Looks at the Lilacs" (*CP* 48–49), "Bouquet of Belle Scavoir" (*CP* 231–32), "From the Packet of Anacharsis" (*CP* 365–66), "Bouquet of Roses in Sunlight" (*CP* 430–31), and *The Bouquet* (*CP* 448–53), represents reality — "floridest reality," as Stevens would say (*CP* 366). In all these instances the poet depicts how reality escapes perception and retains its otherness. In this sense, Stevens' sense of reality comes close to Lacan's real order. However, in the last of the poems mentioned above, the "bouquet" is treated in a different way, as the poet both places it beyond the reach of desire and makes a vigorous attempt at its fullest possible perception and cognition. If the "chief connotations" in the "meditations on pain and evil" of *Esthétique du Mal* (*CP* 313–26) are "Italian in character" (Patke 166), those in the meditations on the real of *The Bouquet* are French — in both the senses (that is, literally and romantically). Stevens has always used "French" in the sense of the "romantic." The first half of the first line of the poem puzzles the reader; the significance of the word "medium" is not realized unless one thinks of its Frenchness. In French, it belongs to the jargon of psychology and means "psychic." One has to look at the "bouquet" from this vantage point.

Reality being an activity of the imagination (*OP* 110), section I of *The Bouquet* describes it as of psychoanalytic nature, since it resists perception. However, one desires its perception or knowledge that comes suddenly, without notice, and momentarily illumines the inner world that thus experiences a temporary *jouissance*. This "sense" of reality is immediately filtered through the grid of the imaginary. From "Anecdote of the Jar" (*CP* 76), we know Stevens uses the "jar" to represent the imagination. Thus, the bouquet metaphorically exists in the imagination. Metaphor is related to condensation and metonymy to displacement. The bouquet standing in the imagination may seem to be its displacement from the outer to the inner, which would also be a condensation of the outer and the inner, or its continuing to stand in an actual jar (a physical object as container) may suggest its displacement from the reach of the imaginary. It seems that the poet is doing two things at the same time: stressing the objectivity or otherness of the "bouquet" as it continues to stand in the actual jar even after illumining the inner world and offering metonymic pleasure, and suggesting that it immediately takes on the attributes of the imaginary, effecting a condensation of the real and the imaginary, thus existing metaphorically in the mind (imaginary). Taking both possibilities into account is necessary since metonymy is essential for metaphor (*É* 157).[25]

Metonymy, strictly speaking, is the evasion effected by an object or signifier that retains its otherness, although it may seem to have been symbolized (if it is an object) or dialectized (if a signifier). The bouquet in the jar is a complex image since it suggests both metonymic otherness and metaphoric symbolization of the bouquet. In such metaphorization of the real, the imaginary functions as innocuously as the unconscious in the sense that there is no conscious or deliberate imagining involved. This sense of reality is thus always a result of "the way/We feel" (*CP* 430) or of the way we unconsciously imagine, just as lightning is never sensed as a scientific phenomenon, but always *as* its effects on us. This is only for a moment, but it can reappear in the conscious as soon and as suddenly; it is a kind of reflection on (or of) the conscious of the "sense" of the real experienced during that moment and, therefore, is artificial. Yet Stevens considers it important, for it helps the mind to grow.

Stevens sees the mind itself as an artificial construct, since it is largely made up of the effects the real has on it and the senses thereof (see *NA* 83, 140, 141). This is more true of the unconscious. In sensing the real that is without, one senses the unconscious itself. This is how one gets to know about the Other (as) eye or I. In approaching it, section II says, one enters the inner world, the North of the mind. The Other is the place of "meta-men" and "para-things," or simply of the real. Stevens' sense of "homecoming" here has much to do with Freud's "*Wo Es war, soll Ich werden.*" The very feeling contained in Stevens' expression anticipates the *moi*'s coming to the place of *Es*, the real subject of being. Even though *Es* is in radical otherness to the *moi*, it is still the subject of the same human being. Thus, despite their otherness, the meta-men and para-things are still men and things that comprise the unconscious. In other words, Stevens is emphasizing the fact that the real cannot be separated from the actual and the immediate. There are meta-men and para-things because there are men and things, just as there is *Es* because there is *moi*; however, one might say that meta-men/*Es* or para-things/real exist *as* repressed or *as* absences. Accordingly, as will soon be seen, the poet emphasizes the importance of the actual world from time to time in this poem. It might be that Stevens felt that we have already lost the real through the Fall of the first humans, and that if we still feel related to it, it is through the actual world of objects as signifiers of that which is lost.[26] Should we feel alienated from even this physical world of ours, what would be our fate? This anxiety is betrayed in one of Stevens' remarks, as it reveals the narrowing sense of the world in which we live and praises imagination for enabling us "to live our lives" (*NA* 150).

The feeling of alienation from the real increases over time (*CP* 171), increasing our sense of insecurity and jeopardizing the possibility of living. What is in our hands now is to rediscover our relation with the nature and the other (i.e., the actual world), even though the relation is that of conflict. The Other, being the place of all knowledge (S XX 96–97, 105), knows that the reality changed after we Fell; we have become impotent, as we are denied pure perception of the real. However, we must overcome it. Stanzas 5, 6, and 7 of section II suggest how this can be achieved. The poet here strengthens the relation between man and the Other, the meta-man. It is interesting to see that this requires mediation by the actual world. The Other is to be aligned with the meta-man. It is difficult to see why Stevens does not use "meta-man" instead of "meta-men." In section XVI of *Chocorua*, he refers to the Other in singular form and at the same time stresses its plurality; in fact, as said earlier, he treats singularity and plurality, or particularity and universality, of the Other without differentiating between them. Here, too, one should avoid the mistake of taking "meta-men" strictly as plural. In fact, one might argue here for the poet's maturity. I think that Stevens' "major man" and "major men" may be compared with the Other as both particular and universal simultaneously (e.g., see *CP* 335). Even Lacan's concept of the Other is polyvalent—that is, as the past, as the other people, as language, as the mother, as the phallus, as object(a), as *das Ding*— all these are the Other insofar as they retain their radical otherness in relation to the subject.

Things of a psychoanalytic and a physical nature (the French *choses* are English "things") are contrasted. The former belong to the psychical world within, and the latter to the physical world without; the latter have fixity about them (concrete reality) in comparison with the things of psychical nature (perceptions, images, impressions), which are flexible in the sense that they are more susceptible to change. The poet is aware of the fact that the "real" real is not seen as such by the mind, but as changed, however slightly, by the feelings and emotions. Yet it is a pleasing spectacle of the real within the mind. The feeling ensuing from this spectacle is one of joy since it reduces the otherness of one's self to oneself and brings the two closer; it is a feeling of being, properly conveyed by Freud's enigmatic "*Wo Es war, soll Ich werden.*" This is how our impotence can be overcome with the help of the actual world. The passage speaks of how perception of the real is responsible for the feeling of being. It also marks the *moi*'s "fading": (e)motion is caused by the imaginary activity; the *moi* being the imaginary subject that is literally moved—both spatially and emotionally—it fades. This fading or disappearance (*aphanisis*) of the *moi*-as-self enables the establishment of the much-desired relation with the Other, recalling Freud's statement quoted above. One of the two selves in Stevens' line is the "Ich," the *moi* of Lacan, and the other is the *Es*, the real subject that resides in the unconscious—the meta-man, as Stevens would call it. In fact, this poem is in many ways resonant with the Lacanian concept of sublimation, which involves the function of the *Triebe*. It is the *Triebe*, or "drive," that is responsible for the *moi*'s fading. Lacan says that sublimation satisfies the drive (S VII 110). The object that the poem sublimates is the bouquet.[27]

Stanzas 8 and 9 of section II describe how a thing from the physical world outside becomes a thing of psychoanalytic nature as the Other beholds the idea of that thing. Like the window, the door is a mode of perception; the lake signifies the conscious, and the white duck symbolizes the real object. One sees the real and its image is created in the conscious; it then vanishes into the unconscious, existing there as an idea. The seeing, here, is not simply seeing as the eye but also as the gaze (*le regard*), which in Lacan is one of the causes of desire functioning to fill the void in being. Defining the gaze, Lacan says that in our scopic relation with things, "something" constantly "slips ... and is ... eluded in it" (S XI 73). Stevens has already described this "something" that "slips" throughout the previous two stanzas. Looking at something does not satisfy us — we always seek something more or something else there, something that is beyond the actual object seen, such that not only the subject but also the object fades. The perception of that something eludes the conscious, which is nonetheless aware of this elusion and therefore is able to tell "of the image spreading *behind it* in idea" (emphasis mine). The Other, who is behind it, however, does not separate the image and its idea. Thus, the gaze that is "out there" is also "in here," in the Other (see ERS 44). In a beautiful play on "tell," Stevens tells us that the object only signifies, informs or represents something to the conscious, and that the conscious speaks "of the image spreading behind it." That "behind it" is ambiguous: behind the image or behind the conscious itself? The former is indicative of the mnemic trace left in the mind and the latter of the gaze.

The gaze as "seeing oneself seen" is obviously not applicable here. However, the very fact that the Other sees speaks of the Other's gaze. "[T]he image spreading behind it in idea" illustrates the Lacanian notion, in relation to the act of seeing, that one does not see what one intends to see (S XI 103). The white duck is not the object of desire in the poem, for that object is beyond it. Stevens therefore does not end the argument with the perception of the white duck, but with the Other perceiving the idea behind it as its real. The gaze of the Other is important for Stevens. Ragland-Sullivan comments that the gaze (regard) can create "an awareness of unconscious motivation and intentionality" within the consciousness (94). The object of desire is therefore the gaze of the Other, a desire for recognition by the Other. Though Stevens does not speak of it directly, the primacy of the Other beholding is obvious here. Although the poet's arrest by the gaze of the Other sounds insalubrious, the whole poem is valuable due to the experience in the perception of the ultimate real, the "idea" of it existing in the field of the Other, symbolized in "the bouquet."

The real is the habitat of the duck, which is both outside and inside the mind. The bouquet belongs to this complexity of place. In stanza 10, the poet distinguishes between the duck and the bouquet. The former suggests the unmediated, pure corporeality, while the latter suggests the ultimate, real object of desire; in indicating the unity of their place, the poet is also speaking of the otherness of that place in relation to the subject's place. The verb "comes" is not innocent, for Stevens could easily have used "belongs"; it suggests the literal coming of the bouquet from the realm of the unknown to that of the known, which is why it is different from the duck, which does not need to "come," as it is available to seeing. It is possible that the bouquet does not belong as such to the place of the duck even though it comes from that place since, like the duck, it does not at all belong to the corporeality. Stevens' use of contrasting expressions may also be noted: while the duck vanishes in stanza 8, the bouquet "comes." This is why the duck does not receive as lofty treatment as does the bouquet, which is described using French terminology that offers "pleasure" (*L* 792).

What follows is a picturesque illustration of the bouquet as "the fore of lofty scenes": If white is the color of pure reality without meditation, red is the color of reality mediated by human meditations on it. The "white" and "red" form the background on which the bouquet is placed. Stevens often uses the image of the window to signify the perceptive communication between the inside and the outside; however, the window here is not of the "house" or "room" (self) but of the "land," of the corporeality outside. There is no mention of the house, unlike in Frost's "Tree at My Window" (*Collected Poems* 318). It may safely be assumed that the bouquet is on the other side of the "window," beyond the corporeal. This is the place of the real. The placing also highlights the radical otherness of the bouquet—hence it is *above* the "red" and "white" (recall "the fore of lofty scenes"). The pure (white) and humanized (red) realities form the background, of which the bouquet is the "fore"; thus, it is sublimated.

The pure and humanized realities form the concrete outlines of peace and happiness as they become, or seem to become, animate, and lead to a consciousness blurring their distinction so that there is no difference between the meditated reality and the pure, unmediated reality. This is the effect of the potential of the bouquet. In other words, the meditated and unmeditated realities owe their "anima" to the bouquet. The implication is that everything else is a metonym of the bouquet, thus asserting the permanence and centrality of this "floridest real." If the world seems beautiful and meaningful, it is because of the bouquet, which is essentially of a psychoanalytic nature; hence, it can be recognized but not real-ized.

Lacan says that one's status as subject owes itself to one's *aphanisis* (disappearance) since it is a form of alienation (there is no subjectivity without alienation). It is this *aphanisis*, or fading "in the ... locus ... of the unconscious" (S XI 221), that is implied when Stevens speaks of the failure of consciousness to distinguish between the humanized and the pure reality and treats them as one. Here in the poem, the subject fades before and toward the real, and this gives access to "the thing intact."[28] This relational, contingent structure of the subject is effected by the "drive"; Lacan prefers this word for Freud's *Triebe* owing to the possibility of the punning "drift" and "derive." "Drift" speaks of the fading effect and "derive" of the precipitation or establishment of the subject in those relational dynamics. There is no doubt that the alienated desire is the cause of the "drive"; since desire is always the "desire of the Other," the "drive," a means of satisfying desire, functions always in relation to something apart from the body of the subject. The drive is associated with what are called "erotogenic zones," which are parts on the surface of the body from where, mythical as it may sound, that which the subject desires has escaped. These parts, therefore, are on the border between the subject's body and the other. From Lacan's list of these parts (see *É* 314–15), the slit between the eyelids is more important here, since Stevens emphasizes the scopic drive in the poem. The whole poem is an exercise in the poetic analysis of the scopic drive. The "bouquet" is not an actual object as such, but it represents the desire's aim. And it is achieved (in a sense) at the cost of the subject's fading. Thus, the "bouquet" may be regarded as object(a), the signifier of being itself (*OP* 109).

Lacan's object(a) has two sides to it. In one sense, it is that which is always already lost for the subject who spends all his life in rediscovering it, but can never fully or permanently achieve it; in another, the term also signifies those objects in the actual world that provide some measure of satisfaction of the subject's desire but are essentially substitutes for the radically lost original object. Stevens' "bouquet" has little to do with the second meaning. It represents that ultimate object which the desire aims to attain; this is implied in the expressions that describe it as "the fore of lofty scenes" and as "coming from the duck's place," expressions that further separate the bouquet from "the seen." Thus, like object(a), the bouquet is rediscovered to some extent in the mind but, as stanzas 14 and 15 suggest, it is lost just as soon. If these lines are marked by the sense of loss, they also mark at the same time the metonymic process of desire as the mind clings to whatever of the ultimate real remains, in whatever forms. These remains and forms, these *objets petit a*, belong to the actual world. Thus, the desire is oriented in the direction of the actual world in which one lives and expects to watch the glimpses of the bouquet in this world's beautiful things and happenings, depicted in the last stanza of this section, that prophesy poetry.

Stevens' faith in the love for this phenomenal world of ours owes a lot to his belief that its objects have a link with "the thing intact." Thus, as section III begins, Stevens concentrates on the proper outlook to appreciate this variegated world. While the "Latest Freed Man" emphasizes the authority and influence of the external world, *The Bouquet* emphasizes the way the beholder views that world. Stevens' poetry maintains a perfect balance between the importance of both the outside and the inside, or fails to swerve in favor of any one of them in particular. However, it often favors only one at a given point in the poetry. The present poem, as opposed to the "Latest Freed Man," favors the beholder's way of looking. Moreover, it is not only a question of beholding the outside world by man but also of "regarding" the aim of desire by the Other, which is human just as Lacan's Other is also the other people. Even if one feels here that by meta-men the poet could be referring to the great minds of human civilizations that have tried to paint the ultimate object of human desire, it is more likely that Stevens is speaking of the Other here, since what those sages have said has become part of our unconscious, for their *enunciations* are our "pre-history," which is crucial in psychoanalysis. Stevens says that the object of human desire is individuated (i.e., humanized or made part of human reality), and in this way is estranged from the real order by the desire for the Other's desire. Here, Stevens is in perfect accordance with Lacan in saying that the real is symbolized, made part of human reality, as it is severed from the real order by our desire and language. This is how the "bouquet" becomes a symbol, a social reality. And yet it retains its sovereignty; it is not an ordinary (secondary or "binary") signifier, but the signifier in the real (the "master" or "unary" signifier [for more information on the "unary" signifiers, see Lemaire 135–52]). Excepting the first four lines, the whole of section III depicts the bouquet as such a cogent signifier.

Lacan uses the word "symbol" more in a linguistic than literary sense (see ERS 170); therefore, it may be replaced with "signifier." Stevens seems to be using the word in much the same way. Thus, to speak of primary symbols is to speak of primary signifiers. These signifiers fix the meaning of a text or speech; their role is to bind the discourse together (S III 289). The term Lacan uses for such a signifier is *point de capiton*. However, Stevens' "bouquet" represents the most fundamental *point de capiton* or the ultimate signifier, which may be said to be the anchoring point of all human discourse that replaces or represses that signifier in a metaphoric way. In other words, it is that signifier which gives rise to all human discourse as if the human discourse is continually engaged in acceding to and interpreting that signifier. In Lacan, the phallus is the ultimate *point de capiton*. In this sense, Stevens' "bouquet" may be likened to the phallus; the etymological root of "bouquet" is *bois*, meaning "wood," suggestive of the image of the erect penis. Indeed, much of Stevens' poetry as discourse can be shown to be "suspended, 'vertically,' as it were, from that point" (*É* 154). Lacan's term "phallus" has its origin in what he calls the *Name-of-the-Father* and, in both, the father and the penis are not excluded. We know that Stevens regretted what happened between him and his father around the time of his marriage. I have already discussed the sense of guilt that he must have carried with him for a very long period of time after his father's death. Lacan links the sense of guilt with neuroses (see S III 288), which is concerned with the repression of certain signifier(s) from the subject's conscious discourse.

Thus, even if the "bouquet" is treated as an object of desire before section III and as the ultimate signifier in section III, it represents the phallus — both as "thing" and as signifier. However, even the forever lost object(a) is both an object and a signifier, precisely because it is always metaphorically replaced by surrogate objects; this is very much like the phallic signifier being replaced by all other signifiers. The "bouquet" thus may also be likened to the lost object(a). At one point, the poet also calls it "the thing intact," which might make one think of *das Ding* (desire itself). In fact, Lacan never clarifies the distinction between the phallus-as-imaginary, object(a), and *das Ding* except perhaps in terms of the masculine and the feminine desires; Hamlet and Antigone's deaths cannot really be separated since both result from desiring what cannot be had — call it the phallus or object(a) or *das Ding*. All of them are "intimately exterior" or "extimate" to the subject (S VII 139), who never tires of trying to rediscover his desire and thus to graft himself onto the real from which the castrating effect of the symbolic order has separated him.

Although it is not possible for the subject to rediscover the lost object *in fact*, the possibility of rediscovery — indeed, the illusion of that possibility — keeps him going in that direction. In this attempt he experiences certain moments that give him a semblance of the satisfaction of having found the object. During such a moment he feels or is closer to the lost object. This is the moment of *jouissance* for the subject. Appropriately, the last three stanzas of section III celebrate this moment. The experience of the object restores one's faith in the present, in the time and world in which one lives. The moment is described as "an apanage/Of indolent summer not quite physical." The French word *apanage* means "privilege," "monopoly," or, to use Stevens' word, "sovereignty." "Indolent summer" would seem an oxymoronic expression in the context of the experience; however, one would do well to see the etymology of "indolent": "in" (without) + *dolere* (pain), which is suggestive of a happy mood. "Summer" is always associated with happiness, strength, maturity, and so on; Stevens uses it to represent reality as well. "Summer not quite physical" should, therefore, suggest "psychical summer."

It is useless to paraphrase the poet's lines here; it is more a matter of sensing the happy mood and the effects of the experience in general. However, the last stanza has something else that may be discussed. The first and the last lines of the stanza suggest how the (illusion of) rediscovery of the lost object makes the actual world more interesting. Lacan says that for Freud all human perception depends upon the "fundamental hallucination" caused by the lost object and that we owe the phenomenon of "attention" solely to this hallucination (S VII 53). The objects and experiences of the actual world have any function only insofar as they reflect something of the lost object. This is what binds the world together for the subject; the organized world with its objects is a sort of reference system hallucinated due to the primordially lost object (S VII 53). In short, the world functions like a set of signifiers, which is why the sense of its organization, like a signifying chain, is pleasurable; like a chain of signifiers, it offers the subject a meaning of the order of subjective determination. This is how one constitutes one's world; otherwise it would be a nonhuman world—an inhuman world, in fact. In order to keep one's interest in this world, it is necessary to have the experience of this kind, described on so many occasions in Stevens' poetry. Each time, it is described differently and with difficulty—the language often struggles with syntax and fills with anacolutha, the sentences seem not to stop, and the sense groups within these sentences are extremely evocative and are properly "sense" groups as such, almost each of which betrays the feeling of joy and freedom. Is not the poet here speaking of the subject's freedom from the symbolic castration, which must be given up for him to real-*ize* himself, to map himself onto the real?

Stevens seems to have a word to say here to other subjects—that this experience in real-*izing* one's self is the privilege of a happy mental attitude ("an apanage/Of indolent summer not quite physical"). Illustrating this concept with examples taken from James Thompson and Walt Whitman, Stevens appreciates the latter's strength (*NA* 119). Thompson's lines in this illustration present a bleak picture of the outside world, as opposed to Whitman's harmonious view of it. For Stevens, melancholy is weakness and happy attitude strength. The "bouquet" of Stevens, then, is the privilege of a happy and positive attitude. The (sense of) rediscovery of the original lost object fills the world through its representations and/or interpretations in the symbolic order of language and through the imaginary relationship dynamics that give rise to its "doubles." These interpretations and doubles are caused by the perception of the "bouquet," and help the subject organize the world in a meaningful way.

In section IV, Stevens speaks of these doubles or para-things that the imaginary gives rise to. The "colors" referred to here point to the "colors" of "summer not quite physical" from the previous section. Thus, here the "colors" belong in the mind and are evocative of the aspects of psychic reality, as in section IX of "The Blue Guitar." When seen with the mind's eye, they betray their origin much as the petals of the bouquet cling to it even after falling away in section II. Since the origin of one's psychic reality is that forever lost object (and also of one's physical reality, since that object was also the parental Other's desire), they reflect something of it. That is not all. They spread the bits of that hue around the unmeditated, nonhumanized reality outside, which, thus "hallucinated" by the lost object, tends to acquiesce to the imagination. This is how the outside reality is humanized and assumes the red color. Even so, the humanized reality is not very human since it is independent of the human and is complete and full. If this reality does not need human intervention for its fullness, why is it present in our lives? Does it wish to tease us for our incompleteness? Stevens' bitter feeling of our "imperfection" is betrayed once again (*CP* 194).

In French, *facture* means "invoice" or "list of goods"—hence a representation or image of the goods. The image of an object in the mind is always "leafed"; thus it stands there as transformed into a "para-thing." These leaves are inner representations of the real, which are nevertheless fundamental to the mind or to the imaginary because these images of the real are very important for our identity and the perceptual basis (ERS 143). However, Stevens is referring to the single image, that of the originally lost object, of "the thing intact." This image must be the most fundamental. This is what Lacan indicates in Seminar VII when he speaks of the "fundamental hallucination" (53), which helps the subject relate the objects of the actual world and thus organize his world. This is nothing but symbolization of the real—imaginary symbolism, in fact, since the process of symbolization of the real begins at the level of the imaginary.[29] However, the very meaning of symbolization is to vanquish the real or actual by bringing it into the human domain. It is a kind of underdetermination of reality. Even so, the object, however underdetermined, exists in the mind as knowledge and intellect. Its image in the mind (the symbol) *in*-sists, because, as a symbol, it is "an imaginary figure in which man's truth is alienated" and any amount of "intellectual elaboration ... cannot disalienate it" (A. Vergote in Jameson 351 from Lemaire). Yet the poet desires to capture the object as it is, to map himself onto it, not to symbolize and thus have it in a sort of degenerate form as the mind "colors" it; however, since that is not possible, (whatever) perception of the object when the desire is most intense is described in terms that betray a feeling of unhappiness—in fact, a very happy unhappiness.

Stevens was a poet who accepted human limitations. He therefore describes the images in the mind in ambiguous terms: the past-tense form of "farce" could have been used as both noun and verb. Its use as noun seems to suggest absurdity of the images of the real; however, as the past-tense form of the verb, it also suggests that they are "filled." The very next word seems to have been formed from the French *fini* and the English "kin." The French *fini* is used in two senses: (*i*) "accomplished" or "well finished" and (*ii*) "finite" or "limited." The English "kin" is also used in two senses: (*i*) as noun, it shows relation or similarity; and (*ii*) as suffix, it is used to form diminutive nouns. Thus, the poet is simultaneously underdetermining the nature of images and valuing them for their importance in human life: they may be absurd and meaningless in comparison with the real, but they are stuffed or filled with it — hence they incorporate the real; they may fall far short of the real, yet they have a relation with or are similar to the real, for it is images that are responsible for *our* (perception of) reality, and hence must be looked upon as full, accomplished, complete. The word could also have been derived from the French *fin*, meaning "ultimate" or "crux," and the English "kin." Even this indicates the poet's appreciation of the images. His use of the sound /f/ with reference to the imaginary is noteworthy: in section XI of "The Blue Guitar" and "Study of Images I," images are described as responsible for the *méconnaissance* using the same sound. Being a fricative, /f/ gives the feeling of holding the egressive pulmonic air that nonetheless must escape; the reality is evasive in much the same way. Yet Stevens must uphold the imaginary (images and imaginary processes), since these processes help us compose (our) reality. There would be no reality except for the imaginary. The imaginary *is*, and the images *are* (CP 463). Whatever the images may be, they do exist in the mind — they are positively there. Stressing the authenticity (the existence) of images, he further says that they are not unreal or ostentatious displays in the mind or the imaginary domain; they do not have momentary existence like a "splash," but instead exist much like the things that have concrete existence. The next sentence clearly says that the real "bouquet" is a part of the whole field of images and imagination, and "hallucinates" the world of experience. Stevens is thus seen to elevate the bouquet to the level of God.

The final section of the poem seems to be a picturesque presentation of how realism is baneful to reality (*OP* 166). The traditional realism that reason and objectivity believe in seems to be at the background. The "soldier" in this section represents a realist driven by the mechanical device of reason. He expects to find someone in the "house"; his approach is very methodical and mannered, and yet baneful: even though the door of perception (hence imagination) is not locked, yet as part of his "manner*ism*" he first rings the doorbell before knocking. Then he enters the "house" and calls in expectation of a response. This is very much a scientific way of approaching the truth through stages of verification. He receives no response whatsoever; hence the conclusion that there is no one present. His aggressiveness, like that of a man of reason, cannot be missed. The table with the bouquet on it is a sure sign of an existence within the "house," yet his reasoning (if no one responds to his different calls, then there is no one) prevents him from believing it. Thus, he destroys the structure of reality within the "house" rejecting it aggressively. His disbelief in this structure does not allow him to see that someone might be there, might show up if he is willing to wait or just to believe that someone must be residing in the "house." He enters and searches in the house instead of waiting there by suspending his disbelief; instead of looking within, he looks without. Entirely convinced that no one is there, he leaves. Perhaps he was looking to find the Other within the "house." However, his mistake was his objective approach. The Other belongs in the real order, and the real cannot be seen or said without subjective involvement. Stevens perhaps felt that the readers would not believe what he wrote in the first four sections — that they would ignore the bouquet, the ultimate truth of man, if they kept verifying the existence of the Other objectively, aggressively, and impatiently, like the "soldier." This is why the final section is written in such a manner that it does not look like an integral part of the poem except for the mention of the bouquet. Through it, Stevens suggests that the perception of the bouquet, of the ultimate truth of human existence, is something that happens suddenly, on its own, and not something that we achieve by effort (*CP* 386).

There is another possibility of interpretation here. It is obvious that this section places more importance on the "someone who might be living in the house" than on the bouquet. It is the Other who is more important. This could be supported by Lacan's dictum that "the desire of man is the desire of the Other." That is, the agency of the Other is instrumental for the subject to have any desire at all. Without any belief in the existence or role of the Other, the subject will shun his own desire, like the soldier.

Although Stevens symbolized the ultimate object of desire with the "bouquet," it was finally granted the status of a signifier, of a substitute for that which is not, thereby shifting the ultimate object of desire further beyond. It is like losing the sense of wholeness again and beginning to desire the object afresh (*CP* 358). However, for a man who has embarked himself on the greatest possible achievement (*CP* 508), it is not possible to stop there in company with Ludwig Richter of "Chaos in Motion and Not in Motion" (*CP* 357–58). His desire therefore must go ahead in its search for the shifted aim. This is how the "bouquet" succeeds to the "rock" in the poem *The Rock*, where an attempt will be made to capture the object and cause of desire ever more fully. *The Rock*, therefore, enjoys the status of "green's green apogee" in his opus (*CP* 373).

Stevens has often used symbols like "stone," "mountain," and "rock" to evoke that which goes by the name of the real in Lacan. The psychoanalyst includes the unconscious and the Other in the real order; similarly, the poet has *Chocorua*, where the "neighbor" evokes Lacan's Other as the external as well as internal authority governing the human subject. Lacan's difficult object(a) is the subject's alienated being and the aim of desire; Stevens' "rock" is the symbol, much like Lacan's object(a), of that aim (by realizing) which the subject "supposes" to realize his being. Both object(a) and the "rock" are thus the fantasmatic partner ("neighbor") of the subject who desires. Because the "rock," like object(a), is of an essentially elusive ilk, most critics of the poem confess the difficulty of apprehending it, with the exception of Miller,[30] who approaches the poem from the deconstructionist perspective. However, since the "rock" is, strictly speaking, *the thing* of psychical experience, a psychoanalytic approach would be of greater help.

The composition of *The Rock* could have begun in late 1949; it was published in 1950. This completes seventy years of the poet's life. In seeking to go seventy years back, he certainly evokes the infantile or even the pre-natal unity with the mother, and the wholeness it afforded; in fact, it can only be the *sense* of that unity, the *jouissance* of the sense of oneness or wholeness. This is the time before the subject comes to be barred, the time of freedom from the arrest in the symbolic. However, now seventy, the poet laments that this freedom is no more because he has long since been living as barred from the *jouissance* of that unity with the mother. Psychoanalytically speaking, that unity itself is the "being," which is now merely an illusion since the subject is forever alienated from it. The separation from the (m)Other also prepares one for an entry into the symbolic order; it is this symbolic Other that, after birth, limits and "arranges" us for ourselves through cultural strictures. Even though the mother still exists "housed" inside oneself as a rem(a)inder of that oneness, she does not respond to or satisfy our desire. This crass emptiness is the *manque-à-être* (the lack/want-of-being) in Lacan. This is how Stevens describes the primordial traumatic moment of loss and laments.

This, however, does not portend bleakness; on the contrary, it asserts our humanity, since "to be human is to be subjected to a law which decentres and divides" (*FS* 26). It is one of the ironies in Stevens' work that deserves inclusion in Marjorie Perloff's essay. After seventy long years, the poet comes to the conclusion that our faiths, the mothers, and their "houses" (along with their influences), exist no more. If this is so, then whatever we did with our imagination and language in order to achieve them was all (in) vain. Both the imaginary and symbolic exploits that we engaged ourselves in are therefore meaningless. This is because both have failed to attain that for which they strove. In all this absurdity, however, there is one thing that the poet acknowledges: the desire. Desire is more satisfying, hence real (in comparison with the imaginary and symbolic exploits), as it unites two desiring human beings into a single consciousness, enabling them to experience the ecstasy thereof, reminiscent of Donne's "Ecstasie" (99–102).

However, for the two human beings to unite, there must be some hypothesis shared equally by both. Without equal belief in it, they will not be able to unite. It is necessary that both be desiring beings themselves; for them to be so, it is a prerequisite that they be alienated from that hypothetical truth or certainty. Hypothesis is a matter of thought, which makes present that which *is* as absence, but also, insofar as Lac*analyse* is concerned,[31] as that which once *was*. Freud says something similar in his "Negation" (see "Negation" 237–38; also see the modified translation in Fink 93). The hypothesis Stevens speaks of is a representation of something that is not present now, but there is the desire—"reality testing," as Freud calls it—to refind it in order to prove the hypothesis that the object represented thereby still exists "out there." Stevens' emphasis on desire and two human beings, and the secret allusion to Donne's "Ecstasie," are enough to suggest that it is the object(a) as the lost mother-child unity that is sought here, since both the human beings have lost it, so it thus exists only as a hypothesis for them. The sharing of this hypothesis lends them a reality even as it brings them together. Here the poet is suggesting the importance of the mutual relationship as profitable to both; by virtue of their unity, each of them affords the other happiness. However, who is the "other" here: the wife/beloved or the mother? The poet seems to be confusing the desire as "further separation" with the desire for the (m)Other.

Object(a) is always already lost, leaving a nothingness; nevertheless, this nothingness functions as a signifier—thus giving rise to the possibility of there being a signified—since it sends the subject in search of that which created it and which must be "assumed" in its equivocal senses. "The Snow Man" did not suggest this possibility; it was written when Stevens was just introduced to the "nothing" as a result of the signifier's repression. It was only very late in life, after—and as a result of—his long struggle to overcome its repression, that one can see some meaning emerge for him from the "nothingness," like "a helping from the cold" (*CP* 438). In this sense, Stevens shows improvement as an individual and development as an artist. The very anticipation of there being such an object is heartening. This is the importance of that illusive object, the desire for which is so strong that it gives rise to all kinds of interpretations and meanings that gloss and cover over this "rock." Yet these fictive coverings are no less important since their relation to the "rock" is capable of providing a sufficient measure of satisfaction. The original lost object is thus replaced with its glosses, which proliferate and root in the mind the sense of being that object itself.

In this way, the first section comes very close to Lacan's object(a) as the cause of desire and being. At the beginning of this section, it is presented as the traumatic cause; around the middle, it becomes a rem(a)inder of the dyadic mother-child unity as the object of desire; toward the end, it is glossed as something that the subject must either become or internalize; and throughout this section it is interpretable as both the lost object capable of yielding the subject's being and the product of the dialectization of a master signifier. The "nothingness" is the master signifier in this section and is directly mentioned as such. Its dialectization is effected through bringing it into a relationship with other signifiers that exist in the forms of the hypothesis and the "other" human being, who could be a female as the *objet petit a* as a signifier.[32] In fact, the processes of both dialectization and metaphorization are involved here; one might even say that both are the same, since there is a "condensation" of the two human beings, resulting in a metaphorical spark and effecting a metonymic realization of that hypothesis.

The experience the poem reproduces is essentially that of an individual, but it is also a collective or universal experience, since all human beings experience it. This vindicates the poet's use of the pronoun "we"; perhaps it is part of the impersonality in his poetry, or it may reveal his desire to be accepted by the readers—a desire to identify with them. Therefore, the reference to "man" in the second section, "The Poem as Icon," and the "we" of the first section are interchangeable. Section II begins on the note of the desire's insatiability. The "rock" is man's desire, but symbolic glossing of it is not sufficient; it must function to recover man. Each time Stevens uses the word "cure" in the space of the next three lines, its connotation shifts. Man ails due to the absence of the "rock," and he will be recovered by re(dis)covering the actual world: "ground," "earth," "human body," and "the real" are the same thing (for example, see the opening lines of "Anatomy of Monotony" [*CP* 107–8]; also recall the two "clods" from the first section of *The Rock*). One is a patient—from the psychoanalytic point of view—if there is a "loss of reality"; one recovers, the Lacanian school believes, by mapping oneself onto the real. Thus, re(dis)covering the real is indicative of the "restoration" of the real, thus curing the self; this is not far from suggesting a reinstitution of the (sense of) "self." This is an "unforgettable" cure; here, the word "cure" almost takes on the meaning of *jouissance*.

Likewise, the word "leaves" is also used in two senses, which are mutually inclusive: as actual leaves of paper on which the poem's words take the place of the "rock," and as the by-product in the form of fictions of the "rock." In any case, Stevens is here referring to the symbolic order of language and culture, which is productive in itself and, therefore, can be helpful for the ailing human. We are subjects of the Other as symbolic; Stevens seems to believe in the restoration of reality through the symbolic order, since he knew that it is words that create the world for us (*CP* 345). Lacan, in fact, regards the entry into the symbolic order (i.e., castration) as a necessary precondition for such a "cure" (*É* 323–24; also see Fink 72). This also vindicates Stevens' emphasis on the final belief in a supreme fiction, since the fiction is inseparable from words or language. Though the fiction covers over the "rock," it is no less important than the "rock" itself; it is the icon in language of the "central poem" that the clairvoyant men of "Primitive Like an Orb" celebrate (*CP* 441). The "leaves" and their fictions might be "late plurals," but they still give a sense of the real that is evoked through their flora, recalling Stevens' "florid" poems. They enmesh and beautify the otherwise coarse real much as, in Miller's example, the blank page is hidden by the thin line one writes on it ("Stevens' Rock" [1976b] 337). Stevens is also aware of the dimension of time: in bringing spring, summer, and autumn together, he evokes timelessness, the zero hour. As he says in "The Blue Guitar," it is time that separates us from the "rock" (*CP* 171). The "rock" itself is timeless, and it is only our distancing from it that gives rise to time; the fictions of the rock help annihilate or reduce the time's dark as they replicate or even re-create it. Therefore, they are worthy of the poet's praise, which grants them the status of "the poem, the icon and the man." Since the poem's words are chosen out of desire, they are immensely satisfying; since the fiction they create is the final belief, it is like the sacred image; and since the fiction is a human creation, it is related with his life—it is himself. It is capable of restoring both the real and us.

In the sixth stanza of this section, in declaring that "there is nothing else," Stevens is also almost directly suggesting the permanent lack of the "rock" or object(a), and also the human dependency on the words that (re)cover it.[33] Thus, the fictions of the rock continue to be created, yielding fruit. In other words, man keeps approaching the "rock" merely through this cycle of "leaves." This is why they are more important for us, more important than even the "rock" itself, which would be useless otherwise. Object(a) as the "rock" is the cause of the subject's being; he is destined to approach it by renouncing his castration by the symbolic order, which is not merely signifiers and fictions but also that which helps the subject come face to face with his being; it is through the symbolic that he acquires desire and is able to dream of the object of desire. Therefore, even though the object(a) *is not*, what is important is the subject's renunciation of the symbolic castration. It is (t)his giving up of castration that allows a precipitation of the self (or subject) through the emergence of the real subject of being (budding of the purest "I"), and thus also allows one to procure some modicum of the fantasized object and attain a new sensibility that enriches man's sense of being and existence in general. It is what arouses desire, which helps annihilate the distance from the "rock." The symbolic order is, therefore, what quickens the body and roots the mind. Since it is from within the symbolic that the subject knocks, dashes, and breaches through to the real, and since object(a) *is not*, the predicate that "there is nothing else" is justified. It is enough that one lives the life of desire, for desire bears fruit of the "final found" by annihilating the sense of alienation.

This is the moment of "being," which soon vanishes. The poet's words then interpret the experience. In other words, the "rock" is glossed over and thus is brought into increasing signifierization through language. During this process, however, the poem takes the place of the "rock" that thus vanishes. Each word, each expression, as it were, cures the subject of the incompleteness that stands between him and the "rock" as his being. Each gloss of the "rock" is immensely satisfying and therefore important. In this way, the "rock" comes to exist as a multiplicity, not as One or Absolute. This plenty of the symbolic order makes the symbolic universe of humanized reality more beautiful. The acceptance of this plurality, as opposed to the eternal quest for the hypothetical absolute, is more valuable; this is the essence of the first stanza of "On the Road Home" (*CP* 203–4). While "The Man on the Dump" (*CP* 201–3) puts an end to the search for that unending, eternal quest, "On the Road Home" celebrates the humanized or symbolic world. It is only when one accepts the debt of the symbolic that the real can be approached and appreciated. This alone imparts the feeling of homecoming in the otherwise permanent lack of the absolute truth, the One; the final stanza of "On the Road Home" rejoices over what the symbolic can offer. In this way, the plural symbolic world that language represents attains significance as it is rejuvenated. This, in turn, cures the real and us. Therefore, the poem as the fiction of the "rock" is simultaneously both sacred and human.

Section III is the "night's" hymn of the "rock"; here the "night," man's interior world (*CP* 333), meditates and pays its tribute to the "rock." In "Anecdote of the Jar," the "jar" owes its grayness and bareness to its deification (*CP* 76). The "rock" has also attained that status. Stevens' "rock" is like the religious imagination of God as the maker of man. In the penultimate stanza, it is described as the human origin and endpoint/objective. In Lacan's thought, it is the cause of being and (the object of) desire. Man begins from the "rock," but where does he go? Just as the child's sense of wholeness keeps vanishing throughout his growth, so is man led away from the "rock." The word "descent" is ambiguously used here, perhaps deliberately so, since the word does not only mean a "going down," "decline," or "fall," but also (retroactively or diachronically) brings in view the "origin." Thus, in going away from the "rock," man also becomes aware of the distance traveled from it, which he strives to reduce. The rock thus has dual functions, which are highlighted again through examples that involve both origin and end. However, the poet is not ignorant of the fact that the time required for the journey between the origin and end changes the origin, or differentiates the origin from the end.

The time goes with space—hence the thought of space between the two points.

The "rock" symbolizes *jouissance.* Its grayness characterizes its godlike indifference or sternness, its difficult aspect. It is not so kind as to be completely available or knowable. This aspect is associated with the evil, perhaps also corroborating Lacan, who views *jouissance* as evil. Each particular of the physical world is viewed as a reflection of the "rock." Just as there would be no ego without the o/Other, the physical world is meaningless without the "rock." Yet its difficult, even dangerous, aspect persists; at times, its evil nature is revealed. To understand the bipolar nature of the "rock," one has to turn to Lacan, who sees *das Ding* as both the aim of desire and the desire of death, as the *jouissance* object and death, as good and evil at the same time.[34] It might be noted that the poet ends the poem with an evocation of death.

In fact, in the final section the rock is glossed over with many expressions that are oxymoronic, paradoxical in their content, as in Manichean binaries, reflecting the bipolar nature of that foreign desire. The poet's awareness of the differential space between the bipolarities suggests that everything is contained within the two poles, that nothing is excluded from that space. This is how the poem meditates upon the most interior world of man as the poet meditates upon the most fundamental aspect of human existence: it is thus a "night's hymn of the rock." From its start to the end, the poem can be regarded as the "intensest rendezvous" (*CP* 524) with *the truth* of existence and being, which, for Stevens, includes death as well (*CP* 444); it begins with man's origin in the mother and ends with sleep, suggestive of birth and death, respectively. The "rock" contains both these ends and the space between as the life of desire.

Epilogue

Arthur Rimbaud, in his "Lettre du Voyant," proposed that the poet must become a *voyant*, so that "by [his] sight and insight" (*CP* 473) he might apprehend "the true nature of things and self" (Brereton 195). While it is not hard to believe that Stevens could have known the French poet's work and thought, we must see that he was *by nature* such a *voyant*. Rimbaud's remarks might have just given him confidence, since the French poet, afterward, rejected his own theory of the poet as *le grand maudit* on the grounds that it was a mistake, but Stevens probably found it very appealing, as if it suited him best. His poetry suggests that he embraced the theory lovingly—whether he knew it or not—and practiced it. He *was* what the French poet wished the poet to be. One becomes a *voyant* by "a deliberate disordering of all the senses," but Stevens did not have to make deliberate attempt—he was what Rimbaud calls the "arch-sufferer, the arch-criminal, the arch-damned soul [*maudit*]" (Brereton 196). Although Shakespeare's Hamlet is not the arch-criminal, he is certainly the arch-sufferer and the arch-damned soul. In both Stevens and Hamlet, what is lost is the phallus; thus, they are comparable in that sense. However, there is a difference in the treatment of the phallus by the poet and in the play.

Stevens speaks of the phallus indirectly in many of his poems, as a signifier without meaning. All these poems reveal his desire for "it." This is what Hamlet bears out until the very end. Both Hamlet and Stevens realize that they lack/desire "it." Hamlet, however, is more keen on having the phallus; his endeavor is constantly directed toward striking "it." In Lacan's view, having or being the phallus is not possible, but one gets that feeling through its "dialectization," since it is a signifier per se. While Stevens shows his awareness that it is a signifier, Hamlet's attempts at striking it suggest that it holds the status of a thing in his fantasy. In other words, the Shakespearean hero seeks it as an imaginary object (-Φ), which in fact does not exist but "ex-sists" since it belongs in the real order. There is nonetheless one common element in both cases: the phallus goes with the father as he vanishes into the field of the Other, from which he cannot return.

Hamlet does not seem to elevate the phallus to sublimity; his desire to strike it keeps suggesting that he feels much closer to it. All his acts suggest that, in his view, his mother and Claudius, his stepfather, had the phallus when they killed his father — that they have purloined "it," and that he must retrieve "it." This is the reason why he cannot distinguish between Claudius and the phallus, and keeps putting off killing his stepfather lest "it" should vanish once again. It is only after he is able to distinguish between the two ("The body is with the King, but the King is not with the body" [Act IV, Scene ii]) that he is really prepared to kill Claudius. His thinking that he must kill Claudius in order to retrieve the phallus suggests that "it" is still the imaginary object of desire for him. In this way, he is constantly in the vicinity (biologically, one might say) of the phallus. Stevens' situation is different in the sense that he never was or felt himself to be in the vicinity of the phallus. Its repression in his unconscious seems to hinge on its foreclosure. This almost turns it into a mythical object of desire for him; its radical otherness with reference to him is the cause of the imagery that sublimates it and makes it into a most sanctified signifier (*CP* 530). This would mean that Hamlet's situation is less "grave" than that of Stevens. Yet the intensity of Hamlet's search or desire for it is greater; his feeling of being in its vicinity sends him on a mad pursuit and makes him turn to impractical ways in order to strike it. This literally sends him to his grave. On the contrary, its near foreclosure in Stevens' case, and his ambivalence in treating "it" as both object and signifier, apparently saved his life.

Although Stevens realizes toward the end of section I of "Prologues to What Is Possible" that the phallus is the prologue to making the impossible possible, poems like *Chocorua* and *The Rock* cause one to think that the poet was really interested in the (m)/Other, which seems to have remained his ultimate desire. This could be the reason why, after all his life-long resistance to God and religious faith, he embraced the austere Catholic God; if not the (m)Other, he seemingly hoped to seek God as the Other of his desire, thus filling the (m)Other's lack with the Catholic God. From the Lacanian perspective, this suggests feminine structural position and potential, for this is abandoning the phallic pleasure in favor of the Other *jouissance*. Studying Stevens' poetry from the viewpoint of feminist poetics might yield rich results; this possibility is supported by Melita Schaum's attempt to collect articles on the feminine in Stevens' poetry. In this sense, the poet's abandonment of masculinity may lead to speculations that Hamlet was better "placed" in the social structure of sexual identity. However, this is forgetting that Stevens protected his virility by identifying himself with feminine, and that Hamlet remained impotent insofar as his desire for the phallus remained unrealized. Ultimately, what matters is one's virility, the ability to create; this is the real that one must never fail to desire. The sexual identity is symbolic, secondary, even sociopolitically motivated, and therefore not real. Thus, it does not matter whether Stevens recovered or not; what is important, as he says in "The Planet on the Table" (*CP* 532–33), is that he could create.

The phallic signifier having been radically repressed in the unconscious, which for Lacan is the discourse of the Other, it is in this Other of speech that the neurotic "locates himself and recognizes himself" (S III 162). The discourse between the neurotic and his Other is essentially directed toward *being* (S III 138). Stevens' poetry reflects the desire to locate and recognize himself in the Other; at times, it also shows the fear of being disowned by the Other, for it is the relationship with the Other that sustains the subject's sense of his own being. "And what ... could be the subject's noumenal being," Moustafa Safouan asks, "if not that aspect of the same body which remains invisible to the subject?" (*FS* 134). Stevens kept searching for and moving toward his noumenal being inside himself and in the physical world, thus belying Baird's view that "Wordsworth's energy flows toward a Kantian *noumenon*. That of Stevens remains within [his] sense of the physical world" (xiv). Stevens, at best, used his sense of the physical to approach his noumenal being.

To conclude, it may be reiterated that it does not matter whether he recovered insofar as he was able to sustain, even intensify, his dialogic relationship with the Other; it was sufficient for him to be with the Other of his desire, since there he could experience "the intensest rendezvous" with his being (*CP* 524). Stevens' desire seeks a union with the Other, to "inhabit the hypnosis of that sphere" (*CP* 480). He thought that his poetry might take him there, where he would be complete and need nothing — not even the ordinary reality around him, with which he could never really establish a happy liaison. Once *there*, he says in "The Poem That Took the Place of a Mountain" (*CP* 512), he should be able to look down upon the ordinary reality. On Mallarmé's poetry, Valéry once said something to the effect that he sought to elevate the printed page to the level of the midnight sky. Stevens did not merely do the same but he also sought to elevate himself to that level. His poetry likewise reflects the desire to make his desire the instance of everyone's desire, so that everyone could attain that level (*CP* 289). To this end, he must first convince others to believe that there is no difference between the irrational and the rational:

> They will get it straight one day at the Sorbonne.
> We shall return at twilight from the lecture
> Pleased that the irrational is rational [*CP* 406].

Shall we...?

Notes

Chapter 1: Prolegomena

1. Brogan and Wagner have directly expressed this doubt. Brogan opines, "If Stevens suffered (and I think he did suffer) from a schism within himself" (15); Wagner, however, is more direct in talking about the intrusion of the poet's "primary process thinking in his secondary process discourse" as "perhaps symptomatic of neurosis or some developmental failure" (86).

2. For Stevens' Puritan background, see chapter 1 of Joan Richardson's *The Early Years.*

3. Garrett Jr. practiced in Reading, Baltimore, New York, and finally Cleveland as a promising criminal lawyer; John practiced in Reading and eventually became a judge of Berks County, Pennsylvania; Wallace himself became a very famous lawyer in surety, worked with different insurance companies in New York, and ultimately settled with the Hartford Accident and Indemnity Company.

4. Stevens' journal entries of 13 September and 7 November 1904 clearly suggest that Elsie was very miserly in writing him back; he even thought of responding with novelistic indifference toward her and wondered whether they would be really be a happy couple (*SP* 142; *L* 77). Once he accused her of being shameless in neglecting him (*L* 109). He frequently had to remind her to write more often (*L* 135, 137). One feels that something was definitely wrong, for Elsie not only did not write him very often but, later, also destroyed most of the correspondence from before 1907. The poet's daughter agrees, for she writes that Stevens was "deeply in love, but ... all was not going well," and that his journal entries from 30 April 1905 onward have an air of "depression and dissatisfaction" (*SP* 146).

5. The previously unpublished correspondence, presently at the Wallace Stevens Collection at the Huntington Library, is included in Richardson's *The Early Years*. Stevens' letters to Elsie contain innumerable suggestions on how Elsie should behave, what she should do or not do, and what she should do to be good to him. Also see Richardson for Elsie's feeling of being criticized by Stevens (*The Early Years* 254–55).

6. Elsie's father, Howard Irving Kachel, whom her mother had married when she was five months pregnant with Elsie, died the year after the marriage. Elsie's legitimacy was already in question. They were very poor and had to live with Elsie's grandmother. After Howard's death, Elsie and her mother stayed on with Catherine Smith's family until her mother married Lehman Wilkes Moll seven years later. Elsie had to give up her school education during the first year and to go to work in order to support her family. She worked in a department store where she played the piano in the sheet-music department; she also gave piano lessons.

7. Stevens' *Harmonium* has been a special focus insofar as mourning and melancholy in his poetry is concerned. But the lines quoted from *Esthétique du Mal*, the directness of self-reviling and self-impeachment in them, and Stevens' remembrance of his father until almost the end of his life all suggest that he kept mourning the loss of the father throughout his life. See Ramazani for Stevens' elegiac verse as nontraditionally elegiac, and modernist in that sense, due to "interlacing its pathos" with irony, satire, and its display of "a tendency for rage and self-reviling" (569).

8. Lacan's concept of the phallus has evolved from the *Name-of-the-Father*, whose function is similar, if not identical, to that of the phallus. The *Name-of-the-Father* is more or less equivalent to the father figure whom the mother regards. Lacan also calls it the "third term," which breaks the dyadic mother-child relationship, and due to which the child comes to be in the triangular dialectic — the Oedipal triad. The *Name-of-the-Father*'s "No" to the dyadic relationship enabled Lacan to bring together into permanent juxtaposition the homonyms *le nom du père* (*Name-of-the-Father*) and *le non du père* ("No"-of-the-Father). Perhaps the difference between the *Name-of-the-Father* and the phallus is that the former is the signifier and neutralizer of the *désir de la mère* while the latter is that of the *désir de l'Autre* (both French expressions in this sentence are essentially ambiguated by the subjective genitive *de*, enabling two ways of reading: "desire *of* the mother/Other for something" and "desire *for* the mother/Other").

9. Here Lacan uses the term *Manque-à-être*, which is translated as "Want-of-being," following Schneiderman's translation of it in consultation with Lacan himself; in the next chapter, I also retain Schneiderman's translation of *aggressivité* as "aggressiveness" instead of "aggressivity" (see Schneiderman, "Translator's Note" vii).

10. Lemaire writes that the obsessional is characterized by his encystic unity with the (m)Other, and that this gives him a feeling of "too great self-adequacy," of "being too much loved"; the hysteric, however, feels the want of that love by the (m)Other since he knows he is not the phallus the (m)Other would enjoy (see 228–29).

11. The neurotic's ego being very strong, and thus very sensitive, the other easily becomes an Other for him. This Other is, however, different from the Other of his desire, which is what he is deprived of— the signifier that he has somehow lost.

12. Stevens had asked Williams several times to stop at Hartford on his way north. Once, when he came to lecture at Hartford, Williams did stop for a night — not at the Stevens home, to his dismay, but in a hotel (B 113). Richard and Betty Eberhart felt that Mrs. Stevens did not like people coming in their house (B 114). Who knows whether the Eberharts were not made to believe that the problem was with Elsie? Samuel French Morse says that Stevens was a gentleman and did not express his unhappiness or anger; instead, he made it look like his fault even though Elsie was responsible for it (B 157–58). Perhaps the frankness demanded by the friendship might have revealed Stevens' secret.

13. Stevens' *Harmonium* is perhaps the most direct expression of a disoriented desire. The "alogical phrases, tropes, and wayward titles" of the volume, along with its "violent verbal disjunctions" and symbolic over- and underdeterminations, are symptomatic of the poet's "deeply disoriented phenomenology of self and world" (Sampson 34, 35).

Chapter 2: Neurosis of Winter

1. The Greek word *métoikos*, Chandran explains, means "a resident alien" (54).

2. While the neglected people of Umuofia in Achebe's *Things Fall Apart* accept Christianity, the hero of the novel, Okonkwo, resists this cultural trespassing with all his might.

3. Hesla's treatment of the poem is preferred as a point of departure since his is the most recent and longest attempt at reading the poem, and intends to "correct ... misreadings" (Hesla 241).

4. See Cook's "Riddles, Charms, and Fictions in Wallace Stevens" and *Poetry, Word-Play, and Word-War in Wallace Stevens*.

5. Miller writes, "Only the snow man, the man who is 'nothing himself,' is free of imagination's fictions and can behold 'nothing that is not there and the nothing that is'" ("Wallace Stevens' Poetry of Being" 155; also see his *Poets of Reality* 277); Keyser says, "If one has a mind of winter for a long time, one will be able to see the winter without thinking of the misery" (596); Susan Weston believes that "the argument of the poem is that one must be a snow man — 'nothing himself'— in order to perceive reality without thinking of any misery in it" (9). Cameron is close to Weston when she speaks on behalf of the poem's speaker thus: "Could he rid himself of all human characteristics, become transparent, he might see the world as it is" (585).

6. It could be said that an experience attains universality at one's first removal from it; however, the concern is how one thinks — for instance, (a) it worries me; (b) it worries you too; and (c) it worries all alike.

7. It is not exactly an afterthought, since it is possible that the thought of misery was lurking in the unconscious before suddenly surfacing to the level of the conscious.

8. Lacan's *moi* suggests the sense of "self" as attached with the ego. Though the poet and the psychoanalyst did not know each other's work, Booker points out that the poet was aware of the phenomenon of "hearing-oneself-speak" (495). As an example, Booker quotes Stevens' lines from *Chocorua to Its Neighbor*; however, the problem of determining who speaks cannot be solved easily, for the poem refers to that speech as "meditation" and "solitaria," suggesting that it is not an articulate speech, and hence not the *je* discourse. In fact, Stevens' poetry proves one of Brooks' statements — that "the structure of literature *is* in some sense the structure of mind ['the mental apparatus']" (337).

9. Although the "subject" or "I" of our discourse is the same as the ego or *moi* (since we are still egocentric people), unless otherwise suggested the noun "subject" represents the human subject (the "I"). Also, in French, *sujet* is a masculine noun. Therefore, and also for convenience, I tend to treat the English "subject" as a masculine noun.

10. In a literary work of art, the sequence of frustration, regression, and aggressiveness is very often reversed, such that it begins at the point of aggressiveness and ends with frustration. However, there are two types of regression: one conforms to Lacan's definition of it, as "the ego's gradual decomposition," and the other is poetic regression through which the work finally returns to the ordinary (often distasteful) reality. In psychoanalysis, things begin with frustration and, through the Lacanian notion of regression, culminate in aggressiveness.

11. *Jouissance* has no English equivalent, and Lacan uses the term with a variety of nuances in his work. In French it means "pleasure" or "enjoyment," but the psychoanalyst also assimilates it with the French word *jouir* (the pleasure derived from sexual orgasm). In yet another sense, he uses it to convey the pleasure derived from meaning, and splits the word as *jouis-sense* (*jouissance* of meaning). There are still more shades of the word's meaning, which will be explained later in this study.

12. The two poems, however, differ from each other: while "Snow Man" prolongs the period of aggressiveness and introduces intervention in the middle, in "A Dish of Peaches" the aggressiveness toward the peaches is immediately followed by the question "Who speaks?," thus gradually building up the frustration from the start as compared with the belated, yet sudden, introduction of the frustrating misery in "Snow Man."

13. Wilden therefore comments, "[T]he *moi* is thus another" (161).

14. Note that Lacan here recalls the equivocal senses of the S: as the *je* and as Freud's *Es*, which represents the *id* that is equivalent to Lacan's Other, suggesting that the Other speaks with the ego, which is the most characteristic feature of a psychotic's discourse.

15. Tom Whalen's article on Stevens' "Valley Candle" (*CP* 51) discusses the "night" as consuming darkness.

16. Lacan's imaginary, symbolic, and real orders may be briefly described, respectively, as the domains of images and image formation, language and culture, and the corporeal world. The real order also includes the effects of the corporeal world on the subject; moreover, it also contains everything that is unknown.

17. Broadly speaking, Lacan's concept of the signifier is the advent of a symbol as a result of the absence of that which it symbolizes and makes part of the social or humanized reality. However, there are two categories of signifiers in Lacan: signifiers that are commonly used in languages and signifiers that belong in the unconscious (signifiers in the real, or unary signifiers). The signifiers of the second category are the master signifiers (designated as S1) that the subject must *dialectize* in order to achieve his or her normativization. The categories are not absolute, for a signifier used in the language spoken by the subject (S2) may lose its meaning and be repressed into his or her unconscious, thus becoming an S1, and an S1 after its dialectization may enable the subject to use it in the language spoken by him or her.

18. The *Name-of-the-Father* is more or less equivalent to the father figure whom the mother

regards (see note 8 of chapter 1 for more information on Lacan's label for this concept). The biological father is dispensable here since anyone who enjoys the status of the father figure in the family can perform the function of prohibiting the child's attachment with the mother. The concept of the signifier phallus, in Lacan, has evolved from the *Name-of-the-Father* through the 1950s and 1960s. Though the two are not exactly identical, their function is more or less the same: to delimit the subject's *jouissance* by intervening as law.

19. The repressed signifier being part of the unconscious, which is the discourse of the Other, it is in this Other — in this Other of speech, in the speech of this "you" — that the subject accosts with his self and being (S III 162).

20. Lacan discusses this while explaining the case of a Hungarian tram conductor and also the case of Freud's most famous patient: Dora (see S III, chapters XII and XIII; see also Freud's "Fragment of an Analysis of a Case of Hysteria" 7: 7–122).

21. In Freud as well as in Lacan, sexual division or identity has nothing to do with anatomical difference; it depends on the phallus, which "either exists or does not exist." Human beings are thus divided only as those who have the phallus and those who do not have it (for more on this division, see *FS* 101, 124). Both Lacan and Freud have been attacked for their "phallocentric" position by their once-followers and feminists.

22. Robert DeMaria's "'The Thinker as Reader': The Figure of the Reader in the Writing of Wallace Stevens" explores the poet's interest in the activity of reading.

Chapter 3: Bits of Blue

1. The astounding similarities of thought between Stevens' "imagination" and Lacan's "imaginary" allow interchangeable use of these terms; thus, they are not distinguished in this study. Similarly, Stevens' conception of "reality" being very close to Lacan's "real" order, I use the two terms interchangeably, though Lacan uses "reality" more often to suggest the humanized, social reality.

2. See Freud's "On Narcissism: An Introduction" (14: 67–102) for detailed understanding of "introjection."

3. Stevens was interested not so much in becoming a philosopher, but rather in philosophers' poetry (*OP* 195). In "A Collect of Philosophy" (*OP* 183–202), he argues that all philosophical ideas are essentially poetic, which perhaps explains why he was a poet and not a philosopher.

4. These experiences include mirror-stage effects oriented toward identity formation, castration, desire, Oedipal intervention, and so forth (see ERS 148).

5. Note that, in the passage from *Credences*, "capture" is related with "captive" not only structurally but also through the common Latin root *capere*. This passage will be discussed in detail later, during the reading of *Credences*.

6. The "moment" is not rational since imagination transfigures things as they are (*NA* 77); this metamorphosed state of things is not factual or rational, and is subject to change without notice.

7. Lacan's notion of the real includes the actual, concrete, corporeal world that exists around humans; however, since there is no term to refer to the metamorphosed state of things except the term "image," and since the poet does not doubt the reality of the image in the mind, the term "real" is retained to signify both things and their metamorphosed state, which cannot really be referred to by that expression since by "real" we designate the *Ding an sich* (the thing in its purity), without any embellishment or deviation. Yet Lacan also uses the term "real" "for the moment of impossibility" of the pure perception of the object "onto which both [the imaginary and the symbolic] are grafted, the point of that moment's endless return" (*FS* 31); in this sense, Stevens' exalted sense of reality as a result of its transfiguration or sublimation is nothing but attaining to that "moment of impossibility." Thus, the metamorphosed, transfigured, sublimated state of things could appropriately be referred to by Lacan's "real." Moreover, Stevens' conception of what he calls "reality" also incorporates the effect it has on the perceiving mind.

In these senses, it is not distinguished from Lacan's "real"; therefore, like "imagination" and the "imaginary," Stevens' "reality" and Lacan's "real" are used interchangeably in this study.

8. Stevens often uses the image of the "room" or "house" — or architectural images — to suggest the world "within" as having a "window" from which the mind sees the world "without" (e.g., see *CP* 9, 57, 210). Perhaps Stevens owes this image to Robert Frost, who uses it in his "Tree at my window" (*Collected Poems* 318) to an effect that is parallel to Stevens' use of it.

9. This is how Vendler explains a similar expression used by the poet with respect to the ancient river Stygia in "The River of Rivers in Connecticut" (*CP* 533; *Words Chosen* 73).

10. Here, as well as in the discussion that follows, capitalization is used in such representations to suggest the largeness of the concerned entities since the poem involves the issue of their enlargement and diminution; the normal type indicates their original state. The "space," being originally vast and large, is capitalized at the start of the discussion itself.

11. However, Stevens does not pose or pause to think of the "nothing" here, probably because thinking itself is a result of the "nothing" for him.

12. Doggett suggests that the "hand" symbolizes creativity (24, 44).

13. Vendler says that in his assertions Stevens "more naturally tends to a middle ground, looking for an accommodation, a sensible ecstasy of pauvred color... ." and thus mitigates what would be bold assertions with qualifications, often making them sound like hypotheses that are "interesting to entertain but of questionable solidity" ("The Qualified Assertions" 163). The need for such mitigation or qualification doubtless reflects anticipation of the other; it arises out of the desire for acceptance of the assertions. At the same time, however, they are assertions proper. Always in the difficulty of *to be*, they also reflect the poet's doubt about the reality or validity of his illusions and hallucinations, the paranoiac knowledge, on which the assertions are based; yet his efforts to make them acceptable are suggestive of a desire to lend them credibility and reality.

14. Stevens himself spoke of the anti-mythological nature of *The Comedian*, further arguing that the poem's protagonist is everyman (*L* 778). Guereschi sees three stages throughout the poem's six sections in order to apprehend the poet's "line of resistance to the mythological" past: "the denial of man's heroic destiny (I, II), the difficulties of apotheosizing Eden (II, III, IV), and the failure of the mythopoeic imagination (V, VI)" (74).

15. "Decreation" is, Stevens explains, going from "the created to the uncreated," and he also says that modern reality is one of decreation, which reveals our powers (*NA* 174–75).

16. Bevis realizes the importance of these stylistic devices in Stevens (113–14).

17. As in "A Dish of Peaches in Russia," the other separates the *moi* from the Other, thus cleaving the mind.

18. Apropos of Stevens' "must," Vendler writes in "The Qualified Assertions of Wallace Stevens" that it is often used when the insistence in the assertions anticipates "fear ... of chaos and disintegration if the assertions are not valid"; that it is "not a word of faith but ... doubt, implying ... an unbearable otherwise"; and that it "reflects obligations or destinies of a less voluntary sort" (167, 168, 166). However, such instances of "must" are very few in number (e.g. "The Snow Man"); in most other instances, its use reflects the impossibility of the assertions *and* the desire to fetch them into the domain of possibility or credibility. His "must" is therefore more a word chosen out of desire than chosen for qualification; this is why it is more a word of faith in Stevens' work than a word of doubt.

19. Though it was Husserl's idea that "an object has being in itself" (qtd. in Leonard and Wharton 85), it could be Stevens' own belief since there is little chance that he was aware of or influenced by Husserl. See also Hines 23–24.

20. Carrier interprets these sentences on the basis of Descartes' famous dictum: "'He' (man) 'is,' (ergo) 'we' (individual men) 'are.' Or possibly: 'He' (the idea of man) 'is' (ergo) 'we' (the images of man) 'are'" (167). However, Descartes' assertion of *sum* is dependent on the movement of the conscious, whereas Stevens' assertion is not dependent. It is a next step that thinks of things other than "I," hence possibly suggesting the relation between "I" and the rest of the things and phenomena that have independent existence and are the other to the "I."

21. Unlike Nietzsche's killing of God, Stevens' killing of Him is a mercy killing, so that

He may be replaced with something equally supreme. Stevens wrote Henry Church about Nietzsche that he distorted the world and rendered it unclear for perception, and quips about Nietzsche's attempt "getting out of focus" (*L* 431–32).

22. The image-making process is viewed as cultivation. "Terrace" is obviously derived from *terra*; the "imaginary" is Stevens' *cultiva terra*, which yields images. ("Cultivation" means improvement or development — for instance, of the mind [*OED*].) Warren Carrier, too, interprets the relevant lines in a similar way, but he takes "mandolins" to represent feelings (168). However, images are prior to feelings; it is the already known or recorded image that helps make sense of its recurrence, or of the recurrence of a similar type of image, which then evokes feelings. In the very first line of "Lunar Paraphrase" (*CP* 107), Stevens says that the imagination (not image) breeds emotions and feelings. Images of feelings could also be prerecorded. It is this record that is used as reference point for perception or for evoking feelings at a later moment.

Chapter 4: *Jouissance*

1. I am indebted to Melville and Fink for their readings of Lacanian formulae of sexuation.

2. As I have already explained in note 8 to chapter 1, the signifier *nom du père* (*Name-of-the-Father*) also includes the suggestion of a "No!" of the father through the homonym *non du père* (*No-of-the-Father*), since it is the father who says "No" to the child's attachment with the mother. The child, thus alienated from the mother, is led to see that it is the father who is the mother's desire (rather than him- or herself). This is how the child comes to respect and participate in the symbolic order of culture. After getting over the family and assuming a role in the society, the *Name-of-the-Father* changes to the phallus. The loss or repression of the phallus may be brought about by the *Name-of-the-Father* or father-figure, and the subject is then left with the (m)Other or, in a male subject, with any other woman of his desire. This is more or less "the time of the Other" ("Desire" 17).

3. Although the time of that unity is not a remembered experience of satisfaction, it is very much there in the unconscious memory, since without this the Oedipal complex or the Oedipal situation will never come to be, and then there would be no possibility of its resolution.

4. See *Hamlet*, Act V, Scene i. In discussing this scene from the play, Lacan says that Ophelia-the-object "regains its immediacy and ... worth for (Hamlet)" ("Desire" 36). In Wallace's case, it was not a question of regaining, as in Hamlet's case, but of gaining Elsie (of course, this gaining was ultimately only an attempt to regain the [m]Other).

5. Here, the symbolic phallus represents the *Name-of-the-Father*, or the law; it initiates the subject on the path of his own desire, relieving him of the desire for the (m)Other. In the absence of the symbolic phallus, the subject is entrapped by the desire for the (m)Other and imagines that the (m)Other has the phallus, which he does not actually see but imagines and desires; or else he imagines that the (m)Other desires the phallus, which he must become or procure *for her*. Here, the subject imagines the phallus to be a thing (that is, real). Hamlet is seen to think of it as a thing that he must restore, or procure for his mother, whereas Stevens sees his mother as having it — this is obvious in the figurations of the phallic mother in the poetry.

6. Wagner rightly observes that the mother in "Madame La Fleurie" is "the pre-Oedipal, phallic mother ... a threat to the male child" (92). It is death insofar as the subject fails to assimilate the "third term" (*Name-of-the-Father* or phallus) and thus to come to be in the symbolic order as a human subject; he or she thus remains in the real, in the dyadic relationship with the mother. The last line of the poem has been excised from the *Collected Poems*, but it was present in Stevens' folder (see Richardson, *The Later Years* 386–87). This line speaks of the punishing mother that castrates.

7. The image of the bush appears later in "Study of Images I" (*CP* 463–64), and there, too, it symbolizes the conscious domain.

8. Fink notes that "exist" is derived from the Greek *ekstasis,* which means "standing outside of or apart from something"; he speaks of "exist" and "ex-ist," the former suggesting existence as intimate and the latter suggesting an existence that is not intimate, but rather "extimate" (122).

9. "The less we speak, the more it speaks to us" (S III 138).

10. The phallic mother-beloved in Stevens may be compared to the phallic Ophelia in *Hamlet.* Hamlet speaks of the phallus and of the object of desire in connection with each other ("Here is metal more attractive") and, like a child would speak to his mother, he asks Ophelia, "Lady, shall I lie in your lap?" (Act III, Scene ii).

11. Patke does not necessarily agree with this view (30).

12. See Patke (27–29) for more information on the significance of the letter C.

13. Eleanor Cook, in her essay "The Comedian as the Letter C," notices this when she writes that "Crispin has already shed" the European notion of divinity external to man (196n8), and also cites from another Stevens poem where God is replaced by man (*CP* 245).

14. Sukenick comes close to saying what the *it* is when he writes that it is an "alien reality, utterly nonhuman, that is represented by the star in 'Nuances of a Theme by Williams'" (50–51).

15. Stevens detests the God of old faith, for He cannot speak and is not visible (*CP* 262). The relevant lines from *The Comedian* evoke Triton, whose body partly resembles man's body, suggesting something human about the unconscious, but this human quality is negligible. Even earlier in the same section, the lines concerning Triton support this interpretation. Thus, Stevens' concept of the unconscious consists of the human and the inhuman or nonhuman. In Lacan's thought as well, the unconscious is full of the other people, though it does not care for the subject's (human) feelings.

16. Like Stevens, Lacan also uses the word "shadow" apropos of the other (S II 244).

17. It is language that separates the subject from the real or the Other (S II 244), and, as I have said while discussing "Re-statement," the introduction of a nonconducive element is actually conducive to romance.

18. Refer to the discussion of "North-South" dialectic in chapter 3 above.

19. Constance Rouke observes that "mythologies do not lend themselves to small or delicate comic intricacies" (qtd. in Guereschi 73).

20. Here, one can apply the theory of the dialectization of the master signifier, treating "being" as the master signifier (S1) and the phallus as the other signifier (S2). Bringing S1 into some relation with S2 is a dialectization of S1. However, the phallus (S2) gains more importance here, since without it the S1 will have no meaning for the subject.

21. Lacan suggests that the subject is deprived of the phallus, and that this loss is responsible for giving the object(a) its function in the subject's fantasy; thus, desire originates from the phallus and aims at the fantasy or object(a) ("Desire" 15, 23).

22. This is how George Orwell's novel *Animal Farm* derides the socialist view. In the last few lines from section IV of *The Comedian,* Stevens echoes Nietzsche's Zarathustra, who despises the preachers of equality: "'Men are not equal.' Nor shall they become equal" (101). We see a similar position taken by Realism in the form of José Ortega y Gasset, who said that it is a "provoking and profound injustice" to consider that "men are actually equal" (7). The idea of equality underlies most modern political philosophies, which Stevens would not accept. However, this does not mean that Stevens is promoting any anti-socialist ideology; rather, it is part of his realism.

23. Icarus is portrayed as the symbol of an aspiring human being in W. H. Auden's poem "Musée des Beaux Arts" (3).

24. For Kermode, the daughters are "without doubt the seasons" (48); for Bloom, too, "these ladies appear to be the poetry of Stevens' seasonal cycle, possibly based ironically upon Keats's *Human Seasons*" (82); Riddel finds "Kermode's suggestion that the chits are the faces of nature's four seasons" fruitful (101), but his own opinion is that they are Crispin's own "progeny" (100), since "chit" also means "sprout" or "shoot" (101); and Sukenick echoes Riddel in saying that "they are merely daughters ... four mirrors of Crispin's self that stir his imagination instead

of merely reflecting it" (59). Susan Weston also finds it easy to believe that they are "daughters instead of poems" (55), thus upholding the opinion of Riddel and Sukenick. Nassar believes that they "represent for Stevens something like four different kinds of poem, from the most ambitious and self-conscious to the most trivially descriptive" (170). Baird goes so far as to say, "Each daughter seems to be a century, an age in the history of the American imagination, symbolized in Crispin himself. Each is a presiding woman-genius of an age, *curled*, marked by acts of imagining barbers" (200).

25. "Turquoise" is greenish-blue; green and blue being colors of reality and imagination, respectively, "turquoise" here suggests imaginary perception of reality.

26. Apropos of Freud's comment brought to Lacan's notice by Valabrega — that desire is fulfilled in the dream (S II 212) — Lacan says that desire introduces fantasy (S II 213); Lacan does not agree that it is ever fulfilled, and neither does Stevens.

27. In a letter, Stevens uses the word "rout" apropos of one's discovery of oneself as multiplicity owing to many influences (*L* 91). Yet here he separates the self and the influences to keep one's identity apart from the influences. This is what Crispin does in establishing his identity, different from that of the contemporary influences.

28. Cook has also suggested this — her word is "embrace" ("'The Comedian as the Letter C'" 201); the issue is overcoming one's alienation from oneself, one of the dominant themes in Stevens' work.

29. Patke praises the poem's "many beguiling aspects for which the undemanding reader can acquire and retain an indulgent affection" (8), while Cook rejects seeing Crispin "as abject failure or as tragedy" ("'The Comedian as the Letter C'" 198).

30. Maureen Kravec points out that "ephebe" is derived from Latin *ephebus* (from Greek *ephebos*: *epi-* "at, upon" + *hebe*, "early manhood"), which, in ancient Athens, was "a young citizen (18 to 20 years) undergoing physical and military training" (166). In *Notes toward a Supreme Fiction*, Stevens exhorts the ephebe to see with complete ignorance (*CP* 380), where the ignorance may point to ignoring other people's desires, talk, conversations, goals, aspirations, and fantasies that one assimilates as a matter of course, as if naturally. We may take this as ignoring the symbolic order itself, or the preexisting conceptions, since these have become "musty" (*CP* 120). This goes well with Stevens' stance, which was always bent toward approaching and apprehending things in their reality.

31. As already mentioned elsewhere, in Lacan to "symbolize" is also to "kill"; "the letter kills" (qtd. in Fink 24, 182nl) in the sense that in symbolizing the real, the symbol introduces a break or fissure into the fullness of the real and creates an absence in that part of it which is symbolized. However, in this poem the symbolization is effected not by the letter but by the eye; hence it is imaginary symbolization, which is called "introjection." Lacan argues that "introjection" is always symbolic (S I 83) — a symbolization with the imagination.

32. Lacan speaks of the human subject in terms of a signifier in Seminar XX (33). He has effectively shown that humans have no existence except in language — in short, as signifiers. This explains why one has a sense of identity *as distinct from others*, which is parallel to the existence of any signifier of a language as dependent on or distinct from other signifiers.

33. For a detailed analysis of the Wordsworth poem, see Deshmane.

Chapter 5: Rubbings of Reality

1. It is hard to resist the temptation to say that the coffee in the cup from Robbe-Grillet's sample passage cools down in the first four or five sentences and freezes by the end of the next half-dozen lines, and by the middle of the passage the reader himself freezes and becomes indifferent to what is being read by him or is before his eyes. While this description is extremely accurate, the reader's interest in, or even the faculty of, creating the same picture in his mind comes to a standstill after the initial efforts (see Ellmann and Feidelson 365–66).

2. The subject, which corresponds with the ego, is an imaginary function; thus, it is the imaginary that makes reality august.

3. In fact, Lacan shows the interdependency among his three orders (imaginary, symbolic, real) in Seminar XX through the Borromean knot (123–36).

4. I owe this interpretation to Raghavacharyulu.

5. Though I have used Stevens' wording for my own purposes, I believe that both Nanzia Nunzio of *Notes* (*CP* 395–96) and the "you" of "To the One of Fictive Music" (*CP* 87–88) represent desire, which is the origin of the imaginary that, in turn, serves as the desire's instrument aimed at its fulfillment. Lacan uses the word "desire" in two senses: to represent the psychical function set in motion by the lack, and to represent that which lacks — the latter usage suggests the lost object as illusion. In this way, there is no desire without the lack; therefore, both senses of the word cannot really be separated. Stevens likewise wrote of the Ozymandias section from the *Notes* that it shows the value of illusion (*L* 431), and he concludes "To the One of Fictive Music" with an apostrophe to the illusive "Unreal" (*CP* 88), thus justifying the lack as desire. "To the One of Fictive Music" also glosses desire as having its origin in our birth and our imperfection or lack (*CP* 87).

6. William Empson rightly observes that "understanding that other people are different is one of the bases of civilization" (94); yet it is only a half of that particular base — the other half is that there is at the same time a sense of identification between or among people. The two halves are interdependent and are well balanced in Stevens' use of the positive degree instead of the comparative or superlative form of "close" in the poem, suggesting that it is a normal process.

7. Santayana believed that "the poetry we see in nature is due to the emotion the spectacle produces in us ... nature ... would be dust and ashes to us if there were nothing sublime and romantic in ourselves to be stirred by it to sympathy" (*Three Philosophical Poets* 35).

8. Bethea points out that glass represents imagination in Stevens, commenting that the poet is the "glass man" who "enriches people's lives by enhancing their imaginations," thus enabling them to create order out of the chaos of life (104). In "The Idea of Order," the lights seem to have a similar function; the female singer's song has created them and the anonymous listener feels aggrandized as a result.

9. In "Landscape with Boat," Stevens suggests that man himself and his subjective responses to the happenings around him, which the "he" of the poem rejects, are real or part of it (*CP* 242).

10. McCollough suggests that desire constantly challenges the established order and hooks itself up with some new object or idea; this way, it gets coded, territorialized. However, "desiring-production" is something that "seeks to outmaneuver these codes by means of endless addition" (100).

11. Since both the guitarist and the audience speak in the poem, the dropping of quotation marks raises the questions of who speaks and who listens, which remain unanswered. It is a question of identity and identification.

12. This is how Andrew Marvell describes virginity in "To His Coy Mistress" (see Gardner 251).

13. Bloom suggests that this section evokes "'the hum of thoughts evaded in the mind'"; yet, surprisingly, he is not inclined to accept that there is either philosophical or psychological stance (312).

14. Stevens' first preference is for the sense of sight and the second is the sense of hearing; therefore, section II speaks of the love between the subject and the Other caused by vision and sound. However, note that it is brought about by the movements in the mind; hence, it is also a gustatory love.

15. Chapels and schools are where some kind of teaching is expected. Chapel also means a branch of a club or society where things as they are will likely be distorted, reminiscent of the coffeehouses of the Restoration period where each day saw somebody's reputation destroyed. Formerly in printing works, there used to be a separate section of printing workers, called chapel, for producing religious texts; if Stevens had this in mind, he might be speaking of printing errors as an inevitable part of those texts.

16. Stevens' crisis seems to be echoed in his "cry." It has two sides to it: it is almost always

a cry of either recognition or the fear of death, both of which seem mutually related. Bloom's etymological tracing of "cry" to its meaning of "imploring the aid of one's fellow citizens" through the Latin *quiritare* (literally, "wailing") and *quiris* ("Roman citizen"), and also of "occasion" ("dying fall"), are noteworthy here (320–21).

17. Perhaps Stevens owes his love for the quotidian to Baudelaire, who "could find in the sounds and sights of Paris the same exhilaration that other poets derived from the mountain or the desert" (Brereton 158–59).

18. Kessler suggests that the bronze man is an image of the dead forms (78).

Chapter 6: Apogee

1. The reality of the human body fades progressively as it keeps getting symbolized increasingly from one's conception itself, and hence belongs more in the symbolic order; its death occurs when it is "fully" symbolized, as if exhausted, and then assimilated into the real order again. This is why the foetus in embryo form and the dead body are almost similar — things that do not "feel the touch of earthly years" or of the symbolic order.

2. In the dialectization of a master signifier, the meaning of the master signifier is realized by the subject and a contact with the lost object(a) is (re)established even though it is lost as soon as it is thus recovered. For more details, see Fink 77–79.

3. Here, I treat *objet petit a* and object(a) as distinct from each other to represent, respectively, the actual object one desires but that can only satisfy the need, and the object constituted as primally lost as a result of one's coming to be in the symbolic order. This distinction is maintained throughout this study. For this distinction, see also Bowie 118–19.

4. In reality, the subject never approaches object(a), which, in this sense, remains at the level of a signifier-in-the-real, like the phallus.

5. Lacan also refers to this as "semiotic *jouissance*": the *jouissance* of meaning ("jouis-sense") derived from *lalangue* (see Fink 194n20). *Lalangue* is the language of symptoms and thus "indicates that part of language which reflects the laws of unconscious processes, but whose effects go beyond that reflection, and escape the grasp of the subject" (*FS* 46).

6. This is the "more than *jouissance*" or "surplus *jouissance*" that the subject is incapable of either experiencing or bearing; it is "something more than pleasure which can easily tip into its opposite" — namely, pain (*FS* 34).

7. Lacan refers to the human beings as signifiers in Seminar XX (33, 39; also see Lee, 176).

8. The neurotic's ego (or, in other words, his imaginary function) being very strong, and thus very sensitive, the other easily becomes an Other for him. This Other, however, is different from the Other of the neurotic desire in the sense that the neurotic desires what he is deprived of — the signifier that he has somehow lost.

9. The poetic act for Stevens is to project "poetry into reality" (*OP* 238–39).

10. In the discussion on *The Comedian*, it has already been suggested that, like Gandhi, the individual's growth was important for Stevens.

11. One more instance of this is in "Apostrophe to Vincentine" (*CP* 53), which has been discussed in chapter 5.

12. Lacan, in fact, translates the latter half of the dictum in terms of a "civilizing" mission, thus endowing the *soll* ("must") with a moral or civilizing connotation (see *É* 128 and note 6 to the essay).

13. The self's unity, constituted by the *moi*'s imaginary function, must be shattered for the subject's reintegration with his being (*É* 137), which lies with *Es* in Freud's dictum.

14. For Lacan's discussion of *Antigone*, see Seminar VII, 243–301 (for more discussion, see Lee 122–32).

15. The corresponding passage is also translated in Lee (125). Lacan here speaks of death as a result of crossing the *Atè* (the limit).

16. In Hamlet's case, it is the question of the phallus — what he seeks is not the phallus-

as-signifier but the phallus-as-thing; however, as an object or thing, it (the imaginary phallus) is essentially in the field of the Other.

17. The *OED* lists these variants of the word: fortalice, fortalys, fortalyce, fortilitie, fortilesse, fortilage, fortelleze, fortelace, fortiless, fortalise. The seventh of these approximates Stevens' spelling; however, from among so many variants, Stevens' choice of this particular spelling shows the very purpose that I am trying to expose here.

18. The "moderate satisfactions" the subject experiences belong in the domain of symbolic order — of Law; Lacan says, "[T]he Law seems to be giving the order, '*Jouis!*,' to which the subject can only reply '*J'ouis*' (I hear), the *jouissance* being no more than understood" (*É* 319). A great deal seems to be compressed in the statement: the Law gives the order to enjoy, but the subject's situation is such that he, being a subject of the Law (and hence at the level of privation), simply listens obediently to the Law even though he enjoys; thus he never disobeys the Law. The *jouissance* here, in being "no more than understood," is tamed. This is very much like the (supposed) freedom given by the traffic rules to enjoy, say, a speed of 80 kilometers per hour ("*Jouis!*"), but that enjoyment is restricted by the rider's awareness of the limit ordained ("*J'ouis*"); the rider is simply made to understand that this limit is enjoyment and that its violation is subject to punishment.

19. It is not a "division" as such because, although object(a) is the Other's desire, it *ex-sists* for the subject in equal radical Otherness as it does for the Other itself. Thus, there is no Other of an Other.

20. The phallus is the "primordial signifier whose very absence makes the activity of all other signifiers possible" (Booker 493).

21. The second stanza might recall the treatment of the activity of hearing from "Of Modern Poetry" (*CP* 239–40), which is full of evocations of the identification process.

22. Vendler's *Words Chosen Out of Desire* discusses how Stevens seeks to go beyond the Romantic poets, especially Keats.

23. Lacan speaks of the phallus as reflecting at the most "on the level of the object" ("Desire" 48).

24. Wagner in vain blames Stevens for his "ordinary analytical abilities" (100).

25. The two processes are really "two elements of one process, since every condensation is also a displacement from S to S1 [i.e., from one signifier to another], and every displacement relies on terms generated by condensation" (Grosz 103).

26. In an article, "The Phallic Phase and the Subjective Import of the Castration Complex," that emerged out of a group of contributors including Lacan himself, it is clearly stated that the neurotic pretends to give up on the ultimate as his desire and holds on to its signifier: the phallus (see *FS* 110). This is so because it is that signifier which sustains the possibility of there being desire; yet the *aphanisis* (i.e., disappearance) of desire makes the neurotic hold on to the signifier of the desire in such a way that the object from the actual world, which can signify that desire, becomes a fetishistic object of his or her attention.

27. In Lacanian thought, insofar as satisfaction of the drives is concerned, the object is not specific even though the object under the subject's gaze is sublimated, as in the case of the satisfaction of a need, where the object is not sublimated but is often very specific (see *FS* 112). Stevens' poem therefore has nothing to do with the bouquet as such even as the poem's argument makes it clear in its lesser emphasis on the bouquet as compared with that on the effects the bouquet has on the mind.

28. "The drive marks the subject's attempt to realize itself in the field of the Other and to find in that field the object which is eternally lacking" (*FS* 112).

29. Frederick Jameson says that "much of what Lacan will designate as Imaginary is traditionally designated by expressions like symbol and symbolism" (352), and further describes the imaginary as "a kind of pre-verbal *register* whose logic is essentially visual" (emphasis mine; 353).

30. Miller catches the essence of the "rock" symbol in *mise en abyme*, "a term in heraldry meaning a shield which has in its center (*abyme*) a smaller image of the same shield, and so, by implication, ad infinitum, with ever smaller and smaller shields receding toward the central

point" ("Stevens' Rock" [1976a] 11); the term therefore suggests the "rock" as that ever-shifting aim of desire which keeps substituting a surrogate object in its place with each shift, and which is thus no more — the nothing that the subject believes *is* something. This is what Lacan calls the object(a).

31. I use "Lac*analyse*" for "Lacanian psychoanalysis."

32. Lacan asks, "[I]sn't what is at stake in creationism a creation on the basis of nothing — thus on the basis of the signifier?" (S XX 41). Insofar as humans have subjectivity, they owe it to the signifier; they have no existence except in the symbolic. Hence Lacan says, "As soon as the subject himself comes to be, he owes it to a certain non-being on which he raises his being" (S II 192); he or she comes to be as a marker at the place of something (being) that is hollowed out and exists thereafter as absence (non-being). Thus, "men, women, and children are only signifiers" (qtd. in Lee 176 from S XX).

33. Stevens recognizes man's being "at the mercy of language" (ERS 175) when he refers to the joy of language as our Lord (*CP* 322), which is close to Lacan's concept of the symbolic or semiotic *jouissance,* also spelled *jouis-sense* (joy of meaning).

34. It has been already suggested that Lacan does not clarify the apparent distinction between the phallus *qua* object, object(a) as object as such, and *das Ding*; however, in his thought, all of them represent the ultimate object of human desire, the being itself, the attainment of which is the attainment of death. Stevens often seems to see it that way since, especially in his later poetry, he muses on the "being" as including both the imagination and death (*CP* 444).

Bibliography

Primary Works: Wallace Stevens

The Collected Poems of Wallace Stevens. New York: Alfred A. Knopf, 1954.
Letters of Wallace Stevens. Edited by Holly Stevens. New York: Alfred A. Knopf, 1966.
The Necessary Angel: Essays on Reality and the Imagination. New York: Alfred A. Knopf, 1951.
Opus Posthumous. Edited by Samuel French Morse. New York: Alfred A. Knopf, 1957.

Biographical Sources: Wallace Stevens

Brazeau, Peter. *Parts of a World: Wallace Stevens Remembered.* New York: Random House, 1983.
Richardson, Joan. *Wallace Stevens: The Early Years, 1879–1923.* New York: Beach Tree Books, 1986.
_____. *Wallace Stevens: The Later Years, 1923–1955.* New York: Beach Tree Books, 1988.
Stevens, Holly. *Souvenirs and Prophecies: The Young Wallace Stevens.* New York: Alfred A. Knopf, 1977.

Primary Works: Jacques Lacan

Écrits: A Selection. Translated by Alan Sheridan. New York: W. W. Norton, 1977.
Feminine Sexuality: Jacques Lacan and the École Freudienne. Edited by Juliet Mitchell and Jacqueline Rose. Translated by Jacqueline Rose. New York: W. W. Norton, 1982.
"Of Structure as an Inmixing of an Otherness Prerequisite to Any Subject Whatever." In *The Structuralist Controversy: The Languages of Criticism and the Sciences of Man,* edited by Richard Macksey and Eugenio Donato, 186–200. Baltimore: Johns Hopkins University Press, 1972.

Lacan's Seminars: All edited/established by Jacques-Alain Miller

Seminar I: *Freud's Papers on Technique (1953–54).* Translated by John Forrester. New York: W. W. Norton, 1988.
Seminar II: *The Ego in Freud's Theory and in the Technique of Psychoanalysis (1954–55).*

Translated by Sylvana Tomaselli, with notes by John Forrester. New York: W. W. Norton, 1988.
Seminar III: *The Psychoses (1955–56).* Translated by Russell Grigg. London: Routledge, 1993.
Seminar VI: "Desire and the Interpretation of Desire in *Hamlet*" (final three sessions). Translated by James Hulbert. In *Literature and Psychoanalysis: The Question of Reading Otherwise,* edited by Shoshana Felman, 11–52. Baltimore: Johns Hopkins University Press, 1982.
Seminar VII: *The Ethics of Psychoanalysis (1959–60).* Translated by Dennis Porter. New York: W. W. Norton, 1992.
Seminar XI: *The Four Fundamental Concepts of Psychoanalysis (1964).* Translated by Alan Sheridan. New York: W. W. Norton, 1978.
Seminar XVII: *The Other Side of Psychoanalysis.* Translated by Russell Grigg. New York: W. W. Norton, 2007.
Seminar XX: *On Feminine Sexuality: The Limits of Love and Knowledge (1972–73).* Translated by Bruce Fink. New York: W. W. Norton, 1998.
"Seminar on 'The Purloined Letter.'" In *Essential Papers on Literature and Psychoanalysis,* edited by Emanuel Berman, 270–99. New York: New York University Press, 1993.

Secondary Works

Achebe, Chinua. *Things Fall Apart.* London: William Heinmann, 1958.
Alvarez, A. *The Shaping Spirit: Studies in Modern English and American Poets.* London: Chatto & Windus, 1972.
Arensberg, Mary. "'A Curable Separation': Stevens and the Mythology of Gender." In *Wallace Stevens and the Feminine,* edited by Melita Schaum, 23–45. Tuscaloosa: University of Alabama Press, 1993.
Auden, Wystan Hugh. *Collected Poetry.* New York: Random House, 1945.
Baeten, Brooke. "'Whose Spirit Is This?' Musings on the Woman Singer in 'The Idea of Order at Key West.'" *Wallace Stevens Journal* 24, no. 1 (Spring 2000): 24–36.
Baird, James. *The Dome and the Rock: Structure in the Poetry of Wallace Stevens.* Baltimore: Johns Hopkins University Press, 1968.
Baron, Robert A., and Donn Byrne. *Social Psychology.* Englewood Cliffs, NJ: Prentice Hall, 1997. (8th edition, 1999.)
Barthes, Roland. "Death of the Author." In *Modern Criticism and Theory: A Reader,* edited by David Lodge, 167–72. London: Longman, 1988.
_____. *S/Z.* Translated by Richard Miller. New York: Hill and Wang/London: Jonathan Cape, 1975.
Bethea, Arthur F. "Stevens's 'The Emperor of Ice-Cream.'" *Explicator* 62, no. 2 (Winter 2004): 103–6.
Bevis, William. *Mind of Winter: Wallace Stevens, Meditation, and Literature.* Pittsburgh: University of Pittsburgh Press, 1988.
Blackmur, R. P. "Examples of Wallace Stevens." In *The Achievement of Wallace Stevens,* edited by Ashley Brown and Robert Haller, 52–80. New York: Gordian Press, 1973.
Bloom, Harold. *Wallace Stevens: The Poems of Our Climate.* Ithaca, NY: Cornell University Press, 1977.
Booker, M. Keith. "Notes toward a Lacanian Reading of Wallace Stevens." *Journal of Modern Literature* XVI, no. 4 (Spring 1990): 493–509.
Bowie, Malcolm. *Freud, Proust and Lacan: Theory as Fiction.* Cambridge: Cambridge University Press, 1987.

Brereton, Geoffrey. *An Introduction to the French Poets: Villon to the Present Day*. 2nd edition. London: Methuen, 1973.
Brogan, Jacqueline Vaught. "'Sister of the Minotaur': Sexism and Stevens." In *Wallace Stevens and the Feminine*, edited by Melita Schaum, 3–22. Tuscaloosa: University of Alabama Press, 1993.
Brooks, Peter. "The Idea of a Psychoanalytic Literary Criticism." *Critical Inquiry* 13, no. 2 (Winter 1987): 334–48.
Buchsbaum, Betty. "Contours of Desire: The Place of Cézanne in Wallace Stevens' Poetics and Late Practice." *Criticism* XXX, no. 3 (Summer 1988): 303–24.
Cameron, Sharon. "Ideas of a Self in Three Poems by Wallace Stevens." *ELH* 43 (1976): 584–603.
Campbell, P. Michael, and John Dolan. "Teaching Stevens' Poetry through Rhetorical Structure." In *Teaching Wallace Stevens*, edited by John N. Serio and B. J. Leggett, 119–28. Knoxville: University of Tennessee Press, 1994.
Carrier, Warren. "Wallace Stevens' Pagan Vantage." *Accent* 13–14, no. 3 (1953): 165–68.
Chadwick, Charles. *Symbolism*. London: Methuen, 1971.
Chandran, K. Narayana. *Singer in the City: Studies in Modern American Poetry*. Hyderabad, India: American Studies Research Center, 1986.
Conrad, Joseph. *Heart of Darkness*. In *Joseph Conrad: Heart of Darkness: A Case Study in Contemporary Criticism*, edited by Ross C. Murfin. New York: St. Martin's Press, 1989.
Cook, Eleanor. *Poetry, Word-Play, and Word-War in Wallace Stevens*. Princeton, NJ: Princeton University Press, 1988.
_____. "Riddles, Charms, and Fictions in Wallace Stevens." In *Critical Essays on Wallace Stevens*, edited by Steven Gould Axelrod and Helen Deese. Boston: G. K. Hall, 1988.
_____. "Wallace Stevens: 'The Comedian as the Letter C.'" *American Literature* 49, no. 2 (May 1977): 192–205.
Corn, Alfred. *The Metamorphoses of Metaphor*. New York: Viking Penguin, 1987.
Davis, Robert Con. *The Fictional Father: Lacanian Readings of the Text*. Amherst: University of Massachusetts Press, 1981.
DeMaria, Robert. "'The Thinker as Reader': The Figure of the Reader in the Writing of Wallace Stevens." *Genre* XII (Summer 1979): 243–68.
Deshmane, Chetan. "Wordsworth's 'A Slumber.'" *Explicator* 64, no. 4 (Summer 2006): 214–18.
Doggett, Frank. *Stevens' Poetry of Thought*. Baltimore: Johns Hopkins University Press, 1966.
Donne, John. *The Complete English Poems of John Donne*. Edited by C. A. Patrides. London: Dent, 1985.
Doreski, William. "Wallace Stevens in Connecticut." *Twentieth Century Literature* 39, no. 2 (Summer 1993): 152–65.
Easthope, Anthony. *The Unconscious*. London/New York: Routledge, 1999.
Eliot, T. S. *Collected Poems*. London: Faber and Faber, 1963.
Ellmann, Richard, and Charles Feidelson, ed. *The Modern Tradition*. New York: Oxford University Press, 1965.
Empson, William. *Milton's God*. London: Chatto & Windus, 1965.
Feirstein, Frederick. "Psychoanalysis and Poetry." *Partisan Review* 64, no. 3 (1997): 433–39.
Fink, Bruce. *The Lacanian Subject: Between Language and Jouissance*. Princeton, NJ: Princeton University Press, 1995.
Freud, Sigmund. "Creative Writing and Day-Dreaming." *Standard Edition of the Complete Works of Sigmund Freud* 9: 143–153.

_____. "The Devil as a Father-Substitute." *Standard Edition of the Complete Works of Sigmund Freud* 19:83–91.
_____. "Formulations on the Two Principles of Mental Functioning." *Standard Edition of the Complete Works of Sigmund Freud* 12: 218–26.
_____. "Fragment of an Analysis of a Case of Hysteria." *Standard Edition of the Complete Works of Sigmund Freud* 7: 7–122
_____. "Group Psychology and the Analysis of the Ego." *Standard Edition of the Complete Works of Sigmund Freud* 18: 65–143.
_____. "Lecture XXXI: 'The Dissection of the Psychical Personality.'" *Standard Edition of the Complete Works of Sigmund Freud* 22: 57–80.
_____. "Negation." *Standard Edition of the Complete Works of Sigmund Freud* 19: 235–239.
_____. "Psychoanalytic Notes on an Autobiographical Account of a Case of Paranoia." *Standard Edition of the Complete Works of Sigmund Freud* 12: 9–82.
_____. "The Uncanny." *Standard Edition of the Complete Works of Sigmund Freud* 17: 217–52.
Frost, Robert. *Collected Poems*. New York: Halcyon House, 1939.
_____. *Complete Poems*. New York: Holt, Rinehart and Winston, 1964.
Frye, Northrop. *Myth and Metaphor*. Edited by Robert D. Denham. Charlottesville: University Press of Virginia, 1990.
Fuchs, Daniel. *The Comic Spirit of Wallace Stevens*. Durham, NC: Duke University Press, 1963.
Gallagher, Ann M. "Stevens' 'Of Modern Poetry.'" *Explicator* 50, no. 2 (Winter 1992): 91–93.
Gallop, Jane. *Reading Lacan*. Ithaca, NY: Cornell University Press, 1985.
Gardner, Helen. *The Metaphysical Poets*. Harmondsworth, UK: Penguin, 1972. (Penguin Classics reprint, 1985.)
Gasset, José Ortega y. *The Dehumanization of Art and Other Essays on Art, Culture, and Literature*. Translated by Helene Weyl. Princeton, NJ: Princeton University Press, 1968.
Grosz, Elizabeth. *Jacques Locan: A Feminist Introduction*. London: Routledge, 1990.
Guereschi, Edward. "'The Comedian as the Letter C': Stevens' Anti-Mythological Poem." In *Critics on Wallace Stevens*, edited by Peter L. McNamara, 72–81. Coral Gables: University of Miami Press, 1972.
Hartman, Geoffrey. "The Interpreter's Freud." In *Modern Criticism and Theory: A Reader*, edited by David Lodge, 412–24. London: Longman, 1988.
Hesla, David. "Singing in Chaos: Wallace Stevens and Three or Four Ideas." *American Literature* 57, no. 2 (May 1985): 240–62.
Hines, Thomas J. *The Later Poetry of Wallace Stevens: Phenomenological Parallels with Husserl and Heidegger*. Lewisburg, PA: Bucknell University Press, 1976.
Jameson, Frederick. "Imaginary and Symbolic in Lacan: Marxism, Psychoanalytic Criticism, and the Problem of the Subject." *Yale French Studies* 55/56 (1977): 338–95.
Jarraway, David R. *Wallace Stevens and the Question of Belief: Metaphysician in the Dark*. Baton Rouge: Louisiana University Press, 1992.
Kelkar, Ashok R. "Ergo Sum: Descartes in an Oblique Light." *Indian Philosophical Quarterly* XXIII, no. 1–2 (January–April 1996): 165–68.
Kermode, Frank. *Wallace Stevens*. Edinburgh: Oliver and Boyd, 1960.
Kessler, Edward. *Images of Wallace Stevens*. New Brunswick, NJ: Rutgers University Press, 1972.
Keyser, Samuel J. "Form and Meaning in Four Poems." *College English* 37, no. 6 (February 1976): 578–98.
Kravec, Maureen. "Stevens's 'Notes toward a Supreme Fiction.'" *Explicator* 53, no. 3 (Spring 1995): 166–67.
Lawrence, D. H. *Sons and Lovers*. Harmondsworth, UK: Penguin, 1948.

Lee, Jonathan Scott. *Jacques Lacan*. Amherst: University of Massachusetts Press, 1991.

Lemaire, Anika. *Jacques Lacan*. Translated by David Macey. London: Routledge & Kegan Paul, 1977.

Leonard, J. S., and C. E. Wharton. *The Fluent Mundo: Wallace Stevens and the Structure of Reality*. Athens: University of Georgia Press, 1988.

Litz, Walton A. *Introspective Voyager: The Poetic Development of Wallace Stevens*. New York: Oxford University Press, 1972.

Lodge, David. *20th Century Literary Criticism: A Reader*. London: Longman, 1972.

Macksey, Richard A. "The Climates of Wallace Stevens." *The Act of the Mind: Essays on the Poetry of Wallace Stevens*, edited by Roy Harvey Pearce and J. Hillis Miller, 185–223. Baltimore: Johns Hopkins University Press, 1965.

Marotti, Arthur F. "Countertransference, the Communication Process, and the Dimensions of Psychoanalytic Criticism." *Critical Inquiry* 4 (Spring 1978): 471–89.

Martin, Thomas L. "Stevens on Subject and Object: 'Someone Puts a Pineapple Together.'" *Wallace Stevens Journal* 18, no. 1 (Spring 1994): 27–49.

Martin, Wallace. "She and/or Sea in 'The Idea of Order at Key West.'" *Wallace Stevens Journal* 26, no. 1 (Spring 2002): 88–98.

Martz, Louis L. "'From the Journal of Crispin': An Early Version of 'The Comedian as the Letter C.'" In *Wallace Stevens: A Celebration*, edited by Frank Doggett and Robert Buttel, 3–45. Princeton, NJ: Princeton University Press, 1980.

McCollough, Aaron. "'Desiring-Production' in Stevens' 'The Idea of Order at Key West.'" *Wallace Stevens Journal* 26, no. 1 (Spring 2002): 99–110.

Mehlman, Jeffrey, trans. "Seminar on 'The Purloined Letter.'" *Yale French Studies* 48 (1972): 38–72.

Melville, Stephen. "Psychoanalysis and the Place of *Jouissance*." *Critical Inquiry* 13, no. 2 (Winter 1987): 349–70.

Merchant, Hoshang. "The Rhapsody of Things as They Are: Endings in Stevens' Poems." *Indian Journal of American Studies* 21, no. 1 (Winter 1991): 79–87.

Miller, J. Hillis. *Poets of Reality: Six Twentieth Century Writers*. Cambridge, MA: Harvard University Press, 1966.

_____. "Stevens' Rock and Criticism as Cure." *Georgia Review* 30, no. 1 (Spring 1976a): 5–31.

_____. "Stevens' Rock and Criticism as Cure, II." *Georgia Review* 30, no. 2 (Summer 1976b): 330–48.

_____. "Wallace Stevens' Poetry of Being." In *The Act of the Mind: Essays on the Poetry of Wallace Stevens*, edited by Roy Harvey Pearce and J. Hillis Miller, 143–162. Baltimore: Johns Hopkins University Press, 1965.

Mills, Ralph J., Jr. "Wallace Stevens: The Image of the Rock." In *Wallace Stevens: A Collection of Critical Essays*, edited by Marie Borroff, 96–110. Englewood Cliffs, NJ: Prentice Hall, 1963.

Milton, John. *Sonnet XIV* ("On His Blindness"). In *Milton: Complete Shorter Poems*, edited by James Carey, 327–28. London: Longman, 1971.

Morrison, Paul. "The Fat Girl in Paradise: Stevens, Wordsworth, Milton, and the Proper Name." In *Wallace Stevens and the Feminine*, edited by Melita Schaum, 80–114. Tuscaloosa: University of Alabama Press, 1993.

Nassar, Eugene Paul. *Wallace Stevens: An Anatomy of Figuration*. Philadelphia: University of Pennsylvania Press, 1965. (Second Printing, 1968.)

Narasimhaiah, C. D. "Modern American Poetry." *Literary Criterion* VI, no. 2 (Summer 1964): 55–88.

Nietzsche, Friedrich Wilhelm. *Thus Spoke Zarathrustra*. Translated by Walter Kaufmann. Harmondsworth, UK: Penguin, 1978.

O'Hara, Daniel T. "Imaginary Politics: Emerson, Stevens, and the Resistance of Style." In *Wallace Stevens and the Feminine*, edited by Melita Schaum, 58–79. Tuscaloosa: University of Alabama Press, 1993.

Orwell, George. *Animal Farm*. Signet Classic edition. New York: Harcourt Brace Jovanovich, 1946.

Patke, Rajeev S. *The Long Poems of Wallace Stevens: An Interpretive Study*. Cambridge: Cambridge University Press, 1986.

Pearce, Roy Harvey. *The Continuity of American Poetry*. Princeton, NJ: Princeton University Press, 1961.

Perloff, Marjorie. "Irony in Wallace Stevens' *The Rock*." *American Literature* 36, no. 3 (November 1964): 327–42.

Pound, Ezra. *Pisan Cantos*. London: Faber and Faber, 1973.

Powell, Grosvenor E. "Of Heroes and Nobility: The Personae of Wallace Stevens." *Southern Review* 72, no. 7 (Summer 1971): 727–48.

Pradhan R. C. "Descartes and Wittgenstein: Two Philosophical Models of Mind." *Indian Philosophical Quarterly* XXIII, no. 1–2 (January–April 1996): 119–39.

Raghavacharyulu, D. V. K. "The Well-Wrought Jar of Wallace Stevens." *Literary Criterion* 6, no. 2 (Summer 1964): 89–92.

Ragland-Sullivan, Ellie. *Jacques Lacan and the Philosophy of Psychoanalysis*. Urbana: University of Illinois Press, 1986.

Ramazani, Jahan. "Elegy and Anti-Elegy in Stevens' Harmonium: Mockery, Melancholia, and the Pathetic Fallacy." *Journal of Modern Literature* XVII, no. 4 (1991): 567–82.

Reddy, Shrikanth. "'As He Starts the Human Tale': Strategies of Closure in Wallace Stevens." *Wallace Stevens Journal* 24, no. 1 (Spring 2000): 3–23.

Rehder, Robert. *The Poetry of Wallace Stevens*. New York: St. Martin's Press, 1988.

Riddel, Joseph N. *The Clairvoyant Eye: The Poetry and Poetics of Wallace Stevens*. Baton Rouge: Louisiana University Press, 1965.

Robinson, Fred. "Poems That Took the Place of Mountains: Realizations in Stevens and Cézanne." *Centennial Review* 22 (1978): 281–98.

Rose, Jacqueline. *The Haunting of Sylvia Plath*. Cambridge, MA: Harvard University Press, 1992.

Rosenmeier, Rosamond. "'Getting Wisdom': The 'Rabbi's' Devotion to *Weisheit* and Its Implications for Feminists." In *Wallace Stevens and the Feminine*, edited by Melita Schaum, 140–54. Tuscaloosa: University of Alabama Press, 1993.

Sampson, Theodore. *A Cure of the Mind*. New York: Black Rose Books, 2000.

Santayana, George. "Carnival." *Dial* 71 (July 1921): 43–47.

_____. *Interpretations of Poetry and Religion*. Edited by William G. Holzberger and Herman J. Saatkamp Jr. Cambridge, MA: MIT Press, 1989.

_____. *Three Philosophical Poets*. Cambridge, MA: Harvard University Press, 1944.

Schneiderman, Stuart, ed. and trans. *Returning to Freud: Clinical Psychoanalysis in the School of Lacan*. New Haven, CT: Yale University Press, 1980.

Selden, Raman. *The Theory of Criticism: From Plato to the Present*. London: Longman, 1990.

Shakespeare, William. *Hamlet*. Edited by George Lyman Kittredge. Boston: Ginn, 1939.

_____. *Romeo and Juliet*. Arden Shakespeare edition. Edited by Brion Gibbons. London: Routledge reprint, 1992 (first published by Methuen, 1980).

Sheshadri-Crooks, Kalpana. "The Comedy of Domination: Psychoanalysis and the Conceit of Whiteness." In *The Psychoanalysis of Race*, edited by Christopher Lane, 353–79. New York: Columbia University Press, 1988.

Simons, Hi. "'The Comedian as the Letter C': Its Sense and Significance." *Southern Review* V (Winter 1940): 453–68.

Soyinka, Wole. "Telephonic Conversation." In *An Anthology of Commonwealth Poetry*, edited by C. D. Narasimhaiah, 149–50. Madras: Macmillan India, 1990.

Stallknecht, Newton P. "Absence in Reality: A Study in the Epistemology of the Blue Guitar." *Kenyon Review* 21, no. 4 (Autumn 1959): 545–62.

Steinman, Lisa M. "The House of Fathers: Stevens and Emerson." In *Wallace Stevens and the Feminine*, edited by Melita Schaum, 190–202. Tuscaloosa: University of Alabama Press, 1993.

Storm, Martha. "Wallace Stevens' Revisions of Crispin's Journal: A Reaction against the 'Local.'" *American Literature* 54, no. 2 (May 1982): 258–76.

Sukenick, Ronald. *Wallace Stevens: Musing the Obscure*. New York: New York University Press, 1967.

Vendler, Helen H. *On Extended Wings: The Longer Poems of Wallace Stevens*. Cambridge, MA: Harvard University Press, 1969.

_____. "The Qualified Assertions of Wallace Stevens." In *The Act of the Mind: Essays on the Poetry of Wallace Stevens*, edited by Roy Harvey Pearce and J. Hillis Miller. Baltimore: Johns Hopkins University Press, 1965, 163–178.

_____. *Words Chosen out of Desire*. Knoxville: University of Tennessee Press, 1984.

Wagner, C. Roland. "Wallace Stevens: The Concealed Self." *Wallace Stevens Journal* 12, no. 2 (Fall 1988): 83–101.

Webb, Timothy, ed. *Shelley: Selected Poems*. London: Dent Everyman's Library, 1977. (Reprint 1983.)

Weston, Susan B. *Wallace Stevens: An Introduction to the Poetry*. New York: Columbia University Press, 1977.

Whalen, Tom. "'Alone in an Immense Valley': A Note on Stevens' 'Valley Candle.'" *Wallace Stevens Journal* 20, no. 2 (Fall 1996): 229–34.

Wilden, Anthony, trans., with elaborate commentary and notes. *The Language of the Self: The Function of Language in Psychoanalysis*. Baltimore: Johns Hopkins University Press, 1968.

Williamson, Alan. *Introspection and Contemporary Poetry*. Cambridge, MA: Harvard University Press, 1984.

Wimsatt, W. K. *The Verbal Icon: Studies in the Meaning of Poetry*. London: Methuen, 1970.

Wordsworth, Williams. "A slumber did my spirit seal." In *Wordsworth: Selected Poetry and Prose*, edited by John Butt. London: Oxford University Press, 1964.

Index

www.ingramcontent.com/pod-product-compliance
Ingram Content Group UK Ltd.
Pitfield, Milton Keynes, MK11 3LW, UK
UKHW041835100926
8556IPUK00018B/974

9 780786 464579